READING THE POPULAR

JOHN FISKE

READING THE POPULAR

READING THE POPULAR

John Fiske

Boston
UNWIN HYMAN
London   Sydney   Wellington

© 1989 by Unwin Hyman

Unwin Hyman, Inc.,
955 Massachusetts Avenue, Cambridge, Mass. 02139, USA

Published by the Academic Division of **Unwin Hyman Ltd,**
15/17 Broadwick Street, London W1V 1FP, UK

Allen & Unwin (Australia) Ltd,
8 Napier Street, North Sydney, NSW 2060, Australia

Allen & Unwin (New Zealand) Ltd in association with the
Port Nicholson Press Ltd
Compusales Building, 75 Ghuznee Street, Wellington 1, New Zealand

First published in 1989
Second impression 1990

Library of Congress Cataloging-in-Publication Data

Fiske, John.
    Reading the popular/John Fiske.
p. cm.
Bibliography: p.
Includes index.
ISBN 0-04-445436-8.—ISBN 0-04-445437-6 (pbk.)
1. Popular culture. 2. Capitalism.
I. Title.
CB151.F57   1989
306.4—dc20   89-5739 CIP

British Library Cataloguing in Publication Data

Fiske, John, *1939–*
    Reading the popular.
1. Popular culture.
I. Title.
306'.1
ISBN 0-04-445436-8
        0-04-445437-6 (pbk.)

Typeset in 10 on 12 point Palatino by Fotographics (Bedford) Ltd
and printed in Great Britain by Billing and Sons, London and Worcester

For Lisa
For Matthew and Lucy

Contents

Preface

This book is a collection of analyses of texts and sites where people make their popular culture in capitalist societies, together with a theoretical introduction. It is published simultaneously with *Understanding Popular Culture*, the concern of which is to develop the theoretical and political rather than the analytical. This book, then, moves from readings to theories; *Understanding Popular Culture* moves from theories to readings. Each book is designed to be self-sufficient, but I hope, those who read both will find that the readings flesh out and interrogate the theories, and the theories deepen and generalize the readings. But neither book requires the other, so those whose interests center more focusedly on either the theoretical or the analytical should not feel deprived if they confine their reading to one or the other.

One of the advantages of being an academic is that theories travel well, with only a touch of jet lag. Consequently, over the last decade I have been fortunate enough to move freely among the United Kingdom, Australia, and the United States. These essays have been produced during this period; some have been published in earlier versions, others appear here for the first time. They are a bricolage of frozen moments in my thinking about popular culture, a series of snapshots taken by an academic on his intercontinental wanderings in the 1980s. My nomadism has left many traces in both these books, but my experiences in different continents are held together by a common thread running through them—the countries with which I am familiar, and whose cultures I write about, are all white, patriarchal, capitalist ones. Of course, each inflects the common ideology differently, but the differences are comparatively superficial, though fascinating to live through and think about.

This book is more continentally specific than *Understanding Popular Culture*, because analyses are necessarily tied more closely to their social context than are theories. Indeed, the theories that I use are European in origin, they originate in the works of Bourdieu, de Certeau, Barthes, Hall, and Bakhtin, and in *Understanding Popular Culture* I use them as the base upon which to develop my thinking on issues such as the nature of "the people," culture and commodities, popular pleasures, popular texts and discrimination, and the political potential of popular culture. My theories may originate in Europe (as do I), but I use them in both books to engage with the popular culture of English-speaking countries. Shopping malls, video arcades, the tabloids, beaches, skyscrapers, and Madonna circulate their meanings in the United States, Australia, and the United Kingdom, but I read them with a European eye. My work as an academic is as much a social product as that of a builder of motorcars. The history of cultural studies, my academic history, and my personal history all intersect and inform one another, and produce me as a speaking and writing voice at the end of the 1980s. Those familiar with my earlier writings will inevitably find echoes in these books, though all previously published work has been rewritten to a greater or lesser extent. I hope, therefore, that such echoes are amplified enough for them not to be merely repetitious.

My histories and the multiple voices of my colleagues, friends, antagonists, students, teachers, and others constitute the resource bank that I raid in order to speak and write: I take full responsibility for the use I make of them, but without them nothing would have been possible. I wish both of these books to be a grateful acknowledgment to all who, however unwittingly—or even unwillingly—have contributed to them. The vast majority of these I cannot name: some, whose contributions are in their own words, are referenced directly; others who have contributed in different ways I wish to thank here.

My first thanks go to Lisa Freeman, my editor at Unwin Hyman, whose critical encouragement and knowledge of the world of books have had a significant influence upon what has finally appeared in print; I only wish it were more common for academics and publishers to work together so fruitfully. I must also give special thanks to Larry Grossberg for his painstaking and productive criticism. Others who have helped include

Graeme Turner, Jon Watts, Bob Hodge, Mary Ellen Brown, Bobby Allen, David Bordwell, Todd Gitlin, Dan Leab, Jane Gaines, Susan Willis, Liz Ferrier, and Paul Adams. My secretarial colleagues, Rae Kelly in Perth and Evelyn Miller and Mary Dodge in Madison, have contributed as much as my academic colleagues, and I thank them for their friendly expertise. I hope these two books will give some pleasure to all who have contributed in one way or another to their production, and I look forward to many more years of friendship and collaboration.

Chapter 3 first appeared as "Surfalism and Sandiotics: The Beach in Australian Popular Culture," *Australian Journal of Cultural Studies* 1 (2), 1983, and parts of it appeared in J. Fiske, R. Hodge, and G. Turner (1987) *Myths of Oz: Readings in Australian Popular Culture* (Boston: Unwin Hyman).

Chapter 4 is an expanded and edited version of "Video Games: Inverted Pleasures" (co-written with Jon Watts), *Australian Journal of Cultural Studies* 2 (1), 1984.

Parts of Chapter 5a appeared in "British Cultural Studies," in R. Allen (ed.), *Channels of Discourse* (Chapel Hill: University of North Carolina Press), whose permission to reprint is gratefully acknowledged. Chapter 5b is an edited version of "Romancing the Rock" (co-written with Mary Ellen Brown), *ONETWOTHREEFOUR* 5 (Spring), 1987.

Chapter 6 is a combination of edited extracts from "Everyday Quizzes Everyday Life" in G. Turner (ed.), *Australian Television* (Sydney: Allen & Unwin) and "Women and Quiz Shows" in M. E. Brown (ed.), *Television and Women's Culture* (Sydney: Currency Press), both of which are in press.

I also wish to acknowledge the following sources for the illustrations: the *National Times* and the *Australian Journal of Cultural Studies*. Although every attempt has been made to trace the illustrations' sources, in some instances we have not been successful. For this we apologize and would welcome claims for acknowledgment in subsequent editions.

CHAPTER 1

Understanding Popular Culture

POPULAR CULTURE

This book consists of a number of analyses of popular culture in practice. In their various ways they all, I hope, shed some light on the meanings and pleasures we generate and circulate as we live our everyday lives. Culture is the constant process of producing meanings of and from our social experience, and *def.* such meanings necessarily produce a social identity for the people involved. Making sense of anything involves making sense of the person who is the agent in the process; sense making dissolves differences between subject and object and constructs each in relation to the other. Within the production and circulation of these meanings lies pleasure.

Culture making (and culture is always in process, never achieved) is a social process: all meanings of self, of social relations, all the discourses and texts that play such important cultural roles can circulate only in relationship to the social system, in our case that of white, patriarchal capitalism. Any social system needs a cultural system of meanings that serves either to hold it in place or destabilize it, to make it more or less amenable to change. Culture (and its meanings and pleasures) is a constant succession of social practices; it is therefore inherently political, it is centrally involved in the distribution and possible redistribution of various forms of social power. Popular culture is made by various formations of subordinated or disempowered people out of the resources, both discursive and material, that are provided by the social system that disempowers them. It is therefore contradictory and conflictual to its core. The resources—television, records, clothes, video games, language—carry the interests of the economically and ideologically dominant; they have lines of force within them that are hegemonic and that work in favor of the status quo. But hegemonic power is necessary, or even possible, only because of resistance, so these resources must also carry contradictory lines of force that are taken up and activated differently by people situated differently within the social system. If the cultural commodities or texts do not contain resources out of which the people can make their own meanings of their social relations and identities, they will be rejected and will fail in the marketplace. They will not be made popular.

Popular culture is made by subordinated peoples in their own interests out of resources that also, contradictorily, serve the economic interests of the dominant. Popular culture is made from within and below, not imposed from without or above as mass cultural theorists would have it. There is always an element of popular culture that lies outside social control, that escapes or opposes hegemonic forces. Popular culture is always a culture of conflict, it always involves the struggle to make social meanings that are in the interests of the subordinate and that are not those preferred by the dominant ideology. The victories, however fleeting or limited, in this struggle produce popular pleasure, for popular pleasure is always social and political.

Popular culture is made in relationship to structures of dominance. This relationship can take two main forms—that of resistance or evasion. The girl fans of Madonna (Chapter 5a) are resisting the patriarchal meanings of female sexuality and constructing their own oppositional ones; the boys in video arcades (Chapter 4) are similarly making their own resistant meanings of human-machine relations and power structures. But surfers (Chapter 3) are evading social discipline, evading ideological control and positioning. Evasion and resistance are interrelated, and neither is possible without the other: both involve the interplay of pleasure and meaning, but evasion is more pleasurable than meaningful, whereas resistance produces meanings before pleasures.

Making popular culture out of television news, for instance, is possible and pleasurable only if the subordinate can make their meanings out of it, otherwise the news would be part of dominant, hegemonic culture only. So the news of a snow storm (Chapter 7) or of Israeli troops quelling an uprising by Arab youths (Chapter 8) can be made popular only if it offers meanings that are relevant to the everyday lives of subordinate people, and these meanings will be pleasurable only if they are made *out of* the news, not *by* the news. These productive pleasures of making one's own sense are different in emphasis from the evasive, offensive pleasures of the body experienced by surfers or video game players.

Popular culture is always in process; its meanings can never be identified in a text, for texts are activated, or made meaningful, only in social relations and in intertextual relations. This activation of the meaning potential of a text can occur only in the social and cultural relationships into which it enters. The social relationships of texts occur at their moment of reading as they are inserted into the everyday lives of the readers. Shopping malls are quite different texts for women and for unemployed youths, because their social relationships differ in each case (see Chapter 2): for women, malls are legitimate, unthreatening public places, that are opposed to both the street and the home; for unemployed youths, they are a place to trick "the system," to consume the images, warmth, and places of consumerism, without buying any of its commodities. The meanings of shopping malls are made and circulated in social practices.

But they are also made intertextually: bumper stickers announcing, "A woman's place is in the mall," coffee mugs decorated with the words "mall rats," or T-shirts that proclaim the pathology of the "shop-a-holic" can be used defiantly, skeptically, critically, and variously, according to their many uses—a father giving a T-shirt to his teenage daughter would set up a series of meanings that would differ significantly from those generated by it as a gift from one of her friends. The culture of shopping malls, as of Madonna, as of the beach, cannot be read off the primary texts themselves, but only in their social uses and in their relationships with other texts. The postcards we send are as much a part of the meaning of the beach as our use of it to expose ourselves to the sun and sight of others; Madonna's posters are as much a part of her meanings and pleasures as her songs and videos. The fan decorating her bedroom with Madonna icons, the wanna-bes (Madonna look-alikes) striding down the sidewalk, are agents in "Madonna culture," their texts (the bedroom, their bodies) as signifying as any of Madonna herself. The meanings of popular culture exist only in their circulation, not in their texts; the texts, which are crucial in this process, need to be understood not for and by themselves but in their interrelationships with other texts and with social life, for that is how their circulation is ensured.

POPULAR PRODUCTIVITY AND DISCRIMINATION

The art of popular culture is "the art of making do." The people's subordination means that they cannot produce the resources of popular culture, but they do make their culture from those resources. Commodities make an economic profit for their producers and distributors, but their cultural function is not adequately explained by their economic function, however dependent it may be on it. The cultural industries are often thought of as those that produce our films, music, television, publications, and so on, but all industries are cultural industries to a greater or lesser extent: a pair of jeans (see *Understanding Popular Culture*, Chapter 1) or a piece of furniture is as much a cultural text as a pop record. All commodities are consumed as much for their meanings, identities, and pleasures as they are for their material function.

Our culture is a commodity culture, and it is fruitless to argue against it on the basis that culture and profit are mutually exclusive terms—that what is profitable for some cannot be cultural for others. Behind such arguments lie two romantic fantasies that originate at opposite ends of the cultural spectrum—at one end that of the penniless artist, dedicated only to the purity and aesthetic transcendence of his (for the vision is a patriarchal one) art, and at the other that of a folk art in which all members of the tribe participate equally in producing and circulating their culture, free of any commercial taint. Neither of these fantasies has much historical basis, and neither of them is any help at all in understanding the popular culture of capitalist societies. The cultural dimensions of industries are where their dominance is at its shakiest: they know that people have to eat, to wear clothes, to be able to transport themselves, but they are much less sure in determining what or why they want to eat, wear, or travel in. The cultural industries, by which I mean all industries, have to produce a repertoire of products from which the people choose. And choose they do; most estimates of the failure rate for new products—whether primarily cultural, such as movies or records, or more material commodities—are as high as 80–90 percent despite extensive advertising (and the prime function of our enormous publicity industry is to try to ensure the cultural circulation of economic commodities—that is, to exploit the cultural dimension of commodities for the economic profit of their producers). But, despite all the pressures, it is the people who finally choose which commodities they will use in their culture.

These pressures are not merely economic. The beach, for instance, is not a commodity to be bought and sold, and neither are the public rest areas of shopping malls or the view of Sears Tower from the freeway. But the absence of economic power does not mean the absence of social or hegemonic power. As I show in Chapters 3 and 4, attempts to control the meanings, pleasures, and behaviors of the subordinate are always there, and popular culture has to accommodate them in a constant interplay of power and resistance, discipline and indiscipline, order and disorder.

Much of this struggle is a struggle for meanings, and popular texts can ensure their popularity only by making themselves inviting terrains for this struggle; the people are unlikely to choose any commodity that serves only the economic and ideological interests of the dominant. So popular texts are structured in the tension between forces of closure (or domination) and openness (or popularity). In *Understanding Popular Culture*, Chapter 5, I theorize some of the forces of openness; in this book I try to trace them at work. So popular culture is full of puns whose meanings multiply and escape the norms of the social order and overflow their discipline; its excess offers opportunities for parody, subversion, or inversion; it is obvious and superficial, refusing to produce the deep, complexly crafted texts that narrow down their audiences and social meanings; it is tasteless and vulgar, for taste is social control and class interest masquerading as a naturally finer sensibility; it is shot through with contradictions, for contradictions require the productivity of the reader to make his or her sense out of them. It often centers on the body and its sensations rather than on the mind and its sense, for the bodily pleasures offer carnivalesque, evasive, liberating practices—they constitute the popular terrain where hegemony is weakest, a terrain that may possibly lie beyond its reach.

Popular texts are inadequate in themselves—they are never self-sufficient structures of meanings (as some will argue highbrow tests to be), they are provokers of meanings and pleasure, they are completed only when taken up by people and inserted into their everyday culture. The people make popular culture at the interface between everyday life and the consumption of the products of the cultural industries.

The aim of this productivity is, therefore, to produce meanings that are relevant to everyday life. Relevance is central to popular culture, for it minimizes the difference between text and life, between the aesthetic and the everyday that is so central to a process- and practice-based culture (such as the popular) rather than a text- or performance-based one (such as the bourgeois, highbrow one) (see *Understanding Popular Culture*, Chapter 6). Relevance can be produced only by the people, for only they can know which texts enable them to make the meanings that will function in their everyday lives. Relevance also means that much popular culture is ephemeral —as the social conditions of the people change, so do the texts and tastes from which relevances can be produced.

Relevance is the intersection between the textual and the social. It is therefore a site of struggle, for relevances are dispersed, and as divergent as the social situations of the people: the popular text, therefore, has to work against its differences to find a commonality between divergent social groups in order to maximize its consumption and profitability.

There is also a struggle over relevance itself, particularly in the function of news in popular culture. Though there are many similarities between entertainment and information, and hard-and-fast distinctions between them are as useless as they are popular among TV schedulers, power does work differently in each. There are few who now believe that it is in the national interest to control the entertainment of the people so as to improve their taste (which means, in practice, to do away with popular tastes and reduce them all to bourgeois ones), but there are much more solidly grounded arguments that there is information the people *need* to have if democracy is to flourish. A politically ignorant or apathetic electorate will be unable to produce high-caliber politicians. So television news, for example, is caught in the tension between the need to convey information deemed to be in the public interest and the need to be popular. It attempts to meet these contradictory needs by being socially responsible in content, but popular in form and presentation, and thus runs the risk of being judged boring and irrelevant from one side, and superficial and rushed from the other. It is caught between competing relevancies at the national (or global) level and at the local level of everyday life, and can be judged to be successful only when it manages to merge the two into one. In Chapters 7 and 8, I trace the interplay of power, knowledge, pleasure, and popularity in the news as social responsibility and discipline meet popular productivity and relevance.

POLITICS

Popular culture is the culture of the subordinate who resent their subordination; it is not concerned with finding consensual meanings or with producing social rituals that harmonize social difference, as the liberal pluralists would have it. Equally, however, it is not the culture of subordination that massifies or commodifies people into the victimized dupes of capitalism, as mass cultural theorists propose. Different though these two arguments are, they both find in popular culture only those forces that work in favor of the status quo—the liberal pluralists may define this in terms of a consensus, and the mass culturalists in terms of the power of the dominant classes, but neither argument allows popular culture to work as an agent of destabilization or as a redistributor of the balance of social power toward the disempowered. They are therefore inadequate.

Popular culture is structured within what Stuart Hall (1981) calls the opposition between the power-bloc and the people. The power-bloc consists of a relatively unified, relatively stable alliance of social forces—economic, legal, moral, aesthetic; the people, on the other hand, is a diverse and dispersed set of social allegiances constantly formed and reformed among the formations of the subordinate. The opposition can also be thought of as one between *homogeneity*, as the power-bloc attempts to control, structure, and minimize social differences so that they serve its interests, and *heterogeneity*, as the formations of the people intransigently maintain their sense of social difference that is also a difference of interest. It can be thought of as the opposition between the center and the circumference, between centripetal and centrifugal forces, or, more belligerently, as the conflict between an occupying army and guerrilla fighters, as de Certeau (1984) and Eco (1986) characterize it. But the relationship is always one of conflict or confrontation; the hegemonic forces of homogeneity are always met by the resistances of heterogeneity.

These resistances take various forms that differ in their social visibility, in their social positioning, and in their activity. It could be argued that the least politically active are the bodily pleasures of evasion, the dogged refusal of the dominant ideology and its discipline, and the ability to construct a set of experiences beyond its reach. Surfers and video game players "lose" their socially constructed identities and therefore the structure of domination-subordination in their moments of *jouissance* when the intensity of bodily concentration-pleasure becomes orgasmic (see Chapters 3 and 4). Other evasive, offensive pleasures are those of the carnivalesque, of exaggerated, liberating fun (see Chapter 6 and *Understanding Popular Culture*, Chapters 3 and 4) that inverts social norms and momentarily disrupts their power.

There are arguments that such evasive or carnivalesque pleasures are merely safety valves that finally serve to maintain the current structure of power by providing licensed, contained, controlled means of expressing resentment. There are similar arguments against the political effectivity of semiotic or interior resistances that occur within a realm of fantasy that is constructed outside and against the forces of ideological subjection (see Chapter 5b). These arguments hold that because such resistance occurs within the realm of the individual rather than that of the social it is defused, made safe, and thus contained comfortably within the system. But what these arguments fail to take into account is the politics of everyday life that occur on the micro rather than macro level; they fail equally to account for the differences and potential connections between interior, semiotic resistances and sociopolitical ones, between meanings and behaviors, between progressiveness and radicalism, between evasive and offensive tactics. These are the issues and relationships that are central to the politics of popular culture, and theories that fail to address them can never offer us adequate insights.

Theories of ideology or hegemony stress the power of the dominant to construct the subjectivities of the subordinate and the common sense of society in their own interests. Their power is the power to have their meanings of self and of social relations accepted or consented to by the people. At the most basic level, evading this power or inverting it is an act of defiance, for any expression of meanings that establish conflictual social differences maintains and legitimates those meanings and those differences. The threat to the power of the dominant is evidenced by their constant attempts to control, delegitimate, and disparage the pleasures of the people. But despite centuries of legal, moral, and aesthetic repression (see *Understanding Popular Culture*, Chapter 4), the everyday culture of the people, often transmitted orally, has maintained these evasive, resistant popular forces without which more active resistances would have no base and no motivation. Evasion is the foundation of resistance; avoiding capture, either ideological or physical, is the first duty of the guerrilla.

The basic power of the dominant in capitalism may be economic, but this economic power is both underpinned and exceeded by semiotic power, that is, the power to make meanings. So semiotic resistance that not only refuses the dominant meanings but constructs oppositional ones that serve the interests of the subordinate is as vital a base for the redistribution of power as is evasion. The ability to think differently, to construct one's own meanings of self and of social relations, is the necessary ground without which no political action can hope to succeed. The minority who are active at the macro level of politics can claim to be the representatives of a social movement only if they can touch this base of semiotic resistance of people "thinking differently." Without this, they can all too easily be marginalized as extremists or agitators and their political effectiveness neutralized. The interior resistance of fantasy is more than ideologically evasive, it is a necessary base for social action.

But such action does not occur only at the organized macropolitical level; it occurs, too, in the minutiae of everyday life. Indeed, the politics of popular culture are much more effective and visible at the micro than the macro level, for this is their most sympathetic terrain.

Semiotic resistance results from the desire of the subordinate to exert control over the meanings of their lives, a control that is typically denied them in their material social conditions. This, again, is politically crucial, for without some control over one's existence there can be no empowerment and no self-esteem. And with no sense of empowerment or self-esteem there can be none of the confidence needed for social action, even at the micro level. So Radway (1984) found a woman romance reader whose reading empowered her to the extent that she felt better able to resist the patriarchal demands made upon her by her marriage, and D'Acci (1988) found women fans of *Cagney & Lacey* of all ages who reported that the sense of self-empowerment produced by their fandom enabled them to promote their own interests more effectively in their everyday lives (see *Understanding Popular Culture*, Chapter 7). So the provocation offered by Madonna (Chapter 5a) to young girls to take control of the meanings of their femininity produces a sense of empowerment in one of the most disempowered of social groups that may well result in political progress in their everyday lives—in their relationships with their boyfriends or parents, in their refusal to give up the street to men as their territory.

Such political gains in the specificities of everyday life are progressive rather than radical. They enlarge the space of action for the subordinate; they effect shifts, however minute, in social power relations. They are the tactics of the subordinate in making do within and against the system, rather than of opposing it directly; they are concerned with improving the lot of the subordinate rather than with changing the system that subordinates them.

This is controversial territory, for there are those who would argue that such tactics finally serve to strengthen the system and to delay any radical change in it. If this argument is followed to its extreme, it would propose that the more the subordinate suffer the better, because their suffering is more likely to provoke the conditions for radical reform. This may well be theoretically correct, but it is hardly popular. It also rests upon a caricature of capitalism, that the system is not only unfair in its distribution of power and resources (which it *is*), but also totally inhumane in its exploitation of the weak (which it is not, in general, although U.S. capitalism does treat certain groups such as those who are both poor and mentally sick with something close to total inhumanity).

The reverse side of theories proposing that popular culture is at best a safety valve and at worst an opiate is the implication that a different sort of culture could provoke radical social reform. Such assumptions, unstated though they frequently are, are utopian. It is material historical conditions that produce radical reform; evasive and semiotic resistances can maintain a popular consciousness that can fertilize the growth of those conditions and can be ready to exploit them when they arise, but they cannot in themselves produce such conditions. But the resistances of popular culture are not just evasive or semiotic: they do have a social dimension at the micro level. And at this micro level they may well act as a constant erosive force upon the macro, weakening the system from within so that it is more amenable to change at the structural level. One wonders, for instance, how effective the attempts to improve the legal status of women would have been if it had not been for the constant erosion of millions of women working to improve the micropolitical conditions of their everyday lives. It is arguable that the needs of the people are better met by progressive social change originating in evasive or interior resistance, moving to action at the micropolitical level and from there to more organized assaults on the system itself, than by radical or revolutionary change. Western patriarchal capitalism has proved remarkably able to prevent the social conditions that provoke effective radical action, and to contain such radical attempts that have been made upon it. It appears to be much more vulnerable to guerrilla raids than to strategic assaults, and it is here we must look for the politics of popular culture.

CHAPTER 2

Shopping for Pleasure

MALLS, POWER, AND RESISTANCE

Shopping malls are cathedrals of consumption—a glib phrase that I regret the instant it slides off my pen. The metaphor of consumerism as a religion, in which commodities become the icons of worship and the rituals of exchanging money for goods become a secular equivalent of holy communion, is simply too glib to be helpful, and too attractive to those whose intentions, whether they be moral or political, are to expose the evils and limitations of bourgeois materialism. And yet the metaphor *is* both attractive and common precisely because it does convey and construct a knowledge of consumerism; it does point to one set of "truths," however carefully selected a set.

Truths compete in a political arena, and the truths that the consumerism-as-contemporary-religion strives to suppress are those that deny the difference between the tenor and vehicle of the metaphor. Metaphor always works within that tense area within which the forces of similarity and difference collide, and aligns itself with those of similarity. Metaphor constructs similarity out of difference, and when a metaphor becomes a cliché, as the shopping mall-cathedral one has, then a resisting reading must align itself with the differences rather than the similarities, for clichés become clichés only because of their centrality to common sense: the cliché helps to construct the commonality of common sense.

So, the differences: the religious congregation is powerless, led like sheep through the rituals and meanings, forced to "buy" the truth on offer, all the truth, not selective bits of it. Where the interests of the Authority on High differ from those of the Congregation down Low, the congregation has no power to negotiate, to discriminate: all accommodations are made by the powerless, subjugated to the great truth. In the U.S. marketplace, 90 percent of new products fail to find sufficient buyers to survive (Schudson 1984), despite advertising, promotions, and all the persuasive techniques of the priests of consumption. In Australia, Sinclair (1987) puts the new product failure rate at 80 percent—such statistics are obviously best-guesstimates: what matters is that the failure rate is high. The power of consumer discrimination evidenced here has no equivalent in the congregation: no religion could tolerate a rejection rate of 80 or 90 percent of what it has to offer.

Religion may act as a helpful metaphor when our aim is to investigate the power of consumerism; when, however, our focus shifts to the power of the consumer, it is counter-productive. Shopping malls and the cultural practices, the variety of shoppings that take place within them, are key arenas of struggle, at both economic and ideological levels, between those with the power of ideological practice (Althusser), hegemony (Gramsci), or strategy (de Certeau) and those whose construction as subjects in ideology is never complete, whose resistances mean that hegemony can never finally relax in victory, and whose tactics inflict a running series of wounds upon the strategic power. Shopping is the crisis of consumerism: it is where the art and tricks of the weak can inflict most damage on, and exert most power over, the strategic interests of the powerful. The shopping mall that is seen as the terrain of guerrilla warfare looks quite different from the one constructed by the metaphor of religion.

Pressdee (1986), in his study of unemployed youth in the South Australian town of Elizabeth, paints a clear picture of both sides in this war. The ideological practices that serve the interests of the powerful are exposed in his analysis of the local mall's promotional slogan, which appears in the form of a free ticket: "Your ticket to a better shopping world: ADMITS EVERYONE." He comments:

The words "your" and "everyone" are working to socially level out class distinction and, in doing so, overlook the city's two working class groups, those who have work and those who do not. The word "admits" with a connotation of having to have or be someone to gain admittance is cancelled out by the word "everyone"—there are no conditions of admittance; everyone is equal and can come in. (p. 10)

This pseudoticket to consumerism denies the basic function of a ticket—to discriminate between those who possess one and those who do not—in a precise moment of the ideological work of bourgeois capitalism with its denial of class difference, and therefore of the inevitability of class struggle. The equality of "everyone" is, of course, an equality attainable only by those with purchasing power: those without are defined out of existence, as working-class interests (derived from class *difference*) are defined out of existence by bourgeois ideology. "The ticket to a better shopping world does not say 'Admits everyone with at least some money to spend' . . .; money and the problems associated with getting it conveniently disappear in the official discourse" (Pressdee 1986: 10–11).

Pressdee then uses a variation of the religious metaphor to sum up the "official" messages of the mall:

The images presented in the personal invitation to all in Elizabeth is then that of the cargo cult. Before us a lightshaft beams down from space, which contains the signs of the "future"; "Target", "Venture"—gifts wrapped; a table set for two. But beamed down from space they may as well be, because . . . this imagery can be viewed as reinforcing denial of the production process—goods are merely beamed to earth. The politics of their production and consumption disappear. (p. 12)

Yet his study showed that 80 percent of unemployed young people visited the mall at least once a week, and nearly 100 percent of young unemployed women were regular visitors. He comments on these uninvited guests:

For young people, especially the unemployed, there has been a congregating within these cathedrals of capitalism, where desires are created and fulfilled and the production of commodities, the very activity that they are barred from, is itself celebrated on the alter of consumerism. Young people, cut off from normal consumer power are invading the space of those with consumer power. (p. 13)

Pressdee's shift from the religious metaphor to one of warfare signals his shift of focus from the powerful to the disempowered.

Thursday nights, which in Australia are the only ones on which stores stay open late, have become the high points of shopping, when the malls are at their most crowded and the cash registers ring up their profits most busily, and it is on Thursday nights that the youth "invasion" of consumer territory is most aggressive. Pressdee (1986) describes this invasion vividly:

Thursday nights vibrate with youth, eager to show themselves:—it belongs to them, they have possessed it. This cultural response is neither spectacular nor based upon consumerism itself. Nor does it revolve around artifacts or dress, but rather around the possession of space, or to be more precise the possession of consumer space where their very presence challenges, offends and resists.

Hundreds of young people pour into the centre every Thursday night, with three or four hundred being present at any one time. They parade for several hours, not buying, but presenting, visually, all the contradictions of employment and unemployment, taking up their natural public space that brings both life and yet confronts the market place. Security men patrol all night aided by several police patrols, hip guns visible and radios in use, bringing a new understanding to law and order.

Groups of young people are continually evicted from this opulant and warm environment, fights appear, drugs seem plentiful, alcohol is brought in, in various guises and packages. The police close in on a group of young women, their drink is tested. Satisfied that it is only coca-cola they are moved on and out. Not wanted. Shopkeepers and shoppers complain. The security guards become agitated and begin to question all those seen drinking out of cans or bottles who are under 20, in the belief that they *must* contain alcohol. They appear frightened, totally outnumbered by young people as they continue their job in keeping the tills ringing and the passage to the altar both free and safe. (p. 14)

Pressdee coins the term "proletarian shopping" (p. 16) to describe this window shopping with no intention to buy. The youths consumed images and space instead of commodities, a kind of sensuous consumption that did not create profits. The positive pleasure of parading up and down, of offending "real" consumers and the agents of law and order, of asserting their difference within, and different use of, the cathedral of consumerism became an oppositional cultural practice.

The youths were "tricksters" in de Certeau's terms—they pleasurably exploited their knowledge of the official "rules of the game" in order to identify where these rules could be mocked, inverted, and thus used to free those they were designed to discipline. De Certeau (1984) points to the central importance of the "trickster" and the "guileful ruse" throughout peasant and folk cultures. Tricks and ruses are the art of the weak that enables them to exploit their understanding of the rules of the system, and to turn it to their advantage. They are a refusal to be subjugated:

> The actual order of things is precisely what "popular" tactics turn to their own ends, without any illusion that it will change any time soon. Though elsewhere it is exploited by a dominant power . . . here order is *tricked* by an art. (de Certeau 1984: 26)

This trickery is evidence of "an ethics of *tenacity* (countless ways of refusing to accord the established order the status of a law, a meaning or a fatality)" (p. 26).

Shopping malls are open invitations to trickery and tenacity. The youths who turn them into their meeting places, or who trick the security guards by putting alcohol into some, but only some, soda cans, are not actually behaving any differently from lunch hour window shoppers who browse through the stores, trying on goods, consuming and playing with images, with no intention to buy. In extreme weather people exploit the controlled climate of the malls for their own pleasure—mothers take children to play in their air-conditioned comfort in hot summers, and in winter older people use their concourses for daily walks. Indeed, some malls now have notices welcoming "mall walkers," and a few have even provided exercise areas set up with equipment and instructions so that the walkers can exercise more than their legs.

Of course, the mall owners are not entirely disinterested or altruistic here—they hope that some of the "tricky" users of the mall will become real economic consumers, but they have no control over who will, how many will, how often, or how profitably. One boutique owner told me that she estimated that 1 in 30 browsers actually bought something. Shopping malls are where the strategy of the powerful is most vulnerable to the tactical raids of the weak. And women are particularly adept guerrillas.

CONSUMING WOMEN

Bowlby (1987) takes as a premise "Women shop." Within this condensed truism, she finds a number of problems to do with the socially produced definitions of both women and shopping and with the connections between the two. While pondering some of these problems, I was browsing through a shop (where else?) selling cards and gifts. Three items took my eye. One was a bumper sticker proclaiming "When the going gets tough, the tough go shopping"; the second was a birthday card that said, "Happy Birthday to a guy who's sensitive, intelligent and fun to be with—if you liked to shop you'd be perfect"; the third was a card designed for no specific occasion whose front cover showed a stylish, modern young woman and the words "Work to Live, Live to Love, and Love to Shop, so you see . . . " the dots led to the inside and the words "if I can buy enough things I'll never have to work at love again."

These slogans are all commodities to be bought, and while from one perspective they may be yet more evidence of the power of consumerism to invade and take over our most personal lives in that they are seducing us to abrogate our ability to make our own utterances to a commercially motivated producer—the ultimate incorporation—we must recognize that these are not only commodities in the financial economy but also texts in the cultural economy. The meanings that are exchanged are in no way determined by the exchange of money at the cash register. Culturally all three are operating, with different emphases, in two semantic areas—those of gender difference and work versus leisure—and are questioning the distribution of power and values within them.

Each slogan is a feminine utterance, and each utterance depends for its effect upon its foregrounded difference from patriarchal norms. The bumper sticker sets its user apart as different from the "normal" (i.e., masculine) user of the saying's normal form—"When the going gets tough, the tough get going"—so as to distance her from its competitive masculinity (it is used typically to motivate sportsmen, soldiers, and, by extension, businessmen). In so doing, it manages simultaneously to mock such masculine power and to transfer it to a female practice, so that success in shopping becomes as much a source of power as success in sport, war, or business. Shopping entails achievement against a powerful oppositional force (that of capital) and the successful shopper is properly "tough." The user of such a slogan would pronounce "Women shop" in a quite different tone of voice from that used by, for instance, a dismissive patriarch. Shopping is seen as an oppositional, competitive act, and as such as a source of achievement, self-esteem, and power.

The uses of the message's masculine original deny the difference between work and leisure: masculinity is appropriately and equally achieved in sport, war, and work, and conflates these into the single category of the public domain, which it colonizes for the masculine, implicitly leaving the domestic or private for the feminine. Its feminine appropriation, then, speaks against the confinement of femininity to the domains of nonwork, nonpublic, and the "meaning" of the household, the meaning of the domestic, as the place of leisure, relaxation, and privacy—all of which are patriarchal meanings in that they deny the social, economic, and political meanings of the unwaged labor of women in the house.

Opposite the card shop was one selling kitchen equipment; hanging prominently in the window was an apron (the sign of women's domestic slavery) bearing the slogan "Woman's place is in the mall." Of course, one reading of this positions women as mere consumers in patriarchal capitalism, but the slogan also opposes "mall" to "home," and offers up oppositional meanings—if "home" means for women domestic slavery and the site of subordination of women to the demands of patriarchal capitalism exerted through the structure of the nuclear family, then the mall becomes the site of all the opposite, liberational meanings. The mall is where women can be public, empowered, and free, and can occupy roles other than those demanded by the nuclear family. Later on in this essay I will summarize Bowlby's arguments that the department store was the first public space that could legitimately be occupied by respectable women on their own, and Williamson's that buying can bear meanings of empowerment. Both of these arguments are clearly relevant to understanding the contradictory meanings of this apron and its slogan.

But my attention has wandered from the greeting cards. Both of the cards described above link shopping and romantic love as practices in which women excel and men are deficient. Even the "sensitive, intelligent" (i.e., nonjock) male recipient of the birthday card is incapable of understanding shopping. And for the other card, shopping has become, defiantly, the way to solve the problems faced by women in both work and love in a culture that patriarchally attempts to organize both in the interests of men. The conclusion, "If I can buy enough things I'll never have to work at love again," is nonsensical; it deliberately uses the logic of patriarchal capitalism to come to a nonsensical conclusion, the pleasure of which lies in exposing the nonsense for women of the dominant (i.e., patriarchal, capitalist) senses of commodities, work, and love.

The connection made by the two cards between shopping and romantic love may, at first sight, seem odd. But as capitalism developed throughout the nineteenth century it produced and naturalized first the nuclear family as the foundation social unit, and second a new and specific role for women within this unit and thus within the social formation at large. The woman became the domestic manager of both the economic and emotional resources of the family. The romance genre developed (see Chapter 5b) as a form of emotional training of women for their wifely role within the capitalist nuclear family. The development of the feminine as the sensitive, emotional, romantic gender was a direct product of the capitalist economy, so there are clear historical reasons for the interlinking of the romantic and the economic within the definition of the feminine that we have inherited from the nineteenth century.

The popular TV game show *The New Price Is Right* shares many characteristics with the slogans on the cards and bumper sticker. Most obviously it takes women's skills as household managers, their knowledge of commodity prices, and their ability to assess relative values, and gives to them the power and public visibility that patriarchy more normally reserves for the masculine. These skills and knowledges are taken out of the devalued feminine sphere of the domestic, and displayed, like masculine skills, in public, on a studio set before an enthusiastic studio audience and millions of TV viewers. In "normal" life, deploying these skills meets with little acclaim or self-esteem— the woman is expected to be a good household manager and all too frequently her role is noticed only when she is deemed to have failed in it. On *The New Price Is Right*, however, her skills and successes are not just acclaimed, but receive excessive applause and approbation from the excited studio audience. The excess provides a carnivalesque inversion of the more normal silence with which such skills are met in everyday life. Such silence is, of course, a means of subjugation, a form of discipline exerted by patriarchy over the feminine; their excessively noisy recognition is thus a moment of licensed liberation from the normal oppression, and women's pleasure in it derives from a recognition that such skills and knowledges can produce positive values despite their devaluation in the patriarchal everyday. *The New Price Is Right* and "When the going gets tough, the tough go shopping" are both cultural resources that can be used to speak and assert the feminine within and against a patriarchal "normality." Similarly, the inadequacy of the sensitive, intelligent birthday boy when it comes to shopping would debar him from success on *The New Price Is Right*.

Successful contestants on the show receive expensive commodities or cash as their prizes. In another carnivalesque and therefore political inversion, the woman's skills are rewarded not by spending less of the family money (i.e., that earned by the man), but by money or goods for *her*. Feminine skills do not just *husband* (*sic*) masculine earnings and thus benefit the family, but actually produce rewards for the women. Similarly, in the "live" versions of this and other games sometimes played in shopping malls, the entry "ticket" is typically a receipt from one of the shops in the mall. The proof of having spent opens up the chance of winning. The receipt as money is a carnivalesque inversion of economic subjugation.

The deep structure of values that underlies patriarchal capitalism now needs to be extended to include earning as typically masculine, and, therefore, spending as typically feminine. So it is not surprising that such a society addresses women as consumers and men as producers. We may summarize the value structure like this:

The Masculine	The Feminine
Public	Private (domestic and subjective)
Work	Leisure
Earning	Spending
Production	Consumption
Empowered	Disempowered
Freedom	Slavery

Bowlby (1987) makes some interesting points about how shopping enables women to cross the boundary between the public and the private. In her history of the Paris store Bon Marché and its origins at the end of the last century, Bowlby notes that the "diaries" the store gave to its customers as a form of promotion contained detailed information about how to reach the store by public transport:

> That this should have been practically available to the bourgeois lady marks a significant break with the past: department stores were in fact the first public places—other than churches or cathedrals—which were considered respectable for her to visit without a male companion. But this also signified, at another level, a stepping out from domestic bounds. (p. 189)

The value to women of a public space to which they had legitimate and safe access is not confined to the late nineteenth century. Ferrier (1987) makes a similar point about contemporary malls:

> For women there may be a sense of empowerment from their competency in shopping operations, their familiarity with the terrain and with what they can get out of it. The space is designed to facilitate their shopping practices, and in our built environment

there are few places designed for women. The shoppingtown offers public conveniences, free buses, parking, toilets, entertainment, free samples, competitions. In the shoppingtown, women have access to public space without the stigma or threat of the street. (p. 1)

She goes on to associate the freedom malls offer women to reject the gendered opposition of public versus domestic with the equal opportunities to reject the gendered opposition between work and leisure, and the economic one of for sale (i.e., public) versus bought (i.e., private):

The shoppingtown, with its carnival atmosphere, seems set to collapse the distinction between work and leisure. . . . The consumer is allowed to wander in and out of private space to look at, handle and try out products that she does not own. In a department store it is possible to wander through privately owned space, holding or wearing someone else's property as if it were your own, without asking to do so, often without even having to go through the usual social intercourse appropriate to being a guest in someone's place. Boundaries between public and private become ambiguous. (p. 2)

Women can find sources of empowerment both in "their" side of the structured values that patriarchy has provided for them (see above) and in their ability to escape the structure itself. Similarly, Bowlby (1985) finds evidence that spending the "man's" money can be a resisting act within the politics of marriage. She quotes a typical piece of advice given to a congressman's wife by Elizabeth Cady Stanton in her lectures in the 1850s:

Go out and buy a new stove! Buy what you need! Buy while he's in Washington! When he returns and flies into a rage, you sit in a corner and weep. That will soften him! Then, when he tastes his food from the new stove, he will know you did the wise thing. When he sees you so much fresher, happier in your new kitchen, he will be delighted and the bills will be paid. I repeat—GO OUT AND BUY!

Bowlby comments:

Significantly, the injunction to buy comes from woman to woman, not from a man, and involves first bypassing and then mollifying a male authority. To "go out" and buy invokes a relative emancipation in women's active role as consumers. (p. 22)

This is an example of de Certeau's (1984) dictum that subordinated people "make do with what they have," and if the only economic power accorded to women is that of spending, then being a woman in patriarchy necessarily will involve feminine "tricks" that turn the system back on itself, that enable the weak to use the resources provided by the strong in their own interests, and to oppose the interests of those who provided the resources in the first place.

In the same way that language need not be used to maintain the social relations that produced it, so too commodities need not be used solely to support the economic system of capitalism, nor need the resources provided by patriarchy go solely to the support of the system. The conditions of production of any cultural system are not the same as, and do not predetermine, the conditions of its use or consumption.

The gendered structure of values given above constitutes not only a way of constructing the social meanings of gender and of inserting those meanings into social domains, but also a means of discipline through knowledge. The "knowledge" that, for instance, femininity finds its meanings in the domestic, in consumption, in leisure, in the disempowered, is a means of disciplining women into the roles and values that patriarchy has inscribed for them. Yet shopping, while apparently addressing women precisely as disempowered domestic consumers, may actually offer opportunities to break free not just from these meanings, but from the structure of binary oppositions that produces them. So Ferrier (1987) can argue:

It seems that the successful consumer system must have ambiguous boundaries; between leisure and work, public and private space, inside and out, desire and satisfaction, to attract consumers and to make shopping pleasurable. The shoppingtown is in some ways an extension of the consumer's domestic space, and at the same time a totally separate "new world". As Hartley (1983) points out, power resides in the interface between individuals in ambiguous boundaries. In the ambiguous boundaries of the shoppingtown, there is space for fantasy, for inversions, for pleasure. The pleasure and power are linked with the acts of transgression that are sanctioned. (p. 4)

COMMODITIES AND WOMEN

Judith Williamson (1986a) incisively analyses the problems that left-wing cultural critics face when grappling with what she calls "the politics of consumption." She argues that in our society the conditions of production are ones over which people have no control, no choice about if or where to work, or about the conditions under which to work; consumption, however, offers some means of coping with the frustrations of capitalist conditions of production. It thus serves both the economic interests of the producers and the cultural interests of the consumers while not completely separating the two. The cultural interests of the consumers are essentially, Williamson argues, ones of control. Mainly this is a sense of control over meanings: "The conscious chosen meaning in most people's lives comes much more from what they consume than what they produce" (p. 230). Consumption, then, offers a sense of control over communal meanings of oneself and social relations, it offers a means of controlling to some extent the context of everyday life. The widespread use of VCRs is a case in point. In Morley's 1986 study of lower-middle- and working-class families' use of TV, he found that every household, even those with no wage earners, owned a VCR, which was used both to time-shift TV programs and to play rented films: in the first case the VCR allowed control over scheduling, in the second it allowed control over programming.

Williamson (1986a) argues that in a capitalist society buying and ownership not only offer a sense of control, but form the main, if not the only, means of achieving this:

> Ownership is at present the *only* form of control legitimized in our culture. Any serious attempts at controlling products from the other side—as with the miners' demand to control the future of *their* product, coal (or the printing unions' attempts to control their product, newspaper articles, etc.) are not endorsed. Some parts of the left find these struggles less riveting than the struggles over meanings in street style. Yet underlying *both* struggles is the need for people to control their environment and produce their own communal identity; it is just that the former, if won, could actually fulfil that need while the latter ultimately never will. (p. 231)

It is also worth noting not only that the pleasures of control are found in the ownership of commodities through which people can create or modify the context of everyday life and thus many of the meanings it bears, but also that the consumer's moment of choice is an empowered moment. If money is power in capitalism, then buying, particularly if the act is voluntary, is an empowering moment for those whom the economic system otherwise subordinates. And any one single act of buying necessarily involves multiple acts of rejection—many commodities are rejected for every one chosen, and rejecting the offerings of the system constitutes adopting a controlling relationship to it. The following anecdote related to me by a woman shopper is both typical and significant:

double think

> When I was a girl my mother would sometimes take me to the shopping town to go shopping for shoes. She'd spend hours in the shoe shop trying on dozens of pairs, having the assistant running backwards and forwards nonstop. Eventually she'd choose one pair to take home, but I knew she wouldn't buy them, she'd always return them next day saying they didn't fit or weren't right or something.

My informant's apparent embarrassment at the "exploitation" of the shop assistant indicates that she understood the relations between her mother and the assistant at the personal level; her mother, however, was operating on the level of the system, the relationships were those between consumer and producer/distributor, and her pleasure was caused by her empowered position in this relationship. These shopping expeditions were "tactical raids" (de Certeau 1984) upon the system, or a highly developed form of "proletarian shopping" (Pressdee 1986).

But there is another dimension of meaning to this anecdote that can also be traced in Williamson's comparison of the context of production with that of consumption, and that is one of class meanings. The woman telling me the anecdote also characterized her mother as traditionally middle-class, so part of her lack of embarrassment over her treatment of the shop assistant can be explained in terms of mistress-servant class relations, and thus appears less politically acceptable than when it is seen as a tactical raid upon the system.

This raises the suggestion that production may be essentially proletarian and consumption bourgeois. The attempt to control the context of production poses a radical threat to capitalism because it positions proletarian interests in direct, naked, uncompromising conflict with bourgeois interests; it thus invites (and receives) the full weight of the bourgeois ideological and repressive state apparatuses to control and ultimately squash it. The social allegiances formed when aligning oneself with those subordinated by the conditions of production are with those most severely subordinated by capitalism, and therefore those whose struggles are least likely to succeed.

Consumption, however, is more a bourgeois act; it appears to support, rather than threaten, bourgeois values, and by forging these social allegiances, the weak do not invite the repressive attentions of the strong, but can catch them "off guard," as it were. Guerrilla tactics are often most successful when the guerrillas do not wear the uniform of "the enemy." Shopping can never be a radical, subversive act; it can never change the system of a capitalist-consumerist economy. Equally, however, it cannot be adequately explained as a mere capitulation to the system. Williamson's (1986a) key point here is that commodities are furnished by market capitalism, and in themselves cannot be radical; but, she argues, traces of radicalism are to be found in the *way* they are consumed and the needs that underlie their consumption: "What *are* potentially radical are the needs that underlie their use: needs both sharpened and denied by the economic system that makes them" (p. 232).

Stedman-Jones (1982), in his study of the culture of the London working classes in the nineteenth and early twentieth centuries, gives us further evidence of this use of commodities not to express radicalism itself, but to meet a need that is potentially radical:

> More generally, evidence about patterns of spending among the London poor suggests that a concern to demonstrate self-respect was infinitely more important than any forms of saving based upon calculations of utility. When money was available which did not have to be spent on necessities, it was used to purchase articles for display rather than articles of use. (p. 101)

The need for "display" is a need for self-esteem and respect that is denied by the conditions of production, but that may be met by the conditions of consumption. This display may involve the purchase of "middle-class" commodities, and thus give the appearance of buying into middle-class values and the social system that advantages them, but Stedman-Jones takes pains to point out that this is not so:

> For the poor, this effort to keep up appearances, to demonstrate "respectability" entailed as careful a management of the weekly family budget as any charity organizer could have envisaged. But its priorities were quite different. "Respectability" did not mean church attendance, teetotalism or the possession of a post office savings account. It meant the possession of a presentable Sunday suit, and the ability to be seen wearing it. . . .
>
> It is clear from these and other accounts that the priorities of expenditure among the poor bore little relation to the ambitions set before them by advocates of thrift and self-help. (p. 102)

The meanings of a respectable suit for the poor are quite different from those for the affluent, even though the appearance of the poor man's suit may derive many features from that worn by his "social betters." The point is that the meanings of commodities do not lie in themselves as objects, and are not determined by their conditions of production or distribution, but are produced finally by the way they are consumed. The ways and the whys of consumption are where cultural meanings are made and circulated; the system of production and distribution provides the signifiers only.

In his ethnographic study of Bostonian Italians in the West End, Gans (1962) found similar patterns of consumption. He found that display of self through clothes was as common among West Enders as among other working-class groups, and that they were adept at making their own fashions out of what the fashion system provided:

> At the time of the study, for example, the "Ivy League" style was beginning to be seen among the young men of the West End. Their version of this style, however, bore little resemblance to that worn on the Harvard campus: flannel colors were darker, shirts and ties

were much brighter, and the belt in the back of the pants was more significant in size if not in function. (p. 185)

Gans's description of this style as "informal and jaunty" points to its "display." It would seem that self-display is, for those denied social power, a performance of their ability to be different, of their power to construct their meanings from the resources of the system. It has within it elements of defiance and of pride in self- and subcultural identities, and it is pleasurable insofar as it is a means of controlling social relations and one's cultural environment. There is a sense of freedom underlying display, and it is this that frequently attracts the disapproval of the middle classes, who are prone to label such performance as vulgar or tasteless. Gans finds that the car contains all these cultural meanings and pleasures for the West Enders:

> The automobile, for example, serves as an important mode of self-expression to the male West Ender—as it does to many other working-class Americans: it displays his strength and his taste. When the man has the money—and the freedom to spend it—he thus will buy the most powerful automobile he can afford, and will decorate it with as many accessories as possible. The size of the car and the power of its motor express his toughness; the accessories, the carefully preserved finish, and chrome are an extension of the self he displays to the peer group. (p. 184)

The complexity and subtlety of the roles played by commodities in our culture are all too easily dismissed by the concept of a "consumer society." In one sense all societies are consumer societies, for all societies value goods for cultural meanings that extend far beyond their usefulness. In this context, Marx's distinction between use-value and exchange-value is less than helpful, for it suggests a difference between a "real" value, that of the material and human labor in goods, and a "false" value that society gives to commodities as it exchanges them.

Baudrillard (1981) claims that the ultimate effect of capitalism, certainly of its late variant in which we currently live, is to confuse the relationship of use-value and exchange-value, and, in fact, to turn a system of use-values into one of exchange-values. Exchange-values are culturally useful: "Through objects, each individual and each group searches out his-her place in an order" (p. 83). The function of commodities, then, is not just to meet individual needs, but also to relate the individual to the social order. Consumption is not just the end-point of the economic chain that began with production, but a system of exchange, a language in which commodities are goods to think with in a semiotic system that precedes the individual, as does any language. For Baudrillard there is no self-contained individual, there are only ways of using social systems, particularly those of language, goods, and kinship, to relate people differently to the social order and thus to construct the sense of the individual.

Sinclair (1987) points out that Baudrillard's poststructuralist account of the meaning of commodities differs from the more structuralist and Marxist ones of Williamson in an earlier work (1978) and Leiss (1978), both of whom conceive

> of a system of persons on one hand made to correspond to a system of goods on the other, with individual subjects finding it increasingly difficult to maintain a coherent sense of unified identity as the satisfaction of their needs becomes ever more fragmented by greater product differentiation. (Sinclair 1987: 55)

Williamson's later work reverses this emphasis, and traces ways in which people can make meanings out of the commodity system, rather than, as here, having their meanings of themselves made for them by that system.

The semiotic function of goods is stressed even more strongly by Douglas and Isherwood (1979), who argue that "consumption is the very arena in which culture is fought over and licked into shape" (p. 57), and that goods "are needed for making visible and stable the categories of culture" (p. 59). They conclude:

> Enjoyment of physical consumption is only part of the service yielded by goods; the other part is the enjoyment of sharing names. . . . Physical consumption involves proving, testing or demonstrating that the experience in question is feasible. But the anthropological argument insists that by far the greater part of utility is yielded not at proving but in sharing names that have been learned and graded. This is culture. (pp. 75–76; quoted in Sinclair 1987: 56)

The important point made by Douglas and Isherwood is that people constantly strive not just to gain access to cultural meaning systems, but rather to exert control over the meanings such systems can produce. Consumption then becomes a way of using the commodity system that gives the consumer some degree of control over the meanings it makes possible. Commodities are not just objects of economic exchange; they are goods to think with, goods to speak with.

> Every society has some kind of map, a grid of the terms available to think in at any given time. In ours, consumer goods are just some of the chief landmarks which define the "natural" categories we are accustomed to. (Williamson 1986a: 227)

Speech and thought, of course, are finally social practices, ways of relating to the social order. Products therefore "map out the social world, defining, not what we do, but the ways in which we can conceive of doing things" (Williamson 1986a: 226). The crucial point that Williamson makes is that

> the world of consumerism is the one we live in—it is too late to opt out: but there are two important questions—one, what we say in the language available, the other, what that language itself means.
>
> For the meanings and uses of products cannot be entirely controlled; they can be appropriated and turned around on the society which produces them. (p. 226)

The active semiotic use of commodities blurs the distinction between use-value and exchange-value, and that between materially based and socially produced values, for all values are arbitrary. The values of commodities can be transformed by the practices of their users, as can those of language, for as language can have no fixed reference point in a universal reality, neither can commodities have final values fixed in their materiality. The practices of the users of a system not only can exploit its potential, but can modify the system itself. In the practices of consumption the commodity system is exposed to the power of the consumer, for the power of the system is not just top-down, or center-outward, but always two-way, always a flux of conflicting powers and resistances.

Consumption is not necessarily evidence of the desire for ownership of commodities for its own sake (that is the dominant ideological meaning of ownership), but is rather a symptom of the need for control, for cultural autonomy and for security that the economic system denies subordinated peoples. While agreeing strongly with Williamson that the problem facing the left is not how to turn people away from consumerism, but how to devise new ways in which the legitimate, and admirable, needs and desires appropriated by consumer goods can be met, we must also recognize that, until (if) the revolution comes, the left does not help its cause by devaluing, denigrating, or ignoring the "art of making do," the everyday practices by which people in subordinated social formations win tricks against the system. Nor can we adequately or productively explain such tricks through the inoculation model (Barthes 1973), by which the system takes controlled doses of the disease of radicalism into itself in order finally to strengthen its resistance to it. At the very least such tricks are tactical victories that maintain the morale of the subordinate, and may well produce real gains in their cultural and social experience.

The desire to investigate the practices of making do, wherein can be found the cunning, the creativity, and the power of the subordinate, has been part of a shift in academia that has transformed much of academic theory and research over the past few years. In this shift some feminist scholarship and popular cultural theory come together to partake in a general academic shift of emphasis away from the "grand narrative" toward the particular, away from the text to the reading, away from the speech system toward the utterance, away from ideology and hegemony to the everyday practices of the subordinate. This shift may be summed up as the movement of interest from structures to practices, "from the totalizing structures and mechanisms of power to the heterogeneous practices of everyday life" (Ferrier 1987: 2).

Feminist scholarship has been particularly acute in exposing both the broad structures of patriarchy and the minutiae within which they are embodied. Similarly, Marxian scholarship has exposed the structures and practices of ideology and hegemony, and structuralism and psychoanalysis have done equally important work on the structures of language and subjectivity. As our understanding of these totalizing structures has become more sophisticated and more satisfying, so the realization is growing that this knowledge tells us only half the story, and of itself it can induce only a pessimistic elitism. It requires an often contradictory, sometimes complementary, knowledge of the everyday practices by which subordinated groups negotiate these structures, oppose and challenge them, evade their control, exploit their weaknesses, trick them, turn them against themselves and their producers.

Women, despite the wide variety of social formations to which they belong, all share the experience of subordination under patriarchy and have evolved a variety of tactical responses that enable them to deal with it on a day-to-day level. So, too, other subordinated groups, however defined—by class, race, age, religion, or whatever—have evolved everyday practices that enable them to live within and against the forces that subordinate them. Scholarship that neglects or devalues these practices seems to me to be guilty of a disrespect for the weak that is politically reprehensible. This is particularly the case in certain strands of Marxian or feminist scholarship that end up in the position of despising—or, at least, looking down on—those for whom they attempt to speak, and those whose sociopolitical interests they claim to promote. Similarly, studies of popular culture that are optimistic and positive, rather than pessimistic and negative, frequently celebrate the ritual functions of popular texts and thus deny or ignore the ability of disempowered groups to make *their* popular culture, often by oppositional practices, out of industrially provided and distributed cultural resources. Such work has traditionally drawn upon anthropological models (those of Turner or Levi-Strauss) or rhetorical ones (e.g., Burke) to reveal and explain the ritualistic structures of popular culture. In this approach the shift of emphasis from structures to practices has resulted in the move from structural anthropology to cultural ethnography.

CONSPICUOUS CONSUMPTION

One of the commonest practices of the consumer is window shopping, a consumption of images, an imaginative if imaginary use of the language of commodities that may or may not turn into the purchase of actual commodities. This "proletarian shopping" is closely bound up with the power of looking. As Madonna (see Chapter 5a) controls her "look," that is, how she looks to others and therefore how they look upon her, so the window shopper searches a visual vocabulary from which to make statements about herself and her social relations. Looking is as much a means of exerting social control as speaking. Elsewhere, I have argued that shopping malls are a visual feast, a plethora of potential meanings, palaces of pleasures offered particularly to women (Fiske et al. 1987). The connections among femininity, women's subordination in patriarchy, and looking have been well theorized, particularly in regard to film and advertising. In patriarchy, the woman has been constructed as the object of the masculine voyeuristic look, which places him in a position of power over her and gives him possession of her, or at least of her image. Women's narcissistic pleasure, then, lies in seeing themselves as idealized objects of the male gaze; a woman is always the bearer of her own image, sees herself through the eyes of the other. While there is much evidence, particularly in cinema, to support this theory of the gender politics of looking, its ability to explain the pleasures of shopping, of the use of commodities to construct images of self, is more limited.

Despite the fact that the language of fashion shows strong patriarchal characteristics as it swings its focus around the female body—now emphasizing the bust, now the buttocks, now the legs or the waist, but always guiding the eye toward the eroticized areas—the meaning of fashion for women cannot be reduced to such political simplicity, nor can the pleasures offered to women by their own bodies be adequately explained by the giving of pleasure to the masculine other. The pleasure of the look is not just the pleasure of looking good for the male, but rather of controlling how one looks and therefore of controlling the look of others upon oneself. Looking makes meanings; it is therefore a means of entering social relations, of inserting oneself into the social order in general, and of controlling one's immediate social relations in particular. Commodities are the resources of the woman (or man) who is exercising some control over her look, her social relations, and her relation to the social order. The Madonna "wanna-bes" who buy fingerless lacey gloves are not buying the meanings these items would have, for instance, at a Buckingham Palace garden party—they are buying a cultural resource out of which to make their own meanings, to make a statement about their own subcultural identity and thus about their relationship to the social order. It is unhelpful to denigrate such a visual speech act by saying that it is pseudospeech or severely limited speech, in that the language of commodities only allows all the fans to say the same thing.

A number of points need raising in response to this criticism. The first is that if commodities speak class identities rather than individual identities, this does not mean that they are necessarily an inferior language system; such a criticism derives from the ideology of individualism and denies, first, the extent to which individual inflections of class meanings can be made within the commodity system (see the discussion on taste and style below), and, second, the extent to which class meanings are spoken by verbal language, however "creatively" or "originally" it may be used. All language systems relate the user to the social order and thus to others who share that or a similar relationship, at the same time they allow concrete and specific differences in their use by each person. The pleasures of linguistic control traverse the realms of the personal and the social. The pleasures and meanings offered by the plenitude of goods in shopping malls are multiple, and bear the dominant ideology while offering considerable scope for cultural maneuver within and against it. On the economic level such glittering excess provides a daily demonstration that the capitalist system works, and on the ideological level that individualism can flourish within it. A wide consumer choice is not an economic requirement, but a requirement of the ideology of individualism. But exercising choice is not just "buying into" the system: choice also enhances the power of the subordinate to make their cultural uses of it.

Two people wearing the same clothes, or furnishing their houses in the same way, are embarrassed to the extent that they feel that their similarity of taste has denied their individual differences, for the centrality of individualism in our ideology gives priority to these meanings rather than to ones of social or class allegiance. It is not surprising, then, that one of our commonest ways of marking the difference between capitalist and communist societies is by the commodity system and consumer choice. Westerners typically mythologize communist societies as providing very limited consumer choice, and, therefore, of producing a gray, undifferentiated mass of people, instead of the vibrant individuals of the West. The "sheeplike" nature of such people, which leads them to accept such a totalitarian social system, is mapped out inconically in their monotonous grayness, resulting from the lack of consumer choice. Because style and taste have, according to this capitalist myth, no role in a communist system that denies its people the language of commodities as it denies them individual "freedom," then the people in such a system have no control over their social relations, no way of varying or determining their points of entry into the social order.

It is therefore essential for capitalist shopping centers to emphasize the plenitude of commodities—goods tumble over each other in a never-ending plethora of objects, a huge cultural resource bank. Of course, such a plenitude of differences can exist only within an overall similarity—all the goods are, after all, produced at the same historical moment by the same capitalist society—but any sense of individuality is constructed, as are all meanings, upon the play of similarity and difference. Similarity is the means of entry into the social order; difference negotiates the space of the individual within that order.

The difference between style and taste is never easy to define, but style tends to be centered on the social, and taste upon the individual. Style then works along axes of similarity to identify group membership, to relate to the social order; taste works within style to differentiate and construct the individual. Style speaks about social factors such as class, age, and other more flexible, less definable social formations; taste talks of the individual inflection of the social.

Such an interplay of style and taste is given spatial representation in Sydney's Centrepoint. Its three levels are class determined, but within each level is a huge variety of commodities. Individuality is a construction of the social, of language, of gendered experience, of family, education, and so on; commodities are used to bear the already constructed sense of individual difference. They are no truer and no falser than our idiolect, our accent, our ways of behaving toward others in the family, and so on. All such markers of individual difference are social, commodities no more and no less than any other. So the class-differential levels of Centrepoint are used by people whose identity already, necessarily, contains class meanings, and riding the escalators through them becomes a concrete metaphor for class mobility. In late capitalist societies blue-collar workers can earn as much, if not more, than white- or pink-collar workers, so style and taste displace economics as markers of class identity and difference. And insofar as style/taste is symbolic and clearly arbitrary, with little of the material base of the economic, it becomes less determined, more open to negotiation: class identities based on economics offer little scope for negotiation; those based on style are not only more flexible, but also offer the consumer greater control in their construction.

In an earlier study, my colleagues and I argued that in Centrepoint class markers are found in the location of shops within the overall structure and in their design, both of which are spatial metaphors for social relations (see Fiske et al. 1987) The most "democratic" shops—those with low-priced goods that appeal to everyone, such as news agents, card shops, and pharmacies—are on the lowest level and tend not to have windows, but open fronts so the boundaries between their territory and the public concourse are leaky; their goods spill over into the pedestrian areas, minimizing the distinction between the public-democratic and the private-exclusive. On the "middle-class" level—that of the medium-priced, trendy fashion shops selling clothes, shoes, bags, and accessories—the shops mark their boundaries a little more clearly, but not exclusively. They have windows, but racks of shoes or T-shirts often push out onto the concourse. And the windows are packed full of goods, tastefully arranged according to color and style, but bursting with them. They offer a plenitude of differences, a bottomless cup of resources for individual tastes to draw upon. These windows, too, reveal the shop: the multitude of goods in the windows never obscures the even greater number of goods within the shop itself. The lighting of both the shop and the windows is bright and cleverly designed to give an identity to the shop that differentiates it from others and from the concourse. As different individuals construct their images within the similarity of fashion, so different shops construct their identity, frequently by the use of lighting and color, within the overall stylistic unity of the shopping center. Window shopping involves a seemingly casual, but actually purposeful, wandering from shop to shop, which means wandering from potential identity to potential identity until a shop identity is found that matches the individual identity, or, rather, that offers the means to construct that identity. The windows and lighting of these middle-range shops create an identity for them that differentiates them from each other and from the public areas, but then opens them up; their brightness invites the gaze, invites the browser inside.

The "democratic" shops do not stress their own identity, do not differentiate themselves so clearly either from each other or from the public areas. The "middle-class" shops identify themselves as different, but as available to all who have the taste to want the identity they offer. The importance of individual differences increases as we ride the elevators up the class structure. So the "upper-class" shops are individualistic to the point of exclusivity. Their windows have fewer goods in them, signaling the opposite of mass availability; their lighting is more subdued, with highlights on the individual commodity, and the shop behind the window is much less easily seen—sometimes, indeed, it is invisible. The contrast in lighting styles between the middle- and upper-class windows is a contrast in class taste and social identity. The highlight on the exclusive commodity, a fur coat or a haute-couture dress, suggests that the wearer will be in the spotlight, picked out from the others. The overall bright lighting in the middle-class windows suggests that the wearers of the commodities within them will be members of the group that shares that style and taste. In theatrical terms, it is the difference between lighting the star and lighting the chorus line. The windows of these upscale shops exclude the mass viewer and signal the limited availability of their commodities, and thus of the identities they offer.

Centrepoint uses vertical differentiation to materialize class difference, a typical instance of the bourgeois ideological practice of conceptualizing classes as though they existed in a spatial, rather than a social, relationship to each other. So the upper-class shops are "naturally" on the highest floor, the "democratic" ones "naturally" on the lowest. This is a good example of how language constructs rather than reflects social reality, for there is no logical reason, if we wish to conceptualize the relationships among classes in spatial terms, that we should not use, for example, *right, center*, and *left*. There may not be a logical reason for our culture's selection of the metaphor here, but there is, of course, an ideological one. Using right, center, and left as a metaphor would suggest both the arbitrary nature of class differences and their political dimension, whereas using upper, middle, and lower grounds these differences in material reality and makes them appear natural. It also gives them a natural value system—as Lakoff and Johnson (1980) have shown, *up* in our culture is good (it is, after all, where God is) and *down* is bad. The spatial up-down metaphor that we commonly use to express moral and social values has been (literally) made concrete by Centrepoint's system of levels.

PROGRESS AND THE NEW

A key feature of the styles on offer is newness, and shopping malls emphasize newness over almost any other characteristic. The plethora of shiny surfaces, the bright lights, the pervasive use of glass and mirrors all serve to make both the commodities and the center itself appear brand new, as though minted yesterday. In Centrepoint (Sydney) and Carillon (Perth) everything is squeaky clean, never a smear or finger mark on the acres of plate glass, never a dull patch on the shiny walls or ceiling. It all adds up to an overwhelming image of newness, a space with no place for the old, the shabby, the worn—no place for the past, only an invitation to the future. So the publicity for Centrepoint and Carillon is dotted with words like *trend, new, fashion, now, today*; newness and "nowness" mark the threshold of the future, not the culmination of the past.

Newness, of course, is central to the economic and ideological interests of capitalism: the desire for the new keeps the production processes turning and the money flowing toward the producers and distributors. The fashion industry has been frequently and accurately criticized for creating artificial newness and therefore artificial obsolescence to further its own economic interests, and, implicitly, to work against the interests of its consumers. Such a criticism, accurate as far as it goes, does not go far enough, for it fails to question why consumers, largely women, continue to want the new, if this desire is totally against their own interests. The "cultural dope" theory would have to work enormously, not to say impossibly, hard to offer a finally convincing explanation of this.

The desire to be up to date, and there is plenty of evidence that it is a common desire, cannot be created entirely by slick publicity, for advertising can only harness and shape socially created desires, it cannot create them from scratch. At the ideological level, the origins of the desire for the new can be traced back to the ideology of progress that has pervaded the economic, political, and moral domains of post-Renaissance Christian capitalist democracies. Such Western societies see time as linear, forward moving and inevitably productive of change. The forward movement of time and the changes it brings are then made social sense of by the concept of progress, improvement, and development. Other societies in which time is seen as circular rather than linear give a quite different value to the relationships among the past, the present, and the future, and make a quite different sense of newness.

But, of course, ideologies do not suit all groups in a society equally well; indeed, it is their function not to do so. The sense of pleasure or satisfaction occasioned by progress achieved is not equally available to all; rather, it is most "naturally" accessible to the mature, white, middle-class male, and becomes progressively less available as social groups are distanced from the ideological norm. The life opportunities available to, for instance, a young, black, working-class female offer limited chances of experiencing the pleasures of progress achieved, yet people of such a group experience the same ideology of progress as do the "successful."

There is, I suggest, an inverse relationship between the possession of a job that offers the pleasures of progress achieved and the seeking of alternative inflections of these pleasures in trendy fashions and the desire to be up to date. Chodorow (1978), for instance, has argued that men's jobs in patriarchy have tended to be goal-oriented and to offer a sense of achievement, of a job done. Women's jobs, on the other hand, tend to be repetitious and circular, of which domestic labor is the prime example and secretarial labor the commercial equivalent. Chodorow's emphasis on gender difference, however, leads her to neglect class, age, and race differences within men (and women)—so it is the mature, white, middle-class male who is most likely to have the sort of job that Chodorow characterizes as men's. It is also likely that such a man will have conservative tastes in fashion, and will not find pleasure in up-to-dateness; indeed, he will often avoid it. For women, on the other hand, who are likely to have the nonprogressive, nonachieving job of wife-mother, or, if in the work force, are likely to be in more routine, more repetitive jobs, it may be that participation in fashion is their prime, if not their only, means of participating in the ideology of progress. And because progress and the new have been masculinized, the pleasures they offer can receive public acclaim and validation. The stereotype of the dowdy housewife who has "let herself go" is encumbered with negative values partly because she is seen to have missed out on both the progressive and the public.

For a woman in patriarchy, commodities that enable her to be "in fashion" enable her to relate to the social order in a way that grants her access to the progressive and the public. Such a move may not be radical in that it does not challenge the right of patriarchy to offer these pleasures to men more readily than women, but it can be seen as both progressive and empowering insofar as it opens up masculine pleasures to women. Just as the department store was the first public space legitimately available to women, so the fashionable commodities it offers provide a legimated public identity and a means of participating in the ideology of progress.

Similarly, many youth subcultures, for both genders, are characterized by a strong desire for up-to-date tastes, in dress and music particularly. Those whose position in the social system denies them the sort of goal achievements of middle-class jobs frequently turn to style and fashion both as a source of pleasure and as a means of establishing themselves in a controlling rather than dependent relationship to the social order. By the imaginative use of commodities, young people can and do make themselves into icons of street art (Chambers 1986). Commodities provided by an industrialized culture can be used for subcultural, resisting purposes (Hebdige 1979).

So the greeting cards discussed earlier in this chapter are not merely silly. In "Work to Live, Live to Love, and Love to Shop," the female speaker recognizes that working, loving, and shopping are all ways of forming social relations; the utterance inside the card—"If I can buy enough things I'll never have to work at love again"—recognizes that patriarchy's grip on working and love is tighter than its grip on shopping. Thus it is that buying commodities offers a sense of freedom, however irrational, from the work involved in working and loving under patriarchy: working and loving are conflated as chores from which shopping offers an escape.

CHAPTER 3

Reading the Beach

Semiotically, the beach can be read as a text, and by *text* I mean a signifying construct of potential meanings operating on a number of levels. Like all texts, the beach has an author—not, admittedly, a named individual, but a historically determined set of community practices that have produced material objects or signs. By these I mean the beach-side buildings, the changing rooms, the lawns, the esplanades, the vendors' kiosks, the regulatory notices, the steps and benches, the flags and litter bins—all these items whose foregrounded functional dimensions should not blind us to their signifying ones. Like all texts, beaches have readers. People use beaches to seek out certain kinds of meaning for themselves, meanings that help them come to terms with their off-beach, normal life-style. As with other texts, these meanings are determined partly by the structure of the text itself, partly by the social characteristics and discursive practices of the reader—different people use the beach differently, that is, they find different meanings in it, but there is a core of meanings that all users, from respectable suburban family to long-haired dropout surfer, share to a greater or lesser extent.

The beach is an anomalous category between land and sea that is neither one nor the other but has characteristics of both. This means that it has simply too much meaning, an excess of meaning potential, that derives from its status as anomalous. In tribal societies this overflow of meaning on the anomalous is controlled by designating it as sacred or taboo. In our more diverse society the control is exercised less magically, though no less authoritatively. The beach is the place where we go on holidays (Holy Days), a place and time that is neither home nor work, outside the profane normality, and it occupies a similar, if less intensely felt, place in our society as festivals did in earlier ones.

The geographical opposition between land and sea may not be as important for Australians as it was for the maker of Genesis; for us huddled in the developed, urbanized fringe of the continent it is best articulated as City and Sea, or Culture and Nature. The geographical opposition has no meaning until our ideology imposes one, and then it serves to naturalize the ideological. Lévi-Strauss's work demonstrates how all cultures are concerned to articulate this distinction between nature and culture in one way or another, and thus make meanings in and for the culture. I am concerned with how these meanings are articulated in Australia in general and Perth in particular.

But Lévi-Strauss's work also requires us to define the difference between nature and the natural. Nature is pre-cultural reality. It is that external world before any cultural perception or sense-making process has been applied to it. But the natural is what culture makes of nature. In other words, the natural is a cultural product, and nature exists only as a conceptual opposition to culture.

Let us start with the beach as a physically anomalous category between land and sea. Man wishes to mediate this big binary

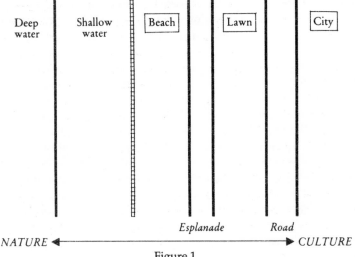

Figure 1

opposition for reasons to do with comfort and the avoidance of terror (motives that gave rise to the creation of Jesus Christ, after all) and so he overlaps the physical structure of Land/Sea with the social structure of Nature/Culture, where he can create mediating categories that are both physical and social. The land, then, becomes culture, the city, civilization; the sea becomes nature, untamed, uncivilized, raw. The beach mediates this terrifying boundary. Figure 1 shows diagrammatically how this is achieved. This is a diagrammatic representation of the structure of a particular beach in Perth, which I will elaborate and name later; for the moment, I wish its anonymity to signal its typicality.

The move from culture, the city, on the right to nature, the sea, on the left is effected through a number of zones. First there is the road, the public site of transition, and the boundary beyond which the car, that crucial cultural motif, cannot pass. Next comes grass, or, more typically and significantly, lawn. Lawns invoke the natural, not nature: the grass is controlled, cropped like a carpet. Lawns are anomalous, mediating between indoors and outdoors, so it is appropriate that on them we find "furniture"—benches that are either painted green to look "natural" or left as "natural" wood. The lawn is the most cultured bit of the beach and is typically used by the old, who need the security of culture, or by the incorrigibly suburban, who import their chairs, tables, rugs, trannies, and sometimes even television to make the outdoors as much like indoors as possible. For most, however, it is an easy transition toward nature, though we will find the occasional "sunbaker" here. The edge of the lawn is marked by an esplanade, a concrete flat-topped wall that marks the boundary beyond which the sea is not allowed to come; like all boundaries, it is a popular place to walk, a moment of balance in a sacred no-man's land outside profane normality. (Notice how joggers patrol the edge of the sea or the banks of the river—and no activity is currently more anomalous than jogging—sacred to some, totally taboo to others.)

By crossing the esplanade we reach the beach, the anomalous category between land and sea, but on the nature side of the Nature/Culture opposition—the fit between the physical and social is good, but significantly not perfect. We need, it would appear, to conceptualize the beach as nearer nature than culture: the beach is natural, whereas the lawn is cultural.

The beach itself tends to be divided by us into significant zones, both horizontally and vertically. These zones are vague, the boundaries ill marked, if not unmarked, and consequently the meanings, the categories, leak one into the other. Just under the esplanade is one narrow zone that provides a set of meanings that serves different functions for at least two very different sorts of people. What they have in common is a negative: they do not see swimming as the main purpose of their visit to the beach (and swimming is the furthest man can penetrate into nature). One group is the dressed mothers and fathers with the undressed children—this is really a group most typically found on the lawn, for whom the meaning of the beach is centered on the home and family (i.e., culture) rather than on nature. The other group is that of the sunbakers, and their meaning, though articulated differently, is surprisingly similar to the suburban family's.

A tan is an anomalous category between *skin* (human, culture) and *fur* (animal, nature). A tanned body is a sign to be read by others, particularly others in the city. It signifies that the wearer, a city dweller, has been into nature and is bringing back both the physical health of the animal and the mental health that contact with nature brings into the artificiality of city life.

The first signifying function of the tan is to bring the natural into culture. The natural, we remember, is not nature, but the culture's construction of it, and thus the tan is achieved via a number of cultural commodities, not least of which are barriers, or screens that protect the body from the dangers of the sun, raw nature, in the same way as the esplanade protects the land from the dangers of the sea. This natural meaning of the tan has also, as do all signs of our culture, a class dimension.

The *National Times* devoted a full-page article to suntanning and sun-screening. Its illustration is significant (Figure 2). The topless sunbaker is middle class—the hat and the connotations of the style of the drawing are adequate class markers. Her (dark) tan needs to be differentiated from the black servant whose color by contrast signals the whiteness (racial) of the sunbaker, and whose class also contrasts with hers. Other signs in the article support the class signification of tan—solarium

The browning of Australia

ROSE SHAPIRO, an English journalist, looks at the peculiar Australian passion for the perfect tan, and, below, GINA SCHIEN gives a guide to the cheapest of the best sunscreens.

Figure 2
The illustration and heading of a full-page article in the *National Times*, December 19, 1982.

tans cost up to $65 to acquire, natural tans of the required quality take up to 10 hours sunbaking a day, sunscreens cost on average $4. Sunbeds are used by "busy working ladies with no time to go to the beach," obviously to signal their desired, if false, membership in the true bourgeoisie, which is a leisured bourgeoisie.

The tan, with its connotations of leisure, money, sophistication, and meanings for others, must be significantly distinguished from the color achieved by the outdoor manual worker, and, of course, it is, by its smoothness and texture and by its evenness over all (or nearly all) parts of the body. As the *National Times* puts it, "It turns out to be all too easy to obtain the uneven coloration deprecatingly termed a 'farmer's tan'. It takes time and commitment to get the all-over allure of a deep and enduring brownness." The "naturalness" of tan serves to naturalize class, leisure, and money, for it is these that provide access to the natural.

Both the suburbanite and the sunbaker are, for different reasons, culture centered, and are thus found either on the lawns or on that part of the beach closest to the security of culture. The language itself is, as always, significant here. The English term *sunbathe* has been transformed in Australian English to *sunbake*. This has, as I would expect, roots in both the physical—the Australian sun is hotter—and the social or cultural. "Baking" is a cultural process; it is a form of cooking, and cooking is, as Lévi Strauss (1969) has demonstrated, a primary means of turning nature into culture. The sunbaker finds a different meaning in the beach from the bather. (Incidentally, the difference cannot be read back into English, for English does not have access to both words as does Australian: meaning resides in difference, and only Australian English possesses it.)

The central zone of the beach and the strip nearest the sea are where the families, the games players, and those who wish to paddle, swim, and jog tend to congregate, for this eases the transition into the first zone of the sea—the shallows, where, again, the very young, the parents, adults, and the elderly bathers find their meaning of the natural. Beyond this, beyond the breaking waves, is the deep sea, used only by strong swimmers, usually youths, those between childhood and full adulthood. Their meaning is one of leaving culture, of accepting the risk and challenge of nature, of testing their strength against that of the sea.

Let us now identify the actual beach I am considering, and thus take into account those features specific to it, but that still have a signifying function that act as examples of specific articulations of the range of meanings we have been looking at. The beach is Cottesloe, and some of its features are added to our basic diagram in Figure 3.

A significant feature is the slab of rock commemorating the landing of the *Naturaliste*, the first arrival of man on this shore. The start of history, the creation of culture out of nature, is appropriately signaled in this sacred anomalous strip. Only two buildings are allowed within these lawns—one sells food, the other houses the toilets. The coincidence is appropriate, for excreta in the terms of structural anthropology are structurally equivalent to food. Both sully the neatness of the boundary between the body and its environment, between nature and culture. Excreta brim over with taboo meanings in the same way food does with sacred ones, and both are commonly heavily ritualized. The shower, too, is worth noting, where fresh water (familiar in our taps and reticulation systems) washes off the sand and salt of sea water, and enables us symbolically as well

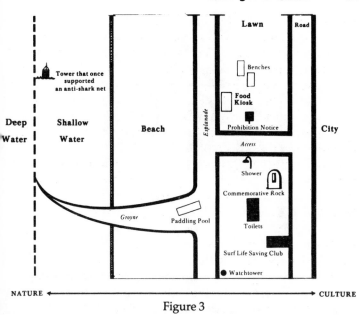

Figure 3

as physically to return from nature to culture. The Genesis opposition of waters of the firmament (fertile, fresh) and waters of the sea (infertile, salt) provides the meaning underlying an apparently functional act. There used to be a beach pavilion here, currently being renovated, which combined all these functions in one building—toilets, showers, changing rooms, and refreshment sales.

Perhaps the most significant sign on the beach is what I will refer to in this article as the prohibition notice, for it provides the perfect example of culture imposing its laws upon nature: no surfboards, no spearguns, no nude bathing, no animals or pets, no vehicles, no litter (see Figure 4).

The first three of these prohibitions are ways of keeping nature at bay. Surfboards, as we shall see later, are a highly meaningful sign in that they violate the boundary between man and fish. Both occupy anomalous categories, but veer to the nature side of the anomaly. Nude bathing similarly takes the undress of the beach too far toward nature and away from culture—nudists call themselves "naturists" and frequently stress how "natural" their hobby is.

Figure 4

There appear to be two main reasons for prohibiting dogs on the beach. One is found in the widespread belief that swimming dogs attract sharks, and the other is the threat of their dirt—and dirt has a special significance in structural anthropology.

Vehicles and litter are signs of the culture that is being excluded from the meaning of the beach. So this notice establishes the differences, the boundaries between nature and beach and between beach and culture in an arbitrary way that may be specific to this beach, but is typical of the exercise of social control.

Prohibiting anomalous activities is exerting ideological closure by controlling the threat of too much meaning. This beach must not, cannot, be allowed to violate the conceptual categories, to signify too much of both nature and culture simultaneously, for that would open the text to radical and oppositional meanings. Beaches such as Cottesloe are not there to offer alternative meanings to culture, but to naturalize it, and to naturalize not just culture, but the center of that culture, which, for Perth at least, is a leisured, family-centered bourgeoisie. The security and comfort of the beach is a natural equivalent of the suburb; this reference to the natural is explained by Foucault (1978) as the reference to a masked social norm. The natural is a culture's production or reproduction of nature, and thus what is perceived as a rule of law of nature is only a displaced or misrecognized rule by which to define social normality. The naturalness (as opposed to nature) of the beach defines the normality of the suburb. But the natural for Foucault does more than justify the norm, it also justifies the disciplining by punishment or other forms of "moral engineering" of those who deviate from it. This notice, with its range of prohibitions, provides not only a negative definition of the norm—that which is not deviant—but also a positive agency of social control or power that defines the structure of relationships and the meanings that go with them to constitute society as culture. The notice's cultural function of controlling the meanings of the beach merges with its social function of controlling the definition of the norm: both serve to deny contradictory interests in the service of an exnominated bourgeoisie.

The four cards shown in Figure 5 were bought at Cottesloe, but depict behavior explicitly banned there. The contradiction is not total, however, because what they depict is not topless sunbaking, but a *staged* performance that is not one of the toplessness, not one of the beach-as-nature, but of the beach-as-ideology. Figure 5a produces a meaning of the beach as a site of male sexuality. The beach is a place for *looking* (SUN, SURF, SAND, and SEE), for possession of the female by the male look.

Figure 5

The girls here are not sunbaking merely to produce a tan to take nature back into the suburbs, nor are they swimming out of culture into nature, but are constituting themselves as bearers of meanings for men.

The beach, with its structure of the natural, legitimates this sexual display and look: the body is permitted a visibility within this anomalous strip that is denied it in more culturally central environments, and the body, of course, is where we are closest to nature. Sexuality may be "natural" in its origins, but the forms by which it is expressed are specifically cultural, however much this may be disguised. This disguise is, however, stripped away in the parodies of middle-class leisure in Figure 5b and c. In b, "I wonder what the poor people are doing," gender dominance is associated with class dominance, and both are naturalized by the iconography of physical (i.e., natural) sex. The connotations of a Roman orgy and/or a sultan's harem add a historical cross-cultural legitimization, so that the card invites the structural association of male with the dominant class, with the emperor/sultan, and of female with the subordinate class, with slave. Figure 5c continues this structure of values. Here the quotation refers to a remark made by Malcolm Fraser that life wasn't meant to be easy. The key words here are "easy" and "hard." "Easy" has to be understood in the context of the Protestant work ethic—by which leisure (when we take it easy) is earned by *hard* work. This is the middle-class, positively connoted meaning. The meaning attributed to the working class by the middle class is of unearned ease, of "bludging." Malcolm Fraser's words are exclusively middle class: there is no possible proletarian meaning of "easy." "Hard" belongs simultaneously to two paradigms—the first is the same verbal one as "easy," the other is that of the sexuality of the body, that of the visual signs in the card. Card d again merges class and gender in the pun on "bums" which inevitably positions the reader as middle-class male: the knowing laugh both constitutes and masks the ideological placement. The male voyeur is even more explicit here than in the word "SEE" in card a. The class factor is present in one of the meanings of the word "bums" (bludgers), but in the cartoon representation of the reader/voyeur it is displaced into signs of Australianness—thongs, shorts, beer belly, and sun hat. Australia is, in its own imagining, a classless (i.e., middle-class) society. In all the cards the naturalness of physical sexuality guarantees and legitimates a class-centered meaning system and provides, like the prohibition notice, a "natural" justification for a masked social norm. Pornography, however soft, is a way of exerting social control over the body, which, being physically part of nature, is thus potentially beyond culture's reach. The beach and the body are naturalized into the bourgeois.

A holiday ad in TAA's in-flight consumer goodies magazine *Gallimaufry* (and what could be more bourgeois than that) lists the ingredients that go to make up "The Beach" (*sic*) as "spectacular surf swimming, fast sun tanning and some very strenuous eye exercise" (*Gallimaufry* 1983). The coyness of the final phrase cannot disguise its identical ideological work with that of the Cottesloe cards, work identified by graffiti noted by Noel Sanders (1982) on the main steps of Bondi beach:

> O baby, what a place to be,
> In the service of the bourgeoisie.

(The words are those of Iggy Pop's 1979 song "The Endless Sea.")

TAA's ad and Bondi's graffiti confirm Cottesloe: the cards contradict it only insofar as they show breasts; in all other respects they support perfectly Cottesloe's appropriation of the beach into bourgeois chauvinism. They not only turn nature into culture, they define by exnomination a particular class and gender as the culture, the site of an ideologically constructed unity of interest that denies the subordinate class/gender a position or interests of their own.

This urbanized culture seeks to extend its control over the meaning of the beach into the sea itself. The groyne, the pillar used to support a shark net, the tower from which the lifeguards watch over the safety of the beachgoers and the paddling pool prohibit waves, sharks, and danger; they prohibit the unwelcome extremes of nature in the same way the notice prohibits those of culture.

But Cottesloe beach is not a complete text on its own; rather, it is a quotation from the syntagmatic string of beaches that constitute "The Beach" for this area of Perth. Extending the text to include the relations of Cottesloe beach with its neighbors to the north reveals a similar set of signifying categories or zones operating vertically rather than horizontally (see Figure 6).

Here, to put it simply, we find the same physical and conceptual movement from culture to nature, only this time in a south to north direction.

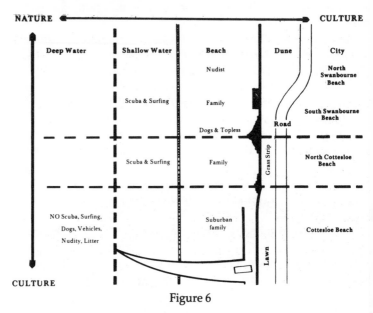

Figure 6

Cottesloe, the family, suburban beach, gives way to North Cottesloe, where surfboards and scuba diving are allowed, but dogs are not. The surf is not particularly good here, so the surfers are young apprentices. Here also, the lawn is reduced to a narrow strip at the top of the cliff, and there is no esplanade. North Cottesloe is more natural than Cottesloe. Further north, by the rocks that mark the boundary between North Cottesloe and south Swanbourne, is a hundred or so meters of beach where younger women go topless and older ones walk their dogs. (Notice that this "scandalous" behavior occurs on a boundary between named beaches.)

There is, however, another beach just south of Cottesloe (Leighton) where dogs and topless sunbaking are both permitted (see Figure 7). The relaxation of cultural control that results in dogs and breasts walking the beach together is worth investigation. The core lies, I think, in the only linguistic category that includes two such apparently disparate natural objects, that is, the category "dirty."

Edmund Leach (1976: 62; quoted by Hartley 1983) has shown how dirt is a condition of boundaries. This derives from excreta, which in a precise physical sense crosses the boundary from man to not-man: excreta are man becoming nature, just as food, ingested, is nature becoming man. Dirty, then, is another characteristic of the anomalous, so dirt has the power and the threat of too much meaning.

Figure 7

Mary Douglas (1966) makes a similar point when she argues that dirt is matter out of place, and that "eliminating it is a positive effort to organize the environment" (p. 2). Dirt is anomalous, "a residual category, rejected from our normal scheme of classifications" (p. 36). The anomalous is seen by her as the threatening, the dangerous, and "attributing danger . . . helps to enforce conformity" (p. 36). The category "dirt" invites social control because of its danger. Dogs are dangerous because they attract not only sharks, but also disease; breasts, because they threaten conventional morality.

On this level, dogs are dirty physically, breasts morally. But in structuralist terms both are dirty because both patrol the conceptual boundary between man and nature. Dogs cross the boundary between man and beasts; breasts, too, signify the boundary between nakedness—the body in nature—and clothes, the body culturized, given meanings. Dress and undress are ways of signifying man's difference from his similarity to the rest of the animal kingdom. The naked body is nature—what man shares with animals—the clothed body is culture. But my point here is that as dogs cross and dirty the physical boundary between man and beasts, so breasts cross and dirty the conceptual one. Both are therefore appropriately banned or permitted together.

I must return from this dirty digression to the beach, and our northward trip up it.

Next is a brief reversion to a family-type beach (no dogs or topless sunbaking), but surfboards and scuba are allowed. Beyond this is North Swanbourne, which is where nudist (or naturist) bathing is allowed. Significantly, the road and city veer away from the beach here, leaving a large expanse of sand dune, partially covered with wild grass—nature's equivalent of the lawn—to mediate between city and sea. The city is physically and conceptually further from the beach here, the beach is therefore closer to nature, and the meaning of the beach is appropriately articulated in nudity.

This double articulation of the conceptual shift between culture and nature means that, on this section of the coastline, at least, culture is located at the bottom right of Figure 6, that is, the lawn at Cottesloe, and nature at top left—the deep sea at Swanbourne.

The beach, then, is an anomalous category, overflowing with meaning because it is neither land nor sea, neither nature nor culture, but partakes of both. It is therefore the appropriate place for anomalous behavior, behavior that is highly significant because it pushes the cultural as far as it can go toward Nature. It explores the boundary of what it is to be social, to be cultured, that is the nonphysical part of the human condition. The anomalies of this behavior can be summarized so far in a diagram:

A	Anomalous Category	Not A
SEA	Beach	LAND
NATURE		CULTURE
NAKED	Topless/Bathers	CLOTHED
FUR	Tan	SKIN
SWIMMING	Surfboard	BOATING
FISH	Scuba	MAN
ANIMALS	Pets (dogs)	MAN

Cottesloe may be the perfect suburban beach for some, safe and culturally controlled. But for others the meaning of the beach must move further away from culture, closer to nature. Craig McGregor's ideal is "a beach with no houses, no tents, no sandmining, no road and no way in except in bare feet, or maybe in thongs, bikini and sunvisor. . . . You can swim naked there. Only albino sand crabs and occasionally, a gaggle of surfboard riders keep you company" (*National Times* January 9–15, 1983). His list of prohibitions are diametrically opposed to Cottesloe's, but his dream of the ideal beach is what, nonetheless, gives Cottlesloe its final appeal. The safe, suburban beach has some symbolic connection with the ideal, isolated beach of nature: both inhabit the same anomalous category and the explicitness and vehemence of Cottesloe's prohibitions signal how close the disruptive force of Nature actually is. I suspect, too, that in our dreams most of us share McGregor's ideal of the beach, but we actually go to Cottesloe.

Jo Kennedy, the rock singer, was cast away with Michael Willesee and two others on a tropical island for a TV program on survival. Standing on a huge, deserted beach, she complained, "I miss the beach—the proper beach with sun tan oil and towels" (*Survival* July 25, 1983). The wild beach and the suburban beach are opposite faces of the same myth. The appeal of the suburbanized beach depends crucially on the fact that the suburbanization is not complete: echoes of that which resists incorporation into the culture still exist to provide a *frisson* of the freedom, the danger, and the potentially subversive challenge that nature mounts against culture. And it is this end of the spectrum of potential meanings that the young tow-haired surfers mobilize to help them establish their position within our culture. For culture is not best understood by a consensus model in which the values at the center are agreed upon and can thus provide the yardstick by which to measure degrees of centrality/deviance. Rather, these values are constantly being contested and are having to defend their centrality, their dominance. So culture is not a relatively harmonious and stable continuum from dominant to deviant, but a confrontation between groups occupying different, sometimes opposing positions in the map of social relations, and the process of making meanings (which is, after all, the process of culture) is a social struggle, as different groups struggle to establish meanings that serve their interests.

The meanings of the beach that serve the family are contested by subcultures such as youth in general and surfers in particular. It is significant how the beach plays an important part in youth culture, because youth, too, is an anomalous category, the one between child and adult. Much of youth culture centers around the beach, sometimes concerned with acquiring the anomalous tan, frequently associated with that anomalous surfboard, and also with the van, that anomalous vehicle, with features of both car and truck, of indoors and outdoors, so it is appropriate that this accumulation of meanings of beach, youth surfboard, van, should have elements of the sacred for its initiates and of the taboo for the rest.

The van is ambivalent in that it has the form of a truck for work, but it is used more like a car for leisure and for other social/sexual purposes. It is mass produced and yet highly individualized, as if to deny its mass production. But the individualization is conventional. The differences between vans are differences of the signifier only. All vans share the same signified, that of youth defining its meaning as neither child nor adult. The owners have to have reached a certain age to own one, to be able to afford one, and to be allowed to drive one legally. They are defining themselves as not children. Yet they are also not adult; the customizing is expensive and conspicuously wasteful so it defines them against the young adult who is typically saving up money to be married, or to put a deposit down on a house, or a mortgage. The conspicuous consumption cuts off the van both from the younger and from the older.

Further, even though vans can be works of art, they are significantly differentiated from the traditional role of art in the capitalist society, which, as Bourdieu (1968) has shown, serves social status and class differentiation as well as economic capital. Van art certainly has the status and class functions, though they serve the deviant, not the dominant, but where van art differs from fine art is in its investment role. Vans are essentially disposable art, the appropriate form for an oppositional youth subculture. In fact, as Enzensberger (1972) has argued about the electronic media, the impermanency itself provides not just an alternative to the bourgeoisie, but a threat:

> The media produce no objects that can be hoarded and auctioned. They do away completely with "intellectual property" and liquidate the "heritage", that is to say, the class-specific handling of non-material capital. (quoted in Hartley 1983)

The van is also anomalous between indoors and outdoors. It is furnished like a house, with carpets, decorations, hi-fi systems, mattresses, and cushions, and yet is outdoors as well. Its furnishings are used typically for sexual promiscuity, which again is part of the deviance of youth, between the nonsexual child and the married, sexually bonded adult. There is a strong association between vans and drive-in movies. A drive-in, too, is anomalous between indoors and outdoors, so the two fit well together. And when vans are in a drive-in, the owners have to signify their difference from the straight family viewer by reversing them, so that the vans are all parked oppositionally to the family cars. Now, we know there is a function for this, in that it enables sex and cinema to be enjoyed at the same time, but the functional dimension is never the only one in social behavior—there is always a signifying dimension. In this case, the signifying dimension is that of establishing difference from the family, composed of adults and children. So the cultural connections, the signifying similarities, among vans and beach and youth are not coincidental. They are all part of a way that a culture, its various manifestations, and its formal institutions fit together in the sort of ideological system that Althusser (1971) called "overdetermination."

On top of the van, as it is driven to Scarborough Beach, is typically a surfboard. The surfboard is perhaps the perfect example of a category anomalous between nature and culture. It is carefully designed, with a scientific approach to the placement of fins and shape of the hull, yet it is also the most minimal object that enables man to float on the sea. The skill and art of the surfer resemble more the way a dolphin interacts with the sea or a bird with the air than man's more normal technological imposition of his will and needs upon nature, typified by the modern giant ships. As befits its anomalous status, the surfboard is both sacred and taboo. To the surfie, it is an object of near worship, and there are strong taboos that prevent girls, or the too young or the too old, from riding it.

We are not interested here in a Freudian reading of the surfboard with male sexuality, but it is worth remarking on the sexist nature of most youth subcultures, where male and female behavior is clearly distinguished, and where males are active and dominant and females passive and subordinate. Vans, motorbikes, and surfboards are conventionally driven/ridden by males and the size, skill, decoration involved in them is part of the male status order. Females are passengers, spectators, there to be won, possessed, flaunted by the male. Surfers' writing mingles accounts of mastering waves with ones of easy mastery of girls. They have an exclusive language for each, language that signals subcultural membership and excludes outsiders, language that performs the vital function of distinguishing *them* from *us*. In this language waves are *tubes, rip curls, double ender pintails*; females are *bushies, garudas*, and *groupies*. But the key term is *hunting*, which applies equally to waves and females. "They were sworn to the cry of '*Hunt* it in the day, hunt it in the dark'. And brave boys keep their promises" (*Australian Surfing World* [hereafter, *ASW*] 190, 1983). Hunting is where man first denotes his mastery over nature: it is the prerequisite of cooking, which, in turn, becomes the resonant metaphor for the process of culturizing nature. And consequently it is seen as a natural activity—man hunting for food, hunting for females, hunting for waves is man behaving "naturally" because he is acting according to his bodily needs.

And this is opening up my main thesis about the meaning of

surfing. For the moment, let me claim that the meaning is to be found in the body, in physical sensation, and that the following ministructure then obtains:

Body: Mind
Physical Sensation: Conceptual Construction
NATURE: CULTURE

'A righthander. So fast it makes Kirra look like a beginner's wave. A small community of surfers, nestled in the cove, looking out onto the point. Arid countryside and stunted growth. No water, less shade. Sunshine, hot air and icy water. The nearest town is 100km away along corrugated gravel tracks. A national park, but no-one at the gate to collect $600 a week to surf here. Just a small group of surfers drawn together to surf one of the world's finest rights.'

Man after man they blurred high in the lip, then dropped like falcons to the depths for the blitzing bottom carve back up to forge the left rail into torqued direction shifts, half the lip exploding through the air. The state of the art. They surfed bloody well.

For the next two hours bullshit reigned from the heavens. Five wave sets, tide coming in, and *the* Sanur-bottom walls disappearing way down the reef in bending perfection. Incredible to bugger youself on a 300 metre ride then paddle out, witness to displays of power and panache in the distance—repeated wave after wave.

Sweat oozed. Like pus from a weeping wound. A smelly heat was raping my senses, bludgeoning memories of a chilly southern autumn. Oppression. Christ. Of dirt and dogs. Of guys and girls in 'Bali' singlets popping blisters in the afternoon sun.

Figure 8

The language of surfing is sensational: it works through and on the senses, the body (see Figure 8). It centers life on nouns and adjectives, the immediate perceptions of the world that relate to the body. Verbs, with their implications of purposeful actions, of structuring time into tenses and modalities, of relating subject and object into the culturally valued world of logic, verbs that so crucially perform the conceptual structuring of culture, are minimized. The short sentences, the disjointed syntax produce a world that is a mosaic of physical sensation, of bodily freedom. The body's (or nature's) life of sensation breaks free from the control of culture, it momentarily disrupts and fractures the seamless world of sense (not, not, not sensation) that is the hallmark and raison d'être of culture. Breaking sentence order, producing sentences without the controlling presence of a verb is breaking the shackles of your primary school English teacher, herself a metonym for the conflation of linguistic and social control. As Barthes (1975b) says, "The sentence is hierarchical: it implies subjections, subordinations, internal reactions . . . any completed utterance runs the risk of being ideological" (p. 50). Opposing the control of the sentence is a way of achieving "pleasure" in the sense that Barthes (1975b: 23) uses it. He writes of pleasure as "something both revolutionary and social . . . it cannot be taken over by any collectivity, any mentality, any ideolect." This resistance of pleasure to ideological control lies at the heart of that paradoxical phrase "the politics of pleasure."

Barthes's move away from his early party political phase to one in which the concept of pleasure takes over from the concept of ideology as the most important one in his thinking is accompanied by his concern with the body of the reader, reading with the body, not the mind. "The pleasure of the text is that moment when my body pursues its own ideas—for my body does not have the same ideas I do" (1975b: 17). When Barthes talks about his body responding to a work of literature, what he is getting at is that there is a part of his response that is natural, not cultural. It is not part of the language system, the cultural experience that he has had, but is much closer to direct physical sensation, which is part of the body. The mind is cultural, culturally determined; the body is natural, physiologically, genetically determined, and Barthes is significantly talking about responding with the body, or reading with the body, to describe that part of the pleasure of reading that he sees as natural or universal. This pleasure (or bliss) of reading he describes using the word *jouissance*, which means both bliss or ecstasy and sexual orgasm. When the body is thus the site of the pleasure of the text, aesthetics merges into eroticism.

Traditional aesthetics seeks the universal or "natural" in the text itself. Barthes is looking to the body and sensation of the reader to find a noncultural dimension to the process of making meaning. This ties in closely with another aspect of Barthes's later work, his insistence that the pleasure derived from reading, like the pleasure derived from sex, comes from the interplay of signifiers. "That is the pleasure of the text: value shifted to the sumptuous rank of the signifier" (1975a: 65). And this links closely with the surf, where the language and the activity foregrounds the signifiers over the signifieds. The signified of "solstice" makes no sense here, but the signifier sounds just fine: "Indigenous night boys in tight fitting fashion hung out of the stereo stalls, pirate sounds destroying what little solstice remained in the streets." The solstice is the moment when day and night are equal; it sounds right, though the signified is wrong. The signifier actually works quite well. Breaking the relationship between signifier and signified is another fracture of social control, for it disrupts the sign, and the sign is culture, the signified is its sense, for this is what culture makes, it makes sense literally and figuratively. The signified is culture, but the signifier is nature, the senses; Barthes's shift of focus from the signified in *Mythologies* (1973) to the signifier in *Pleasure of the Text* (1975b) is a shift from culture to nature, which involves a shift in the definition of politics—a shift from the politics of ideology to the politics of pleasure. The insistence of surf writing on the senses, on the signifier rather than the signified, is a linguistic device that pushes the meaning of surfing closer to nature and further from culture. For the signifier is not a meaning, but a means to a meaning: it is embryonic culture crying for a signified. Resisting this cry is a political resistance because it is resistance against control.

We can now extend our ministructure into something more comprehensive:

NATURE:	CULTURE
Body:	Mind
Physical Sensation:	Conceptual Construction
Signifier:	Signified
Pleasure:	Ideology
Linguistic Disorder:	Linguistic Order
Anarchy:	Control
Danger:	Safety

This opposition between freedom and control, between the signifier and the signified, the body and the mind is an articulation of the struggle to exert power and to resist it. Foucault (1980) talks of the "claims and affirmations . . . of one's own body against power, of health against the economic system, of pleasure against the moral norms of sexuality, marriage, decency" (p. 56). He goes on to describe the response of socially constituted power to the body's resistance to social control as "an economic (and perhaps also ideological) exploitation of eroticism, from sun-tan products to pornographic films. Responding precisely to the revolt of the body, we find a new mode of investment which presents itself no longer in the form of control by repression but that of control by stimulation. 'Get undressed—but be slim, good-looking, tanned!' " (p. 57). Cottesloe's cards and the *National Times*'s advice on sun tanning are equally the culture's attempt to exert control over the body, its incorporation (pardon the pun) of the potentially subversive. White (1979: 106–107) explains how Foucault (1980) sees a prison as a metonym for society because both are agencies of control:

> In the totally ordered, hierocratized space of the nineteenth century prison, the prisoner is put under constant surveillance, discipline, and education in order to transform him into what power as now organized in society demands that everyone become: docile, productive, hard-working, self-regulating, conscience-ridden, in a word, "normal" in every way. . . . [This power as now organized in society] . . . as sovereign in practice as any absolute monarch claimed to be in theory, seeks to make society into an extended prison, in which discipline becomes an end in itself; and conformity to a norm which governs every aspect of life, and especially desire, becomes the only principle both of law and morality.

Pleasure, which affords the escape from this power, the escape from the norm, becomes an agent of subversion because it creates a privatized domain beyond the scope of a power whose essence lies in its omnipotence, its omnipresence. Showing that life is livable outside it denies it.

It cannot be coincidence that the Foucauldian concepts of society as an extended prison, and of pleasure, the satisfaction of desire, the only escape from it, are all present in the ad for

Figure 9

surf suits shown in Figure 9. In the bottom right, the actual prison, its gates labeled No Entry, is contrasted with the laughing (pleasuring) surfies: in the top the signifiers of gates and notice have changed, the signifieds remain the same though more explicitly extended metonymically into a Foucauldian notion of society-as-prison. Here the gate is slightly open and one of the surfers is symbolically (if illogically) escaping over it. Also in the top left-hand corner, almost invisible, almost subliminal, because outside the apparent structure of the ad, outside the photographs, are the words "Shut the Gate." The words and images of fun (pleasure), escape, and surf reveal themselves so clearly in the ad as to deny the need for any analysis of latent structures.

But escape into the surf, into the threat of nature, can mean escape into sharks. Sharks are a motif that merges nature, the body, and physical sensation with a reversal of the hunter: hunted relationship. To us, the culture, they are nature at its most oppositional and one only has to appear off a beach to empty it immediately. But if the relationship of the culture to sharks is one of fear and opposition, we would expect that of the surfie to be different, and so it is. The surfie stays in the water, not without fear, not without danger, but with the sort of recognition that the danger of the shark, the danger of the wave are part of the politics of pleasure. Escaping the control of culture is a risky enterprise, and if culture means security, then nature means risk.

The big wave, the shark, the potential of death is as far as we can get from the safety of culture. The groyne and the shark net at Cottesloe are on the side of life. The surfie risks death, the one element of nature that culture can never overcome, though not for lack of trying.

The surfie is anticulture and pronature in more specific ways than his dicing with death. Our culture—that of competitive capitalism—is individualistic: the surfie is not. Surfies are known and reported by their nicknames— G.D., Crammy, Ricko, G'Day, and Pipeline H—and a nickname signals group identity at least as much as, if not more than, it identifies the individual. Names are not just *of* people, but *for* people. The talk is constantly of "the community of surfers"—community with themselves and community with nature. And typical surfing photos work the same way—time and again they are of huge waves and surf, with the surfie deindividualized into a little speck. It may be argued that this is a function of the technical problems of photographing surfers, but it is not, for closeups are possible.

The table presented in Figure 10 gives the results of a content analysis of 148 photographs in a surfing journal.

The pattern is clear: the largest category is that of de-individualized surfers; the next largest is photos with no surfers

	Individuals Identifiable	Individuals Not Identifiable
Photos of surfies surfing	8	46
Photos of surfies not surfing	12	5
Total editorial photos	20	51
Advertisements showing surfies	34	16
Photos without surfies		27

Figure 10

in them at all, usually of waves, nature, or natives. Even in the close-ups the surfer is not individualized, but becomes almost an abstract statement of man's closeness to nature. The individual is a cultural product—nature is interested only in species, and these photos are photos of species: the surfie, ecologically located in his habitat.

Where the table shows the minimization of the individual most clearly is in the comparison of ads and editorial photos in the same journal. In the ads, 50 photographs show surfers, but 34 of them are individualized and only 16 not. Ads, of course, are culture trying to claw back the deviants from the anarchy of nature into commercial, cultural sense. Individualism is the equivalent in the consumer to choice in the product: each arbitrary cultural production gives meaning to others, and it is interesting to note how surfies are, apparently all too easily, clawed back into cultural centrality once business makes a bid to colonize their meaning. The superficial, artificial differences in the surfboards shown in Figure 11 are there simply to enable the consumer, in making a choice, to construct an individuality. The transformation of surfie into consumer is complete, even if masked by the stylishness of the differentiating decorations. At the same time, of course, the surfboard is transformed into a commodity. A popular culture, with moments of real resistance to the dominant one, is transformed into a mass culture with its commodities, its advertisements, and its centrally created style that can be made instantly obsolete to boost next year's sales. The surfer, who potentially and sometimes actually contradicts beaches such as Cottesloe, is being drawn back into the dominant culture by the very journals, competitions, and manufacturers that apparently serve his interests, but in fact

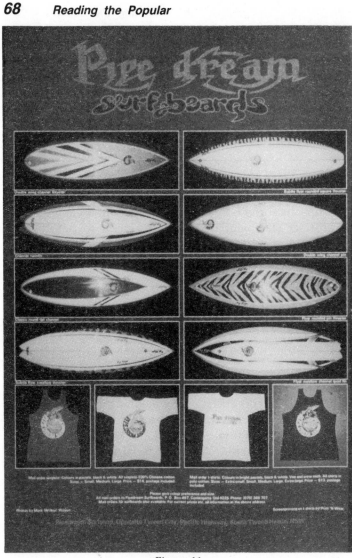

Figure 11

serve those of others whose gain grows as his resistance is diminished.

Volosinov (1973) demands that we rewrite Saussure in order to locate the sign beyond the signifying system as a site of ideological struggle. Meanings always function within the social system and as such are subject to the same struggle for possession as any other locus of power. Signs, through their multiaccentuality, are capable of different meanings for different people, and the struggle for dominance is as much a part of the signifying domain as it is of the political and economic. Thus we can see instance after instance of the signifying institutions of our culture attempting to deny the radicalism of the surfie. When TV news reports their competitions, it draws them back into cultural centrality. Of course, by organizing and participating in national or international competitions, the surfies themselves have set up the contradiction that TV and commerce are all too quick to exploit. Here, notice the difference between a surfie journal's account of the competition and TV news's.

SURFIE JOURNAL

Crammy and Tom were the form surfers in Bali. Tom's finesse at Ulu was highlighted by his flashing roundhouse slashes, and Richard destroyed every wave, allegedly pulling cutback loops at Kuta. Yet if the latter fellow had pulled the first such manoeuvre in an IPS event, i.e., the OM Bali Pro, he could have still scored meagre points due to a trial judging system based on several categories. Many surfers fell victim to this system, notably Nick Carroll with his series of backhand hooks from the Outside Corner. He failed to do any tricks, and steered clear of the smaller waves on the inside (tubes). For my money, Gary Green stole the show on one wave, with respect to Richo's masterful four tubes on one ride. Greeny had inside position against Richo in the quarters. He took a perfect first wave and blew it on the first section. Richo picking it off on the shoulder and scoring max points. Stickm'n had made his first mistake and after his opponent's reaction, the Newport crew wrote him off. Another wave came down to the corner and Greeny took off like a match-stick, straight up and down, reaching the bottom then stalling into a classic soularch, letting the lip pitch over him in the same motion. Three seconds later the Stickm'n emerged, in the same position. With the pressure on, that remains the coolest move in years. (*ASW* 190)

CHANNEL SEVEN NEWS

Voice over shots of surfers: In the final heats of the junior competition surfed in consistent 2m waves at Southpoint, W.A.'s John Schwendenberg gave an outstanding showing against the heavily favoured riders from the East. His surfing today was par excellence and he's given the home state an unexpected but welcome boost. The best W.A. prospects for a national title are in the cadets class where 14 year old Jeff Brown from City Beach and Paul Schneer from Sorrento take on Mickey Brown and Brian Taylor. The West is also waving the flag at the other end of the age scale. . . .

Commentator to camera: At 38 W.A.'s Murray Smith is living proof that there's a lot more to surfing than meets the eye. . . .

Then follows an interview with Murray Smith in close-up in which his face and history are individualized. (Channel 7, Perth, May 5, 1983)

The obvious differences are the naming—the surfie journal uses "tribal" nicknames; TV uses full given surnames with place of origin. The surfie journal refuses to focus on one; the TV finally pulls one surfer, the oldest, out of the water to individualize him. The day before, TV had done exactly the same with the "captain" of the NSW team—not only individualizing him, but giving him a rank in a hierarchy and identifying a community other than a surfing one to which he belonged. The TV concentrates on socially constructed individuals in competition with each other; the journal emphasizes the surfie-wave relationship. TV has colonized the meaning, has tamed the untamed continent and civilized it (cf. the notice on Cottesloe Beach). Surfers are now constructed as individuals competing in the capitalist rat race just like the rest of us, and surfing becomes not the threat of man's reentry into nature, but a sport in which the points awarded by judges become the missing signifieds: they complete the sign and allow culture to extend its control over sensation and the signifier.

The same sort of struggle for meaning surfaces in the

behavior of surfies themselves. The professional is drawn into the international jet set of airports, hotels, and money that sets up a crippling contradiction with the world of tubes and double enders:

> Word spread to Durban, where a dinner party prior to the Mainstay Magnum focussed on the off-beat relationship of Norm's bladder and the carpet of the hotel's disco. (*ASW* 192)

The collision of carpet and bladder, of culture and nature, occurs within the ideological contradiction that makes the struggle for meaning so crucial. This contradiction occurs, naturally enough, within the ads that are an essential part of the contradictory fringe of small and big businesses that surround the core of surfing.

The ad for Fox Wetsuits seems particularly significant (Figure 12). The name itself is crucial. Leach (1972) reminds us that a fox in our structure of animal relationships occupies the same point as does the criminal or deviant in human relationships.

Figure 12

Criminals and deviants occupy the anomalous category between our tribe and their tribe—they are of *us*, but are hostile or threatening like *them*. Similarly, the fox occupies an anomalous category between domesticated animals and wild, alien ones. Hence, according to Leach, the killing of foxes is heavily ritualized and they are consistently portrayed as criminals in folk tales and legends. The anomalous, deviant meaning of the fox makes it a structurally, if not semantically, appropriate name for a surfie's wetsuit. The first paragraph of the ad acknowledges this in the punning use of the word *underground*—significantly and explicitly opposed to *commercial*. The denial of the desire to create "images" is denied by the opening word, for "difference" operates only to create meaning within the system, to provide the illusion of freedom of choice within a determined economic and social relationship, and thus to feed the equally capitalist illusion of the individuality of the consumer. This contradiction continues in the second paragraph, where the pun of "established" brings the deviant back toward the establishment, but by the end of the paragraph the struggle has been lost: "Australia's first full on custom retail wholesale promotional surfsuit."

The heavy use of adjectives in abnormal relationship is a robbery of the deviant surfie syntax, and the stolen form is filled with the content of capitalism. The struggle has been lost, the meaning colonized. Feeble echoes of the contradiction surface later— they "deal direct to the surfing community," and the deal is conceptualized as "100% customer manufacturer relationship."

Many of the ads for surfing equipment stress the craft nature of the industry—to try to disguise the difference between the producer and consumer by stressing their smallness, the way that their boards are designed or used by the professional surfer, who thus becomes a metonym of both producer and consumer and thus masks the industrial process.

The industry itself is aware of the struggle for the meaning of the surf, and to effect its colonization as easily as possible presents itself as noncapitalist, or precapitalist, and thus enables itself to misrepresent its interests as identical with those of the surfers, the colonized—a not uncommon practice in the history of the colonization.

I would be more optimistic about surfing's ability to resist this "clawback," this incorporation, if it didn't offer in its own internal contradictions so many easy purchases for the claws to grab. It was not difficult for TV to relocate surfing within the familiar ideology of sport and thereby to defuse any subversive effect it might have, for this was facilitated by the surfers themselves.

The same sort of weakening contradictions occur within the surfies' own construction of gender relationships. The crucial concepts of body, pleasure, the signifier, nature obviously relate as easily to sex as they do to surf.

From the top lines from the Cape ended thousands of nautical miles in a shuddering climax. An incredible impression cascaded in my brain. Never to be razed. Folds of shimmering glass broke like Harriers in formation clusters, wrapping from a magical point, six in a line. For three weeks I was to be further from the vibe of professional ego-tripping than ever before. A recluse. Windless days and a six feet tall swell sculptured the sea-floor in fine detail. As the tide came in, walls improved set by set until it was dark. And so after 3 hours I was stoked to be buggered, having caught the fourth day of a ten day swell. Sanur had bettered it, bettered it, but J-Bay could only match it. Incessant perfection; freedom to let loose. At the time, the future was masked in gold. (*ASW* 190)

Barthes's (1975a) use of the word *jouissance* to describe the highest type of pleasure (bliss) in reading the text is relevant here, for it is also the word for the ecstasy of sexual orgasm. The description of the surfie-surf sensation is orgasmic—surfing, reading, and orgasm merge in the pleasure of the signifier. Interestingly, too, this quote reveals the contradiction between this pleasure and that of the professional, which is clearly identified as individualistic "ego-tripping"; the ego, we remember, is where reason exerts its control over the libido, the source of desire, and professionalism is where society establishes power over the surfer.

The desires and pleasures of the body—surfing, sex, drugs, alcohol—are where the subversive meanings of the surf are potentially located. But contradictions occur in the unproblematic conflation of surf with sex in its structure. The subversion of surfing lies in its apparent escape from the control of the signified, from social power—the waves, alcohol, and drugs are easily constructed in this way, but sexuality, though it could be, is not. The surfie's sexuality is one of blatant male chauvinism:

bushies, garudas, and so on are there for male power and pleasure. Nowhere do I find any awareness of the difference between a wave and a garuda, of the fact that social relations are denied in one but affirmed in the other. And the women consent willingly to this male hegemony, not only in sexual activity but also in surfing. *Puberty Blues* caught the male chauvinism perfectly with, in the book if not the movie, a welcome tone of feminine resistance to it. No such resistance surfaces in the surfies' own writings; the contradictions are unexplored, unrecognized. This enables passages like this to appear unproblematically in the surfing literature. It demonstrates clearly the normalization of the surf into a comfortable reproduction of a modern marriage, where the educated woman is a domestic manager in a cozy partnership:

> Sponsorship for Glen has had its ups and downs, even with his impressive contest record. His girlfriend Michelle travels everywhere with him, they drive to all the contests in Australia in an old EH Holden wagon. This way they can keep costs down. She has a Bachelor of Commerce degree and majored in Economics at the University of NSW.

> Michelle sees her role in their scheme of things as follows: "I try to help with the practical things so that Glen can surf when he wants to, he believes in heaps of practice. We get along well together because I love the lifestyle, especially travelling. Also I love to watch Glen surf and I've always liked to be near the ocean. I write the letters for Glen and do the initial negotiations with any deals that may be offered. Sometimes people try to bypass me, but Glen and I make the decisions together." (*ASW* 190)

This is, significantly, in a section of the magazine devoted to individualizing the surfers, giving them the treatment normally accorded to stars (the photographs in this section are placed on a background design of stars). All this cannot be coincidental, nor more unfortunate for the subversive potential of the surf.

What the culture is trying to do to the surf is to defuse its potential radicalism. By incorporating it into TV sports and news, into the advertising of banks, or soft drinks, or electronic hardware, it is pulling the surfie back from the brink of becoming nature into the comfortable security of the natural.

The conventional, comfortable signifieds that surfing is given not only deradicalize it, but use its potential radicalism (i.e., its closeness to nature, now misrepresented as the natural) to naturalize the central institutions and meaning systems of the culture. Its meaning is colonized into the service of those who should be most threatened by it. The beach and the surf are worked on by the culture so that their overflowing meanings are controlled and legitimized. The beach, physically and conceptually closer to the city, is more completely colonized. The surf still shows elements of resistance to this imposition of meaning by a culturally dominant class in their own interests. The potential for subversion is still there, because physically and conceptually, the surf is nearer nature, further from the city.

The potentially subversive meaning of the surf derives from this chain of concepts—the body, nature, the signifier, pleasure, and therefore desire seen as articulating an alternative, threatening way of making sense to the one proposed by the official culture. The subversion lies in the denial of control or power as socially constituted.

Barthes has a number of terms through which he addresses this problem of the relationship of signifier and signified, of pleasure and meaning. At times he talks of *figuration* and *representation*, where *figuration* refers to the erotic pleasure of the signifier, while *representation* is that figuration "encumbered with meanings other than desire" (1975b); at other times he distinguishes between *signifiance* and *signification*. Signifiance is the productivity of the signifier, the constant "process" in which the reading subject, freed from the logic of reason, "struggles with meaning and is deconstructed. . . . it puts the writing or reading subject into the text, not as a projection, not even a fantasmatic one, but as a 'loss' . . . whence its identification with *jouissance*: it is through the concept of 'signifiance' that the text becomes erotic (and for that it does not have to represent any erotic 'scenes')" (1981). The productivity of signifiance, by which the reading subject escapes the control of signification by becoming part of his/her meaning of the text, is too fruitful a concept to be confined to literature. The surfie on/in the wave is a subject lost in the signifier—cultural identity deconstructed by the bliss of reading/surfing in the same way as sexual orgasm in the ultimate moment of deconstruction: the limit of sexual politics.

The wave is that text of bliss to the surfie, escape from the signified, potential reentry into nature, constantly shifting, needing rereading for each loss of subjectivity. It contradicts, defines momentarily, the ideological subjectivity through which discourses exert their control. The beach, however, is a text of mundane pleasure, not sacred bliss. It is laden with signifieds, it controls the desire for freedom and threat of nature by transposing it into the natural. It is pornography rather than eroticism, desire institutionalized, given a social location subject to the power of the other who produces its signification, its meaning.

Barthes's formulation of an aesthetics of pleasure sited in the body rather than an aesthetics of beauty sited in the text, and his consequent foregrounding of the signifier, is a tactical attempt to evade the social control of meaning. The body is the Achilles heel of hegemony. So Marxists, structuralists, and semioticians are shifting their attention to this matrix of concepts—the body, pleasure, desire, the signifier—as the only hope for a place outside the empire of ideology, beyond the reach of the social sense that is a disciplinary practice. For only from outside ideology, beyond sense, beyond control can we formulate what possible alternatives might look like. The politics of pleasure may be our only way of situating the forces of social change within the domain of the popular.

CHAPTER 4

Video Pleasures

The West Australian Premier has said that he would like to take an axe to them . . . but President Reagan thinks they are terrific. (*West Australian* May 2, 1983)

Both leaders are referring to video game arcades, and the disagreement between their judgments is evidence of the contradictory attitudes that Western societies hold toward these important agencies of contemporary popular culture.

A study of the press in Western Australia in 1983 and 1984 revealed that social dislike of video arcades is widespread, and that objections to them could be grouped into five categories:

(1) They are addictive for, and thus harmful to, the young.
(2) They cause truancy and divert children's attention away from schoolwork.
(3) They cause petty crime—to pay for their "addiction," children turn to theft and collecting for nonexistent charities.
(4) They are a waste of money—particularly money provided by parents for "better" purchases, such as lunch money and pocket money.
(5) They are a focus for vandalism and hooliganism.

Greenfield (1984) reports similar concerns in the United States, particularly that the games are addictive and wasteful of money—specifically, again, of lunch money.

And yet the Western Australian police are reported as being not worried by the video arcades (*Western Mail* June 2, 1983), the South Australian police commissioned a study that found no evidence to link the arcades with behavioral problems, and Professor Scriven of the Department of Education at the University of Western Australia has been quoted as saying, "The games are a good thing. They are lots of fun and develop some interesting abilities" (*Western Mail* June 2, 1983). President Reagan was a bit more specific; the *West Australian* (May 2, 1983) reported him as praising the games because they developed "incredible hand, eye and brain co-ordination."

Greenfield (1984) cites studies by Brooks (1983) and Mitchell (1983) that cast real doubt on the games' addictiveness. Brooks also found that 80 percent of the kids patronizing the arcades spent less than the price of a movie seat per week, and only 7 percent spent lunch money. Similarly, an industry spokesman is quoted: "Our experience, backed by surveys elsewhere—is that the average person spends less than $1 in a visit to an amusement parlour [arcade]." (*Western Australian* May 2, 1983).

This lack of convincing evidence of the harmfulness of the arcades has been unable to dent concerns that they lead the young to waste time and money, divert them from school, home, and work, and are addictive (which probably means that they offer a welcome means of evading the social control exercised by the home-school-work nexus). For the socially central, whom we may characterize as adults in positions of responsibility, there is widespread concern about the arcades' believed antisocial effect, which is contradictorally coupled with official evidence of their harmlessness. For the subordinate, the young user of the arcades, they offer opportunities of resisting social control and of adopting an alternative cultural stance. Society's disapproval of them is an important part of their meaning, and of the pleasures they offer.

The disapproval of the arcades is a symptom of the recognition that they lie beyond the reach of the social control that a "reasonable" society knows it "ought" to exercise over the young. So it is important to distinguish between the meaning of video games in the home and the meaning of their commercial counterparts in the arcades. The approved context of the home and the absence of any immediate economic exchange makes an enormous difference to the meanings and cultural function of the games.

This study is concerned with games in arcades, and with their place within the map of meanings that constitutes our culture, that is, the sense we make out of social experience. Relating the games to other crucial cultural domains—particularly those of work, school, home, and television—reveals contradictions in this relationship, for they offer disvalued versions of normal social activities: they position the player in interaction with a machine, with its connotative links to the production line, and they position him or her in front of an electronic screen like that of the television set in the home. These similarities of two such normal social activities as manufacturing and television watching cannot be responsible for the arcades' antisocial image, but they provide us with a starting point for our investigation, and this investigation must concern itself with inversions of the normal, not with reproductions of it.

One of the most obvious and most basic inversions of the manufacturing relationship is that the human-machine inter-action produces not goods for the material well-being of *society*, but a resistance, a kind of sense/identity for the *machinist*, and second, that the machinist is not paid, but pays, for the use of the machine. Machines that consume instead of producing can be used as powerful metaphoric interrogations of social norms.

If the machine, whether it be a productive one or a games one, is seen as a metonym for industrialized capitalist society (and it's hard to think of a more fruitful one), then we are justified in arguing that inverted relationships with the machine can be used to articulate inverted relationships with society. In the manufacturing human-machine relationship the machinist has the illusion of being in control of the machine. This control is, of course, an illusion because the machinist has to produce what he or she and the machine are "programmed" to produce; in other words, the human has to work *with* the machine in conformity to the demands of the owner/bourgeois society.

This control may be illusory, but Willis (1981) has documented attempts to make it real:

> Another main theme of shopfloor culture—at least as I observed and recorded it in the manufacturing industries of the Midlands—is the massive attempt to gain informal control of the work process. (p. 83)

Interestingly, for our thesis, he goes on to link adult behavior in the workplace with student behavior in the school:

> Again this is effectively mirrored for us by working class kids' attempts, with the aid of resources of their culture, to take control of classes, substitute their own unofficial timetables, and control their own routines and life spaces. (p. 83)

I, too, wish to develop the similarity of workplace and school as agents of social control, against which leisure is defined. Barthes (1982b) also sees an inverted relationship between parlor machines and the social world of work. Describing pachinko (a Japanese equivalent of pinball), he writes:

> The pachinko is a collective and solitary game. The machines are set up in long rows; each player standing in front of his panel plays for himself, without looking at his neighbor, whom he nonetheless brushes with his elbow. . . . The parlour is a hive, or a factory—the players seem to be working on an assembly line. The imperious meaning of the scene is that of a deliberate, absorbing labour. (pp. 27–28)

Pachinko differs from video games in that the player can win the silver balls necessary to play it—these may be used for more games, or exchanged for small prizes. Barthes continues:

> Here we understand the seriousness of a game which counters the constipated parsimony of salaries, the constriction of capitalist wealth, with the voluptuous debacle of silver balls, which, all of a sudden, fill the player's hand. (p. 29)

This Japanese game, which appears to be played by adult workers, provides a semiotic compensation for a lack of money; the video game, on the other hand, works semiotically within the domain of power and control, not money.

With the video game machine, the machinist works not with the machine, but against it—the time his (gender deliberate) 25 cents buys is extended to the degree that he can resist, work against, the machine. The better the machinist is, the less he pays, and the lower the profit of the owner. This must be a unique phenomenon in capitalism, when the skill and speed of the machinist results in *lower* profits for the owner. The relationship between capital and labor is not finally inverted (after all, only one of them ends up in pocket) but it does allow the machinist the sense of asserting his interests in opposition to those of the owner. This resistance is encouraged and rewarded by the machine—extended periods of good play are rewarded with bonus points, extra lives, or complimentary messages on the screen.

This structure of opposing interests between player and machine owner is explicitly recognized by the editors of Consumer Guide (1982). In their book *How to Win at Video Games*, they write:

> The better you get, the harder they make it. It's a dog-eat-dog world out there. And video games are some of the hottest dogs in town. Manufacturers are developing games that are downright difficult to play. Their idea is to get you spending more money. Even the games that were once simple are being transformed into quarter-eaters. Pac-Man is the classic example. Once you people discovered the secret patterns, you were able to play the machine for 30 minutes or more—on one quarter. Some game owners have started altering their machines to combat their patterns. You've got to learn to fight back. And there's no better way than with this book at your side. (p. 64)

In this investigation we met many games players who told us of their immense satisfaction at making 20 or 40 cents last "for hours." There was a common tendency to boast about and, I suspect, exaggerate the length of time that the player could deny the machine its next coin, and my own experience of playing testifies to the depth of this satisfaction. Frequently, players are consciously aware that in resisting the machine they are asserting their interests against those of the owner. The longer their money lasts, the greater their pleasure at "beating the system," in the all-encompassing sense that that phrase has in the vernacular. Not putting more coins in the slot, the pleasure of not paying for pleasure in a society that has made leisure into a consumer industry, is a self-assertive grasping of economic and temporal control.

There is a further inversion involved at this operational level of the games. The metaphor that "time is money" is so central to our culture that we tend to ignore its metaphorical nature, and think of it as literal. Thus expressions like "saving time" or "wasting time" are rarely seen as metaphors. Lakoff and Johnson (1980) have demonstrated that metaphor is not just an imaginative piece of literary decoration, but that a limited range of metaphors have become so embedded in our culture (call them clichés if you wish to dismiss them) that they have become culturally central sense-making devices. In particular, they seem to be used in Lévi-Strauss's (1979) sense of the "logic of the concrete," that is, they provide material signifiers by which to conceive of, to make sense of, awkwardly abstract areas of our social experience. So money, with its associations of ownership, earning, paying, saving, spending, is used as a vehicle to organize our understanding of time. The political and ideological implications of which metaphors a culture elevates to the rank of uninspected cliché are obvious, but rarely investigated. All I wish to point out here is that a machine that can prove that time is money and, in so doing, "waste" both has the potential for causing profound social offense.

This active waste of that most precious commodity, "money-time," is nonproductive only in the material sense. Video games are machines-for-leisure, and the phrase is only superficially paradoxical. In the same way that machines-for-work produce material commodities, machines-for-leisure produce semiotic commodities. Leisure is essentially a time for self-generated semiosis, a time to produce meanings of self and for the self that the world of work denies. The main productivity of work is obviously that which produces the commodity—the semiotic work of producing the subject is necessarily secondary to, and driven by, the economic. And the economic relations of work always position the machinist subordinately—the subjectivity produced is the subjectivity of a subordinate class, determined by the interests of the dominant.

In leisure, however, there is a chance to indulge in a differently determined semiosis, and we take semiosis to be the common center of all leisure activities. This means that leisure is primarily spent (notice the "time is money" metaphor) producing an inflection of the subjectivity that, while paradigmatically related to that produced by work, is significantly different to it. And the difference resides in the apparent choice and the way that this choice is internally motivated. That is to say, we choose our leisure activities according to personal taste (that which is ours) or at least by our class or subcultural interests. The determinations appear to derive from a similar social position to our own, and the meanings of ourselves and our social relations that are produced appear to be meanings for us, and not for others. The semiosis is self-interested. No wonder, then, that manufacturers have latched onto this self-interest and have attempted to steal it back into their interest by turning leisure into an industry, and by producing and promoting a range of products that, while preserving the illusion of the self-generation of choice, actually ensure that choice is exercised within a paradigm that is consonant with their own interests, and thus readily incorporable.

But the sense of self-interested choice remains for the user, and this is what matters. Video game machines are capable of serving two opposed sets of interests: those of capital and those of resistance. Thompson (1983) makes a similar point in his discussion of the purchase of pleasure as a commodity:

> From the seller's point of view it is rule-governed, rational and calculable, whereas from the buyer's point of view it is rebellious and liberational—in a word, pleasurable. (p. 134)

The interests of capital, of social control, and those of the subordinate, of resistance, can, according to this model, both be served by the same activity. The main ways in which the interests of resistance are served are the production of a noneconomically determined subjectivity, the existence of a control button, and in the provision of an ideological frame so that the resistance is not finally isolating and terrifying.

This subjectivity, which appears to serve the machinist's interests because it is leisure generated, not work generated, may well offer an explanation of the perceived popularity of video game arcades with the unemployed and with truants (for school is the young's equivalent of, and preparation for, work). And the fact that the media construct video arcades as against the interests of work, of school, and of the respectable family is important here, for this dominant construction provides the space for the oppositional semiosis that is the heart of the games-playing activity. Society may not like subjectivities being produced outside the school-work-home nexus, but most of the games players do. Wasting money-time is a positive semiotic act within the politics of pleasure that offers a resistance on two dimensions, for the metaphoric association of time with money works not just on the level of language and thought but also on the level of social practice. The same interests that control the distribution of money in society control the distribution of time. Work and school not only exert minute control over the temporal behavior of the people in them, they also organize the annual and diurnal cycles around their demands. Even within the family, social control is exercised by controlling the organization of time for the subordinate members—mealtimes, homework times, television time, and bedtime are constant constructors of subordination.

But economic resistance must generate a semiotic resistance that is centered in the production of a new subjectivity and a fracture of the old. Economic relations and semiotic relations work together not on the old base-superstructure model, but in the construction of meanings of and for the subject. When these meanings are ones of resistance, pleasure is a major medium for achieving them. Thompson (1983) and Bennett (1983a) both argue that the pleasure principle is a function of the self and of desire (which I will extend shortly to include the body), and that this is necessarily opposed to the reality principle, which is a function of society.

So the resistance to the machine-as-society then becomes the assertion of pleasure over social reality. This is a complex opposition to work with, for while pleasure is a function of the self, at least insofar as it is signifyingly opposed to society, this self must not be seen as a biologically produced individuality, but rather as a culturally determined self-awareness or self-generation. Pleasure is then a function of the subjectivity, that socially and discursively constructed area where the individual's conscious and subconscious work to produce meanings of self and of social experience. Our subjectivity is thus a moment of space in the continuous act of semiosis—the space that is delineated by all previously experienced discourses and meanings-having-been-made, and within which the discourses and meanings meet in each fleeting moment of semiosis.

The popularity of video arcades is greatest among the subordinate, including the unemployed and the truanting student. Also, a larger proportion of nonwhites may be observed in arcades than in many other places of entertainment, and a remarkably small proportion of girls. The most noticeable common factor among the consumer/machinists appears to be that they are the masculine subordinate in a white, patriarchal, capitalist society. We may deduce from this that their subjectivities are the site of potentially disabling contradictions between the socially determined subordination, with its lack of access to power in any form, and the equally, but differently, socially constructed sense of masculinity, with its ideology of dominance. Thus, in sitting down to the video game machine, the vital act is the grasp of the joystick, the touch of the firing button. In this moment "control" passes from society to self, and pleasure becomes possible. This metaphoric transfer of control defuses the contradictions between subordination and masculinity as experienced by the subject as his experience of power(lessness) is shaped by the discourses of economics and gender. What the playing subject is doing, in grasping the controls, is gaining the power to control not just the machine, but his own meanings, and these meanings are intimately connected with masculinity and its relationship to power/subordination.

The anonymous authors of *How to Win at Video Games* recognize how the promise of power motivates the player when they claim that by reading their book he will increase his skill and so "become the Arcade Aristocrat: that majestic person in control of the machines" (Consumer Guide 1982: 4). Their rhetoric may suffer from overkill, but the authors have focused on power and status as the key pleasures offered by the games. Their insight comes from their interviews with "over 50 experts," and their categorization of the games players as "experts" is part of this process of the redefinition of the subordinate that this semiotic granting of power/status achieves. The book contains many comments from players that testify to the sense of power and self-esteem that the games provide. Fran, an 18-year-old from Milwaukee, comments on Centipede:

> I'm embarrassed to accept less than 900 points for killing a spider. You've gotta be good to do it, but I'm good. (p. 14)

A more detailed comment, this time on Pac-Man, by Jim, a 26-year-old from Nashville:

> I sometimes reverse direction just before I eat a killer pill and then turn back and get it. This is tricky because I usually have a bunch of Monsters on my tail. But the rewards are worth it. When you do this, the Monsters all reverse with you for a second, then come back toward you after you eat the pill. That way, you don't run after them, they all come to papa. Big bonus for small action—that's what life's all about, isn't it? (p. 40)

Jim's final comment evidences the need to relate the video game experience to life experience by means of another inversion. Jim's life experience is not, we surmise, one of "big bonuses for small actions," and the consequent unintentional irony of his final cliché, "That's what life's all about, isn't it?" produces immense semiotic richness, for it contains the contradiction between the perceived ideology of capitalism—big bonuses—and the lived experience of the subordinate—no bonuses. The games machines offer to the subordinate the rewards that society reserves for "Them," those few who receive the "big bonuses" that our ideology proposes as the right of everyone. But the machine-as-ideologue, unlike "life," offers these rewards to those who resist it, not to those who conform. The subordinate, appropriately enough, win their pleasures invertedly by resistance rather than through cooperation.

But the machine always wins in the end. Pleasure exists only in opposition to unpleasure, and the pleasure principle only in opposition to the reality principle. Pleasure can, by definition, only arise from, and fall back into, a bed of nonpleasure. It does not function to change society, but to change subjectivity, even if fleetingly. But these fleeting moments of pleasure, when the subjectivity is unified, simplified, and apparently free from social control, may well leave a residue of subversion that remains in the subject, to the discomfort of the social controllers. Certainly, most of the Judeo-Christian system of morality is built on the fear of pleasure and the need to deny it in the name of some greater reality, which always happens to be constructed in the interests of those with social control. The eagerness with which capitalism produced its own version of the denial of pleasure in the Protestant work ethic is further evidence of this point. In the video games arcade, the normal power relationship in which reality/social control dominates pleasure/self-control (literally control *by* self, not *of* self) is temporarily, but significantly, inverted.

This inversion foregrounds the signifier and the body, for social control is exercised through the signified and the mind. The physicality of the body is frequently the only way for the subordinate to evade an ideologically constructed subjectivity, and the flashing mass of signifiers, with their consequent physical reactions, are the roots of the video pleasure:

> One of the most amazing aspects of Defender is the graphics: There are 256 different color combinations that may burst onto the screen at any time. Add to that a variety of noises and a grand parade of shapes and movements and you've got yourself one shining example of video possibilities. (Consumer Guide 1982: 15)

Pleasure, with its foregrounding of the signifier and denial of the signified, then becomes a means of ideological resistance. And the video arcade is the carnival of signifiers: the signifieds pale into insignificance before the insistence of the flashing, darting electronic signifiers. The machines produce messages but no meanings, thus leaving a semiotic space for the player to become author.

Baudrillard (1983) makes a similar point in his discussion of the mass media. He claims that "we are in a universe where there is more and more information and less and less meaning" (p. 86). Here, he is using the word *information* in the sense that it has in communication theory, of the *form* of the message or its signifiers. This accords with my account of the video games as being full of information, but empty of meaning. For Baudrillard, the absence of meaning allows the rejection of a subjecthood defined by the dominant system, and this rejection is more important than resistance:

> The resistance-as-subject is today universally valorised and held as positive—just as in the political sphere only the practices of liberation, emancipation, expression, and constitution as a political subject are taken to be valuable and subversive. But this is to ignore

the equal, or perhaps even superior impact, of all the practices-as-object—the renunciation of the position of subject and of meaning —exactly the practices of the masses—which we bury and forget under the contemptuous terms of alienation and passivity. (p. 108)

He goes on to argue that

the system's current argument is the maximisation of the word and the maximal production of meaning. Thus the strategic resistance is that of a refusal of meaning and a refusal of the word—or of the hyperconformist simulation of the very mechanisms of the system, which is a form of refusal and of non-reception.

This is the resistance of the masses: it is the equivalent of sending back to the system its own logic by doubling it, to reflecting like a mirror, meaning without absorbing it. (p. 108)

Baudrillard's subject here is the mass media, but his ideas seem applicable to video games. Admittedly, video games do not produce the passivity that Baudrillard sees as a positive stance of rejection, but they do act as mirrors and send back to the dominant system meaning without absorbing it. The player of Space Invaders saves society from the aliens only on the nonabsorbent level; in accepting the signifiers only, but sending back the signifieds, he renounces his position as subject and becomes a practice-as-object, a body, that, for the moment of the game, is liberated from the process of ideological construction. This moment of liberation, when the body plays with the signifiers, is the moment of pleasure.

So far, the argument in this chapter has concerned the political economy of semiosis; I now intend to revert to a more traditional textual semiotics. Video games share characteristics not only with machines, but also with television: they have screens upon which symbolic narratives are played out. In this respect we must compare them to television if we are to arrive at a more complete understanding. In the same way that the machinist-machine relationship inverted that found more normally in society, so the player-screen relationship inverts important elements of the more normal viewer-screen one. The existence of the control stick is at the heart of this inversion.

While the reader of the television narrative is able, within limits, to control the meaning of that narrative, he or she cannot physically alter the events as he or she can, and does, in video games. Greenfield's (1984) subjects explained their preference for video games over television:

> They were . . . unanimous about the reason: active control. The meaning of control was both very concrete and very conscious. One nine-year-old girl said, "In TV, if you want to make someone die, you can't. In Pac-Man, if you want to run into a ghost you can." Another girl of the same age said, "On TV you can't say 'shoot now' or, with Popeye, 'eat your spinach now' ". She went on to say she would get frustrated sometimes watching Popeye and wanting him to eat his spinach at a certain time when he didn't. (p. 91)

Video games, of course, allow this reader power to be exercised only within the paradigm of choices provided by the microchip, but within this there is a satisfactingly wide range of choices. The reader-player can delay or hasten the inevitable end, can affect the way in which the end occurs, can play safe or manufacture risks, and can exercise considerable control over the strategy of the game (see Fran from Milwaukee and Jim from Nashville, quoted above). Different games, of course, offer different degrees of control, but the control knob or firing button is always there and its potential is consciously grasped.

This is another vital difference between video games and TV or other forms of popular art. Even though the reader does exert some control over the meanings of the TV narrative, the control is semiotic rather than material. Video game joysticks and firing buttons concretize this control by extending it from meanings to events. The outcome of the video narrative may always be the same, but the means of achieving it is delegated to the player. This lack of narrative authority in the games works with the absence of meaning to evacuate the author, and into that space the player inserts himself. The player becomes the author.

The linguistic link between author and authority is neither accidental or insignificant—nothing in language ever is. Propp (1968) and others (e.g., Wollen, 1982; Silverstone, 1981) working on the structure of popular narrative have shown us the limits to the power of the author: the deep structure of the narrative is determined, the outcome preset, and the author's authority limited to the transformations through which the deep structure is manifest, and the outcome achieved. But our postromantic culture still ascribes to the author a degree of power and self-determination that is both false and widely believed in. In the same way, the microchip provides the deep structure and predetermines the outcome of the video narrative, and the player-author exercises his power only within these determined limits. Grasping the control knob is assuming authority, even if the limits of such control and authority are predetermined.

Another feature of video games is their location in arcades. Unlike TV, they are not at home; unlike machines, they are not at work. And for the young and subordinate, home and work (together with school) are the places where social control is exercised most nakedly. This social control, as we have seen, is a function of the organization of space and of time. So it is significant that the largest chain of video arcades in Perth should have chosen the name Timezone, with its connotations of a nonplace and a nonetime to attract and please those who feel themselves to be nonmembers of society or who at least wish to interrogate that membership.

Yet these consistent invitations to resistance coexist paradoxically with signs of social conformity. These are seen not just in the hortatory notices—no bare feet, neat dress only—but in the surface structure of the games themselves. The resistances they offer typically occur within a manifest narrative of social acceptability—the hero constantly saves society from invasion by aliens, saves others from attacks by ghosts or monsters, or even saves chickens from foxes. In one home video game— Auto Chase, manufactured by Dick Smith—the player controls a robber's car (clearly identified by the traditional motif of a black mask), which is chased through a mazelike road system by three police cars. As it escapes, it has to pick up bags of money (or loot). This explicit identification of the player with the socially deviant is unacceptable, so the instructions go to great lengths to refute it:

YOU DRIVE THE GETAWAY CAR!

On holiday in an evil dictatorship country, you are contacted by the freedom fighters and asked to deliver vital cash reserves to the free world. But first you have to drive around the city and pick up the money bags. Unfortunately the evil secret police have been notified and are out in force to stop you.

The social centrality of the signifieds, unabsorbed though they may be, is crucial. Nowhere do we find video representations of Ronald Reagan or Margaret Thatcher to be blasted out of the skies, nor do cartoon figures of bloated capitalists, schoolteacher bullies, or the fuzz appear as monsters to be avoided or zapped into smithereens. The only arcade game we have heard of that involves a recognizable authority figure is one where Prince Charles has to dodge flying diapers and potties. Failure to dodge results in the contents of the potty being tipped over his head. Significantly, the player "is" Prince Charles, not the hurler of the potty. Part two of the game has the Prince picking his way around cots and nannies to get to Diana, seen lying in bed calling his name. Buckingham Palace is reportedly "horrified" about it (*Daily News* November 6, 1984), but the narrative of the game offers no ideological subversion, just a playful irreverence. The only directly offensive games are ones in which the offensiveness is directed not against the dominant, but against the subordinate; these are games that involve the rape of women, or the Ku Klux Klan catching and lynching "niggers." In a Perth arcade in 1983 there was a stripper game, in which the points scored were "rewarded" by the removal of clothes from a model. By 1984 both the game and the arcade had disappeared.

The evasion and offense that the games offer must be structured against the social control that is being evaded/offended. The pleasures are not the radical ones of rejecting social values entirely, but of resisting the subordination produced by them. The games must contain that which is to be resisted as well as the opportunity to resist it. The video arcades are not, therefore, seething hotbeds of social revolution, for they are popular culture, not radical culture. Hall (1981) argues that popular art must be able to work within the contradictions between the dominant ideological forms and the resistances to them that derive from the social experiences of the subordinate. The work of popular culture, then, provides the means both for the generation of oppositional meanings and for their articulation with that dominant ideology to which they are opposed. Video arcades and the machines in them are bearers of the dominant ideology at the same time they offer the subordinate the means to articulate their resistance to it.

In the arcades this resistance to the social order is given a semiotic materiality for the duration of the game. It takes the form of pleasure experienced physically and thus free from ideological constraint, but there is no evidence to show that it goes beyond a resistance. There is no evidence of an alternative ideology asserting the freedom of pleasure/leisure over the control and constraint of work, and proposing a new social order to achieve this. This is no counterculture of the sort offered by the hippies of the 1960s and 1970s, but evidence only of a masculine, subordinate, oppositional youth subculture whose pleasure derives from the inversion of the dominant social relations and thus of the meanings that constitute that subordination. This inversion is necessarily achieved within the framework of the dominant ideology, and the ideological effectivity of the video arcades resides in their ability to provide a space where an opposing subject can generate oppositional meanings and resistances without denying that dominant frame against which the resistance necessarily defines itself.

For instance, there is, as Bennett (1983) describes in his account of Blackpool pleasure beach, an aggressive display of progress and modernity—fashions for individual games change frequently, and most arcades have a game labeled "The Latest." There are strong connotations of Americanism—the ideology of the future, yet these coexist alongside traditional pinball machines, updated versions of traditional shooting galleries, and even nonelectronic skee ball. The social order that constitutes the ground of resistance is clearly there in its normality—there is none of the carnivalesque disruption of the social order, just some evidence of a much more contained and controlled resistance to it. In the video arcade, the excesses that characterize carnival (Bakhtin 1968), particularly the excesses of the body—eating, drinking, and sexuality— are not only absent, the first two are expressly forbidden. The only excess is the excess of concentration, and this is one that produces not a disruption but a release, which liberates the machine player from the constraints of the signified performing its ideological work upon the mind, and allows a momentarily liberating relationship between the signifier and the body. For the games are played with the body, and excess of concentration produces a loss of self, of the socially constructed subject and its social relations. Subjectivity collapses into the body.

The body becomes the site of identity and pleasure when social control is lost. "Losing oneself" (in a text or game) is for Barthes (1975b) the ultimate "eroticism of the text," and the pleasure it offers is the orgasmic one of *jouissance*, which is experienced at the moment when culture collapses into nature or when the ideological subject reverts to the body (see *Understanding Popular Culture*, Chapter 3). The physical intensity with which the games are played produces moments of *jouissance* that are moments of evasion of ideological control. The muscular spasms and collapse experienced by many players when they finally *die*, when their money is *spent*, are orgasmic. "Dying" and "spending" are, respectively, Elizabethan and Victorian metaphors for orgasm. Video arcades are the semiotic brothels of the machine age.

Madonna

Madonna, who has been a major phenomenon of popular culture throughout the late 1980s, is a rich terrain to explore. Her success has been due at least as much to her videos and her personality as to her music—about which most critics are disparaging. It is also significant that her fans and her publicity materials, along with journalistic reports and critiques, pay far more attention to what she looks like, who she is, and what she stands for than to what she sounds like.

In this chapter, then, I concentrate on Madonna's appearance, her personality, and the words and images of her songs, for these are the main carriers of her most accessible meanings. This is not to say that her music is unimportant, for it is the music that underpins everything else and that provides the emotional intensity or affect without which none of the rest would *matter* to her fans. But it does point to the fact that the pleasures of music are remarkably resistant to analysis, and are equally difficult to express in the words and images that are so important in the circulation of culture.

Before her image became known, Madonna was not a success: at the start, at least, her music was not enough on its own to turn her into a major resource of popular culture. In the autumn of 1984 she was signed to Sire Records, which is "where Warner Brothers put people they don't think will sell" (*Countdown Magazine Special Annual* 1985: 2). She got some dance club play for "Borderline" and "Holiday," but the *Madonna* LP was selling only slowly. *Like a Virgin*, her second LP, had been made but not released. Warner Brothers then gave Arthur Pierson a tiny budget to make a rock video of "Lucky Star." He shot it in an afternoon against a white studio backdrop, and the resulting video pushed the song into the top ten. The *Madonna* album's sales followed suit, and *Like a Virgin* was released for the Christmas market. Both LPs held the number one position for a number of weeks. The film *Desperately Seeking Susan* was released in March 1985, which added an adult audience to the teenage (largely female) one for the songs and videos. The film worked to support the videos in establishing the "Madonna look," a phrase that the media repeated endlessly in 1985 and one that Madonna capitalized on by establishing her Boy Toy label to sell crucifix earrings, fingerless lace gloves, short, navel-exposing blouses, black lacey garments, and all the visual symbols she had made her own.

A concert tour started in April (in the foyers, of course, items of the Madonna look were for sale) and an old film, *A Certain Sacrifice*, that never made cinema release was dug up for the home video market. Also dug up and published in *Playboy* and *Penthouse* were old art school nude photos, and at the end of 1985, her wedding to Sean Penn became a world wide multimedia event, despite its "secret" location. In other words, she was a fine example of the capitalist pop industry at work, creating a (possibly short-lived) fashion, exploiting it to the full, and making a lot of money from one of the most powerless and exploitable sections of the community, young girls.

But such an account is inadequate (though not necessarily inaccurate as far as it goes) because it assumes that the Madonna fans are merely "cultural dopes," able to be manipulated at will and against their own interests by the moguls of the culture industry. Such a manipulation would be not only economic, but also ideological, because the economic system requires the ideology of patriarchal capitalism to underpin and naturalize it. Economics and ideology can never be separated.

And there is no shortage of evidence to support this view. Madonna's videos exploit the sexuality of her face and body and frequently show her in postures of submission (e.g., "Burning Up") or subordination to men. Her physical similarity to Marilyn Monroe is stressed (particularly in the video of "Material Girl"), an intertextual reference to another star commonly thought to owe her success to her ability to embody masculine fantasy. In the *Countdown* 1985 poll of the top 20 "Sex/Lust Objects"

Madonna took third place and was the only female among 19 males (*Countdown*, December 1985:35). All this would suggest that she is teaching her young female fans to see themselves as men would see them; that is, she is hailing them as feminine subjects within patriarchy, and as such is an agent of patriarchal hegemony.

But, if her fans are not "cultural dopes," but actively choose to watch, listen to, and imitate her rather than anyone else, there must be some gaps or spaces in her image that escape ideological control and allow her audiences to make meanings that connect with *their* social experience. For many of her audiences, this social experience is one of powerlessness and subordination, and if Madonna as a site of meaning is not to naturalize this, she must offer opportunities for resisting it. Her image becomes, then, not a model meaning for young girls in patriarchy, but a site of semiotic struggle between the forces of patriarchal control and feminine resistance, of capitalism and the subordinate, of the adult and the young.

The field of cultural studies, in its current state of development, offers two overlapping methodological strategies that need to be combined and the differences between them submerged if we are to understand this cultural struggle. One derives from ethnography, and requires us to study the meanings that the fans of Madonna actually *do* (or appear to) make of her. This involves listening to them, reading the letters they write to fanzines, or observing their behavior at home or in public. The fans' words or behavior are not, of course, empirical facts that speak for themselves; rather, they are texts that need "reading" theoretically in just the same way as the "texts of Madonna" do.

This brings us to the other strategy, which derives from semiotic and structuralist textual analysis. This involves a close reading of the signifiers of the text—that is, its physical presence—but recognizes that the signifieds exist not in the text itself, but extratextually, in the myths, countermyths, and ideology of their culture. It recognizes that the distribution of power in society is paralleled by the distribution of meanings in texts, and that struggles for social power are paralleled by semiotic struggles for meanings. Every text and every reading has a social and therefore political dimension, which is to be found partly in the structure of the text itself and partly in the social relations of the reader and the way they are brought to bear upon the text.

It follows that the theory that informs any analysis also has a social dimension that is a necessary part of the "meanings" the analysis reveals. Meanings, therefore, are relative and varied: what is constant is the *ways* in which texts relate to the social system. A cultural analysis, then, will reveal both the way the dominant ideology is structured into the text and into the reading subject, and those textual features that enable negotiated, resisting, or oppositional readings to be made. Cultural analysis reaches a satisfactory conclusion when the ethnographic studies of the historically and socially located meanings that *are* made are related to the semiotic analysis of the text. Semiotics relates the structure of the text to the social system to explore *how* such meanings are made and the part they play within the cultural process that relates meanings both to social experience and to the social system in general.

So Lucy, a 14-year-old fan, says of a Madonna poster:

> She's tarty and seductive . . . but it looks alright when she does it, you know, what I mean, if anyone else did it it would look right tarty, a right tart you know, but with her its OK, it's acceptable. . . . with anyone else it would be absolutely outrageous, it sounds silly, but it's OK with her, you know what I mean. (November 1985)

We can note a number of points here. Lucy can only find patriarchal words to describe Madonna's sexuality—"tarty" and "seductive"—but she struggles against the patriarchy inscribed in them. At the same time, she struggles against the patriarchy inscribed in her own subjectivity. The opposition between "acceptable" and "absolutely outrageous" not only refers to representations of female sexuality, but is an externalization of the tension felt by adolescent girls when trying to come to terms with the contradictions between a positive feminine view of their sexuality and the alien patriarchal one that appears to be the only one offered by the available linguistic and symbolic systems. Madonna's "tarty" sexuality is "acceptable" —but to whom? Certainly to Lucy, and to girls like her who are experiencing the problems of establishing a satisfactory sexual identity within an oppressing ideology, but we need further evidence to support this tentative conclusion. Matthew, aged 15, not a particular fan of Madonna, commented on her marriage in the same discussion. He thought it would last only one or two years, and he wouldn't like to be married to her "because she'd give any guy a hard time." Lucy agreed that Madonna's marriage would not last long, but found it difficult to say why, except that "marriage didn't seem to suit her," even though Lucy quoted approvingly Madonna's desire to make it an "open marriage." Lucy's problems probably stem from her recognition that marriage is a patriarchial institution and as such is threatened by Madonna's sexuality; the threat of course is not the traditional and easily contained one of woman as whore, but the more radical one of woman as independent of masculinity. As we shall see later, Madonna denies or mocks a masculine reading of patriarchy's conventions for representing women. This may well be why, according to *Time* (May 27, 1985), many boys find her sexiness difficult to handle and "suspect that they are being kidded" (p. 47). Lucy and Matthew both recognize, in different ways and from different social positions, that Madonna's sexuality *can* offer a challenge or a threat to dominant definitions of femininity and masculinity.

"Madonna's Best Friend," writing to *Countdown Magazine*, also recognizes Madonna's resistance to patriarchy:

> I'm writing to complain about all the people who write in and say what a tart and a slut Madonna is because she talks openly about sex and she shows her belly button and she's not ashamed to say she thinks she's pretty. Well I admire her and I think she has a lot of courage just to be herself. All you girls out there! Do you think you have nice eyes or pretty hair or a nice figure? Do you ever talk about boys or sex with friends? Do you wear a bikini? Well according to you, you're a slut and a tart!! So have you judged Madonna fairly?
>
> Madonna's Best Friend, Wahroonga, NSW. (*Countdown* December 1985: 70)

Praising Madonna's "courage just to be herself" is further evidence of the felt difficulty of girls in finding a sexual identity that appears to be formed in their interests rather than in the interests of the dominant male. Madonna's sexualization of her navel is a case in point.

> The most erogenous part of my body is my belly button. I have the most perfect belly button—an inny, and there's no fluff in it. When I stick a finger in my belly button I feel a nerve in the centre of my body shoot up my spine. If 100 belly buttons were lined up against a wall I would definitely pick out which one was mine. (*Madonna: Close up and Personal*, London: Rock Photo Publications, 1985)

What is noticeable here is both her pleasure in her own physicality and the fun she finds in admitting and expressing this pleasure: it is a sexual-physical pleasure that has nothing to do with men, and in choosing the navel upon which to center it, she is choosing a part of the female body that patriarchy has not conventionally sexualized for the benefit of the male. She also usurps the masculine pleasure and power of the voyeur in her claim to be able to recognize her navel, in all its proudly proclaimed perfection, among a hundred others. Madonna offers some young girls the opportunity to find meanings of their own feminine sexuality that suit them, meanings that are "independent." Here are some other Madonna fans talking:

> She's sexy but she doesn't need men . . . she's kind of there all by herself. (*Time* May 27, 1985: 47)

> She gives us ideas. It's really women's lib, not being afraid of what guys think. (*Time* May 27, 1985: 47)

The sense of empowerment that underlies these comments is characteristic of her teenage fans. A group of "wanna-bes," fans dressed in their own variants of Madonna's look, were interviewed on MTV in November 1987 during Madonna's "Make My Video" competition. When asked why they dressed like that, they replied, "It makes people look at us" or "When I walk down the street, people notice." Teenage girls, in public, are, in our culture, one of the most insignificant and self-effacing categories of people; the self-assertiveness evidenced here is more than mere posturing, it is, potentially at least, a source of real self-esteem. The common belief that Madonna's "wanna-bes" lack the imagination to devise their own styles of dress and merely follow her like sheep ignores the point that in adopting her style they are aligning themselves with a source of power.

The "Make My Video" competition showed how frequently the pleasures offered by Madonna to her fans were associated with moments of empowerment. In the competition fans were invited to make a video for the song "True Blue," and MTV devoted 24 hours to playing a selection of the entries. Many of the videos played with the theme of power, often at an unachievable, but not unimaginable, level of fantasy, such as one in which schoolgirls overpowered and tied up a teacher who denigrated Madonna; only by admitting her brilliance was he able to earn his freedom. Another took power fantasy to its extreme: it began with home-movie-type shots of two toddlers playing on a beach; the girl is suddenly wrapped up in a towel in the form of the U.S. flag, while the boy is wrapped in one in the form of the hammer and sickle. The video shows the American girl and Russian boy growing up in their respective countries, all the while telephoning and writing constantly to each other. Eventually she becomes president of the United States and he of the USSR, and they prevent an imminent nuclear war by their love for each other.

Another, less extreme, video made much closer connections between the empowered fan and her everyday life. The heroine sees her boyfriend off at a train station, then turns and joyfully hugs her female friend waiting outside. They dance-walk down the street and shop for clothes in a street market. At home, the friend dresses up in various Madonna-influenced outfits while the heroine looks on and applauds. Each outfit calls up a different type of boy to the door—all of whom are rejected, to the delight of the two girls. The heroine's boyfriend returns, and the final shot is of the three of them, arms interlinked, dancing down the street—then the camera pulls back to reveal one of the rejected boys on the friend's other arm, then continues pulling back to reveal in sequence each of the rejected boys hanging on her arm in a long line. The video shows girls using their "look" to control their relationships, and validating girl-girl relationships as powerfully, if not more so, as girl-boy ones.

In this video, as with the live "wanna-bes" interviewed in the same program, control over the look is not just a superficial playing with appearances, it is a means of constructing and controlling social relations and thus social identity. The sense of empowerment that Madonna offers is inextricably connected with the pleasure of exerting some control over the meanings of self, of sexuality, and of one's social relations.

But, like all pop stars, she has her "haters" as well as her fans:

> When I sit down on a Saturday and Sunday night I always hear the word Madonna and it makes me sick, all she's worried about is her bloody looks. She must spend hours putting on that stuff and why does she always show her belly button? We all know she's got one. My whole family thinks she's pathetic and that she loves herself. Paul Young's sexy sneakers. (*Countdown Annual* 1985: 109)

Here again, the "hate" centers on Madonna's sexuality, expressed as her presenting herself in whorelike terms, painting and displaying herself to arouse the baser side of man. But the sting comes in the last sentence, when the writer recognizes Madonna's apparent enjoyment of her own sexuality, which he (the letter is clearly from a masculine subject, if not a biological male) ascribes to egocentricity, and thus condemns.

Madonna's love of herself, however, is not seen as selfish and egocentric by girls; rather, it is the root of her appeal, the significance of which becomes clear when set in the context of much of the rest of the media addressed to them. McRobbie (1982) has shown how the "teenage press" typically constructs the girl's body and therefore her sexuality as a series of problems—breasts the wrong size or shape, spotty skin, lifeless hair, fatty thighs, problem periods—the list is endless. The advertisers, of course, who are the ones who benefit economically from these magazines, always have a product that can, at a price, solve the problem.

This polarization of Madonna's audience can be seen in the 1986 *Countdown* polls. She was top female vocalist by a mile (polling four times as many votes as the second-place singer) and was the only female in the top 20 "Sex/Lust Objects," in which she came third. But she was also voted into second place for the Turkey of the Year award. She's much loved or much hated, a not untypical position for a woman to occupy in patriarchy, whose inability to understand women in feminine terms is evidenced by the way it polarizes femininity into the opposing concepts of virgin-angel and whore-devil.

Madonna consciously and parodically exploits these contradictions:

> "When I was tiny," she recalls, "my grandmother used to beg me not to go with men, to love Jesus and be a good girl. I grew up with two images of women: the virgin and the whore. It was a little scary." (*National Times* August 23/29, 1985: 9)

She consistently refers to these contradictory meanings of woman in patriarchy: her video of "Like a Virgin" alternates the white dress of Madonna the bride with the black, slinky garb of Madonna the singer; the name Madonna (the virgin mother) is borne by a sexually active female; the crucifixes adopted from nuns' habits are worn on a barely concealed bosom or in a sexually gyrating navel. "Growing up I thought nuns were very beautiful. . . . They never wore any make-up and they just had these really serene faces. Nuns are sexy" (Madonna, quoted in the *National Times* August 23/29, 1985: 9).

But the effect of working these opposite meanings into her texts is not just to call attention to their role in male hegemony— a woman may either be worshipped and adored by a man or used and despised by him, but she has meaning only from a masculine-subject position. Rather, Madonna calls into question the validity of these binary oppositions as a way of conceptualizing woman. Her use of religious iconography is neither religious nor sacrilegious. She intends to free it from this ideological opposition and to enjoy it, use it, for the meanings and pleasure that it has for *her*, not for those of the dominant ideology and its simplistic binary thinking:

> I have always carried around a few rosaries with me. One day I decided to wear (one) as a necklace. Everything I do is sort of tongue in cheek. It's a strange blend—a beautiful sort of symbolism, the idea of someone suffering, which is what Jesus Christ on a crucifix stands for, and then not taking it seriously. Seeing it as an icon with no religiousness attached. It isn't sacrilegious for me. (*National Times* August 23/29, 1985: 10)

The crucifix is neither religious, nor sacrilegious, but beautiful: "When I went to Catholic schools I thought the huge crucifixes nuns wore were really beautiful."

In the same way, her adolescent girl fans find in Madonna meanings of femininity that have broken free from the ideological binary opposition of virgin: whore. They find in her image positive feminine-centered representations of sexuality that are expressed in their constant references to her independence, her being herself. This apparently independent, self-defining sexuality is as significant as it is only because it is working within and against a patriarchal ideology. And the patriarchal meanings must be there for the resisting meanings to work against. *Playboy* (September 1985), on behalf of its readers, picks up only her patriarchal and not her resistant sexuality:

> Best of all her onstage contortions and Boy Toy voice have put sopping sex where it belongs—front and center in the limelight (p. 122)

But even as it recognizes Madonna's patriarchal sexuality, *Playboy* has to recognize her parodic undermining of it, the control she exerts over the way she uses the dominant ideology but is not subjected to it:

> The voice and the body are her bona fides, but Madonna's secret may be her satirical bite. She knows a lot of this image stuff is bullshit: she knows that *you* know. So long as we're all in on the act together, let's enjoy it. (p. 127)

Some of the parody is subtle and hard to tie down for textual analysis, but some, such as the references to Marilyn Monroe and the musicals she often starred in, is more obvious. The subtler parody lies in the knowing way in which Madonna uses the camera, mocking the conventional representations of female sexuality while at the same time conforming to them. Even one of her ex-lovers supports this: "Her image is that of a tart, but I believe it's all contrived. She only pretends to be a gold digger. Remember, I have seen the other side of Madonna" (Prof. Chris Flynn, quoted in *New Idea*, January 11, 1986: 4).

Madonna knows she is putting on a performance, and the fact that this knowingness is part of the performance enables the viewer to answer a different interpellation from that proposed by the dominant ideology, and thus occupy a resisting subject position. The sensitive man watching her "Material Girl" performance knows, as she does, as we might, that this is only a performance. Those who take the performance at face value, who miss its self-parody, either are hailed as ideological subjects in patriarchy or else they reject the hailing, deny the pleasure, and refuse the communication:

> *The National Enquirer*, a weekly magazine devoted to prurient gossip, quotes two academic psychiatrists denouncing her for advocating teenage promiscuity, promoting a lust for money and materialism, and contributing to the deterioration of the family. Feminists accuse her of revisionism, of resurrecting the manipulative female who survives by coquetry and artifice. "Tell Gloria (Steinem) and the gang," she retorts, "to lighten up, get a sense of humour. And look at my video that goes with Material Girl. The guy who gets me in the end is the sensitive one with no money."
> (*National Times* August 23/29, 1985: 10)

Madonna consistently parodies conventional representations of women, and parody can be an effective device for interrogating the dominant ideology. It takes the defining features of its object, exaggerates and mocks them, and thus mocks those who "fall" for its ideological effect. But Madonna's parody goes further than this: she parodies not just the stereotypes, but the way in which they are made. She represents herself as one who is in control of her own image and of the process of making it. This, at the reading end of the semiotic process, allows the reader similar control over her own meanings.

Madonna's excesses of jewelry, of makeup, of trash in her style offer similar scope to the reader. Excessiveness invites the reader to question ideology: too much lipstick interrogates the tastefully made-up mouth, too much jewelry questions the role of female decorations in patriarchy. Excess overspills ideological control and offers scope for resistance. Thus Madonna's excessively sexual pouting and lipstick can be read to mean that she looks like that not because patriarchy determines that she should, but because she knowingly chooses to. She wears religious icons (and uses a religious name) not to support or attack Christianity's role in patriarchy (and capitalism) but because she chooses to see them as beautiful, sexy ornaments. She makes her own meanings out of the symbolic systems available to her, and in using *their* signifiers and rejecting or mocking *their* signifieds, she is demonstrating *her* ability to make *her own* meanings.

The video of "In the Groove" demonstrates this clearly. The song is the theme song of the film *Desperately Seeking Susan*, and the video is a montage of shots from the film. The film is primarily about women's struggle to create and control their own identity in contemporary society, and in so doing to shape the sort of relationships they have with men. The viewers of the video who have seen the film will find plenty of references that can activate these meanings, but the video can also be read as promoting the Madonna look, her style. She takes items of urban living, prises them free from their original social and therefore signifying context, and combines them in new ways and in a new context that denies their original meaning. Thus the crucifix is torn from its religious context and lacy gloves from their context of bourgeois respectability, or, conversely, of the brothel; the bleached blonde hair with the dark roots deliberately displayed is no longer the sign of the tarty slut, and the garter belt and stockings no longer signify soft porn or male kinkiness.

This wrenching of the products of capitalism from their original context and recycling them into a new style is, as Chambers (1986) has pointed out, a practice typical of urban popular culture:

> Caught up in the communication membrane of the metropolis, with your head in front of a cinema, TV, video or computer screen, between the headphones, by the radio, among the record releases and magazines, the realization of your "self" slips into the construction of an image, a style, a series of theatrical gestures.

> Between what is available in the shops, in the market, and the imprint of our desires, it is possible to produce the distinctive and the personalized. Sometimes the result will stand out, disturb and shock the more predictable logic of the everyday. . . .

> The individual *constructs* her or himself as the object of street art,

as a public icon: the body becomes the canvas of changing urban signs. (p. 11)

In this street-produced bricolage of style, the commodities of the capitalist industries are purified into signifiers: their ideological signifieds are dumped and left behind in their original context. These freed signifiers do not necessarily mean _something_, they do not acquire new signifieds; rather, the act of freeing them from their ideological context signifies their users' freedom from that context. It signifies the power (however hard the struggle to attain it) of the subordinate to exert some control in the cultural process of making meanings.

The women in _Desperately Seeking Susan_ who are struggling to control their social identity and relationships are participating in the same process as subcultures are when they recycle the products of the bourgeoisie to create a style that is theirs, a style that rejects meaning and in this rejection asserts the power of the subordinate to free themselves from the ideology that the meaning bears.

Madonna's videos constantly refer to the production of the image; they make her control over its production part of the image itself. This emphasis on the making of the image allows, or even invites, an equivalent control by the reader over its reception. It enables girls to see that the meanings of feminine sexuality _can be_ in their control, _can_ be made in their interests, and that their subjectivities are not necessarily totally determined by the dominant partriarchy.

The constant puns in Madonna's lyrics also invite this creative, producerly relation to the text. Puns arise when one word occurs in two or more discourses, and while the immediate context may give one priority, traces of the other(s) are always present. The pun never makes a final, completed sense of the relationship between these various discourses—it leaves them at the stage of collision and invites the reader first to recognize the pun and second to produce her or his sense out of this meeting of discourse. Within a pun, the play of contradictions and similarities is remarkably free and open. "Like a Virgin" opens with the following lyrics:

I made it through the wilderness
Somehow I made it through
Didn't know how lost I was
Until I found you
I was beat
Incomplete
I'd been had, I was sad and blue
But you made me feel
Yeah you made me feel
Shiny and new

Like a virgin
Touched for the very first time
Like a virgin
When your heart beats next to mine
Gonna give you all my love boy
My fear is fading fast
Been saving it all for you
'Cause only love can last.

In *Understanding Popular Culture*, Chapter 5, I note how the semiotic excess of puns makes them particularly common in popular culture. Madonna's lyrics are no exception. Woven through these lines are puns playing with at least four discourses—religion, particularly religious love, sexuality or physical love, romantic love, and a discourse of street-wisdom, of urban survival. Thus, *made it* has the street-wise meaning of survived or came out on top, but also the sexual meaning of sexual conquest and, in its association with *wilderness*, echoes of Christ's survival and resistance of temptation. It is absent from the discourse of romantic love. *Wilderness*, too, is, in the religious discourse, the wilderness of the New Testament, but it is also the wilderness of contemporary urban life without true romantic love, the secular equivalent of religious love. So we could continue. *Lost* is sexually "lost," a loose woman whose experience is only of sex, not of romance; it is also lost in the streets, and has echoes of Christ or the Israelites lost in the wilderness. *I've been had* similarly has a street-wise and a sexual meaning. So by the time we get to *virgin*, the word has become a semiotic supermarket—the religious virgin, the sexual virgin (which the singer clearly is *not*), the emotional romantic virgin, (which, like the religious virgin, she *is*), and the naive virgin who has "been had" and "lost" in the streets. *Touched* also has religious meanings of "laying on of hands" or "blessing," physical ones of sexuality, emotional ones of true love, and street-wise ones of near madness or loss of control.

The relationship between these discourses is open, unresolved and requires active, productive readers. The similarities and differences among religious love, romantic love, sexual experience, and street-wisdom are left reverberating and active, not closed off. There is no final meaning that says, for instance, that religious love contradicts sexuality but supports romantic love and invalidates street-wisdom. One cannot simply conclude that street wisdom and physical sexuality are rejected, and romantic and religious love affirmed. Romantic love may be placed in a negative relationship to sexuality and urban survival, or it may be a development out of them, a growth for which they provide the soil. Puns do not preach: they raise issues, questions, and contradictions, and invite the imaginative participation (and therefore pleasure) of the reader in their resolution.

The form of the pun always resists final ideological closure: the potential meanings provoked by the collision of different discourses is always greater than that proposed by the dominant ideology. Thus, "Boy Toy," the name Madonna has given to her range of products and the media apply to her, can be read as *Playboy* (September 1985) does when it calls her the "world's number one Boy Toy" (p. 122) or "The compleat Boy Toy" (p. 127). In this reading Madonna is a toy for boys, but the pun can also mean the opposite, that the boy is the toy for her, as she toys with the men in "Material Girl." This is the reading that Madonna herself prefers when she says:

> I like young boys—15 or 16 year olds are the best. I like them smooth and thin. I want to caress a nice smooth body not a hulk. *Madonna: Close up and Personal*, London: Rock Photo Publications, 1985)

The video of "Burning Up" is built around puns, parodic excess, and contradictions. The narrative shows Madonna in a white dress lying writhing on a road, as she sings of her helpless passion for her uncaring lover who is driving toward her in a car, presumably to run over her. Her love for the boy makes her as (apparently) helpless a victim as the stereotyped female tied to the railroad track in many a silent movie. But the last shot of the video shows her in the driver's seat of the car, a knowing, defiant half smile on her lips, with the boy nowhere to be seen. This narrative denial of female helplessness runs throughout the performance as a countertext to the words of the lyric.

So when she sings, "Do you want to see me down on my knees? I'm bending over backward, now would you be pleased," she kneels on the road in front of the advancing car, then turns to throw her head back, exposing her throat in the ultimate posture of submission. But her tone of voice and her look at the camera as she sings have a hardness and a defiance about them that contradict the submissiveness of her body posture and turn the question into a challenge, if not a threat, to the male.

The puns in "Burning Up" are more subdued and less balanced than those in "Like a Virgin," though they also play with the two discourses of the sexual and the religious. The sexual may be given a greater emphasis in the text, but the discourse of religion is not far below the surface as Madonna sings of kneeling and burning, of her lack of shame and the something in her heart that just won't die. This yoking of sexuality and religion appears to be performing the traditional ideological work of using the subordination and powerlessness of women in Christianity to naturalize their equally submissive position in patriarchy, but, as in "Material Girl," the text provides the reader with ample opportunities to undermine the dominant ideology while wryly recognizing its presence in the representation, for again the representation of women's sexuality includes the means of that representation and therefore questions its ideological effectivity. The introductory sequence exhibits this clearly. In the 33 seconds before Madonna is shown singing, there are 21 shots:

(1)   female eye, opening
(2)   white flowers, one lights up
(3)   female mouth, made up (probably Madonna's)
(4)   blue car, lights go on
(5)   Madonna in white, lying on road
(6)   male Grecian statue with blank eyes

(7) goldfish in bowl

(8) close-up of male statue, eyes light up

(9) midshot of statue, eyes still lit up

(10) extreme close-up of eye of statue, still lit up

(11) chain around female neck, tightened so that it pinches the flesh

(12) blurred close-up of Madonna, with the chain swinging loose

(13) laser beam, which strikes heavy bangles, manaclelike on female wrist

(14) laser beam on goldfish in bowl

(15) Madonna removing dark glasses, looking straight at camera

(16) Madonna sitting on road

(17) Madonna removing dark glasses

(18) Madonna lying on her back on the road

(19) the dark glasses on the road, an eye appears in one lens, greenish electronic effects merge to realistic image of eye

(20) Madonna sitting on road, facing camera

(21) close-up of Madonna on road, tilting her head back

This sequence has two main types of image, ones of looking and ones of subordination or bondage. Traditionally, as the eyes of the Greek statue tell us, looking has been a major way by which men exercise power over women, and the resulting female subordination is shown by Madonna's submissive postures on the road. The goldfish caught in the bowl is an ironic metaphor for the woman held in the male gaze. But the laser beam is a modern "look," impersonal, not the traditional male eye beam, and this can cut the female free from her bonding manacles, free the goldfish from the bowl. Similarly, Madonna's singing frees the chain that has previously been tightened around her neck. Later in the video, as Madonna sings of wanting her lover, and wanting to know what she has to do to win him, she tightens and then loosens the same chain about her neck; the next shot is a collage of male eyes, into which Madonna's lips are inserted as she sings. The pattern is repeated; her performance shows how women can be free from the look and the power of the male. Removing the dark glasses as she looks at us is a sign of her control of the look: we see what she allows us to. The glasses replace her lying on the road, but instead of her apparent submissiveness, they gain an active, electronic, all-seeing eye. Similarly, the video of "Lucky Star" opens and closes with Madonna lowering and raising dark glasses as she looks at the camera, again controlling what we see. In "Borderline," the male photographer is a recurring image, as Madonna parodies the photographic model she once was while singing of her desire for freedom. The resulting photograph is shown on the cover of a glossy magazine (called *Gloss!*) being admired by men.

Madonna knows well the importance of the look. This is a complex concept, for it includes how she looks (what she looks like), how she looks (how she gazes at others, the camera in particular), and how others look at her. Traditionally, looking has been in the control of men; Freud even suggests it is an essentially masculine way of exerting control through an extension of voyeurism, but Madonna wrests this control from the male and shows that women's control of the look (in all three senses) is crucial to their gaining control over their meanings within patriarchy.

The ideological effectivity of this is evidenced in a student essay:

> There is also a sense of pleasure, at least for me and perhaps a large number of other women, in Madonna's defiant look or gaze. In *Lucky Star* at one point in the dance sequence Madonna dances side on to the camera, looking provocative. For an instant we glimpse her tongue: the expectation is that she is about to lick her lips in a sexual invitation. The expectation is denied and Madonna appears to tuck her tongue back into her cheek. This, it seems, is how most of her dancing and grovelling in front of the camera is meant to be taken. She is setting up the sexual idolization of women. For a woman who has experienced this victimization, this setup is most enjoyable and pleasurable, while the male position of voyeur is displaced into uncertainty. (Robyn Blair, 19-year-old fan)

The look (in all senses of the word), meanings of self and of social relations, and power or powerlessness are inter-determined concepts—each one requires the other two to complete it. Madonna offers her fans access to semiotic and social power; at the basic level this works through fantasy, which, in turn, may empower the fan's sense of self and thus affect her behavior in social situations. This sort of empowering fantasy is pleasurable to the extent that it reverses social norms, and, when the fantasy can be connected to the conditions of everyday life—when, that is, it is a relevant fantasy—it can make the ideal into the achievable. The first two fan videos described above may be wish-fulfillment fantasies, but the third brings the fantasized ideal within reach of the everyday. The first two evidence the desire for empowerment; the third explores ways of achieving it. Fantasy is not adequately described by writing it off as mere escapism; it can, under certain conditions, constitute the imagined possibilities of small-scale social change, it may provide the motive and energy for localized tactical resistances. Chapter 5b explores further the positive potential of fantasy; for the moment, we need only to note that Madonna's popularity is a complexity of power and resistances, of meanings and countermeanings, of pleasures and the struggle for control.

Romancing the Rock

Rock videos are quintessential television in two main ways. First, they embody in condensed form all the characteristics of television that make it such a popular medium—its "producer-liness" and semiotic democracy; its segmentation; its discursive practices of excess, contradictions, metaphor, metonymy, and puns; and its intertextuality. Second, they appeal specifically to subordinate groups, teenagers in general and within them specific youth subcultures. Madonna's appeal is particularly to teenage girls, and this chapter considers one of her videos, "Material Girl," in some detail and compares it with another designed to appeal to the same market, A-ha's "Take on Me."

Both videos are similar in that both are romances—they refer to the common cultural genre of "romance." The narrative of how girl gets boy is told from the girl's point of view. The viewer is required to bring to bear upon these videos competencies within at least two genres, those of rock video and of romance. In her list of contrasting features of rock video and conventional realist television, Morse (1986) details the main textual devices that video competence has to deal with:

Rock Video	Dominant Realism
nonconsequential images	cause/effect
visual puns that parody accepted cultural values	cultural values taken as a given
juxtaposition of conflicting emotions	consistent emotions for various situations
displacement of time	chronological time
displacement of space	continuity rules (such as the 180-degree rule)

Rock Video	*Dominant Realism*
sometimes abstract	usually logical (uses realistic conventions)
excessive	restrained

The rock video characteristics are essentially those of a producerly, popular text: they require either an active, participating audience or one whose concerns are with image, style and the pleasures of the signifier, rather than those of ideology.

The romance genre is essentially a product of the nineteenth century, the period that produced "sexuality" as a construct and that set up the gender differences required by the new form of patriarchy produced by industrial capitalism. The economic structure of society required women to marry and produce nurture breadwinners. The romance taught them to experience this requirement not in economic or social terms, but in personal, emotional ones. So, the concept of "a romantic marriage" was constructed as an emotional need for women not as an economic requirement of patriarchal capitalism, and romances became a training of women for marriage. Similarly I argue in chapter 6 that TV game shows can be understood, however inadequately, as training women to be happy domesticated consumers; they extend the training beyond the marriage ceremony.

But there is no lasting pleasure in being a cultural dope, and from the start romances, like game shows, contained traces of women's oppositionality. *Jane Eyre* was typical in expressing the strongly felt needs of women for social, economic, and sexual independence, needs that the genre finally submerges into the need to marry, but the marriage is to a sensitized, or feminized, hero onto whom the feminine values of the heroine are displaced so that they are not lost entirely. Within the patriarchal form of the romance narrative, there is evidence of intransigent feminine values that refuse to be totally submerged. The progress of the plot can be seen as the feminization of the originally cold, distant, cruel masculine hero: not until he has been adequately feminized will the heroine marry him. Admittedly, this feminization is achieved by the suffering of the heroine, but the point is that it *is* achieved, and the heroine is not merely a suffering victim: the feisty, spunky sort of heroine whom Radway's (1984) romance fans strongly preferred does not have her spirit broken by her suffering and, in fact, often reacts strongly against it. Women's pleasure in romance comes from this articulation of the tension between masculine and feminine, a tension that survives the patriarchal form of the genre as its equivalent in society has survived centuries of masculine domination.

Television's two genres that derive from the romance—soap opera and some rock videos—show significant changes from their point of origin. Both have minimized the masculine characteristics of romance, particularly its ending in patriarchal marriage, but also its insistence on the suffering of the heroine. Both rock videos and soap opera show women in powerful positions vis-à-vis men. Both differ from romance, too, in being more producerly texts—neither of them reaches a neat point of narrative and ideological closure that attempts to resolve the contradictory voices within it, and both offer up the pleasures of "semiotic democracy," the invitation to the viewer to participate in the construction of meaning, in the process of representation.

Hobson (1982) points out that much of the pleasure women find in soap operas derives from their openness to interpretation—their permission to the viewer to insert herself into the narrative and to play with social conventions, rules, and boundaries, in an active, creative use of the textual conventions and of social rules and knowledge. This creative reading produces a pleasure firmly situated in the subcultural experience of women, which thus evades and resists the dominant ideology. This sort of extraideological pleasure is called "affective pleasure" by Grossberg (1984) and is similar to Barthes's (1975b) *jouissance*. But pleasure is closely related to power; for the powerless, the pleasure in resisting/evading power is at least as great as the pleasure of exerting power for the powerful (see Foucault 1978). Subcultural pleasure is empowering pleasure.

This pleasure is somewhat paradoxical, because teenagers, like women before them, have been systematically cultivated as consumers, and it is popular commodities—records, clothes, concert admissions—that are being promoted through the cultivation of pleasure in rock video. These target groups of teenage girls and women are delivered accurately to advertisers and sponsors. Both rock videos and daytime soaps garner large, demographically specific audiences at little cost to producers and broadcasters. But as I argue in *Understanding Popular Culture* (Chapter 2), the fact that such pleasures serve the *economic* interests of the producers does not prevent them from serving the *cultural* interests of the consumers. This positive, subcultural, socially situated pleasure is quite different from the psychoanalytically oriented concept of desire. It is not based on an *absence-* (or loss-) creating desire that must then be tantalizingly restabilized in equilibrium. Rather, rock videos establish a performative pleasure based on the satisfaction of maintaining a sense of subcultural difference, a social identity that is *not* constructed by and for the interests of the dominant.

VIDEOS AND NARRATIVE ROMANCE

The two rock videos I propose to analyze were both popular in 1985, and both show traces of the conventional romance narrative. "Take on Me" looks to be a typical one-girl-for-one-boy romance tale, straightforward and rather linear, with some compelling animation integrated in logical, if fantastic, narrative. "Material Girl" is Madonna's remake of Marilyn Monroe's "Diamonds Are a Girl's Best Friend" number from *Gentlemen Prefer Blondes*, which in its concrete recognition of the metaphor of woman as ultimate commodity is apparently sexist, fetishistic, and at the same time, in its enveloping narrative framing, conventionally romantic. Both videos are boy-meets-girl, girl-gets-boy romances, though neither ends on an unproblematic note. They have enough traces of the conventional romance for a comparison to be fruitful. Both videos, like romance novels, have young, single, lovely heroines who show signs of independence or feistiness. The hero is conventionally distant, aloof, even cruel, and the progress of the narrative traces the sensitization of the hero and the empowering of the heroine until he is sensitized enough for there to be a meeting on terms that are apparently hers, and over which she exerts some degree of control.

A three-minute video, which has to do more than relate a narrative, can hardly display much narrative progression—video romances do not exhibit the conventions of romance, but rather rely on the viewers' previous knowledge of them. The conventions allow music videos to compress narrative without falling into the trap of obscurity. In "Take on Me" the young heroine is drinking coffee alone in a cheap cafe and reading, interestingly, a boys' comic. The comic contains a narrative about motor racing in which the hero is pursued by two villains. The hero, tough and masculine, is transformed into Morten Harkett, the sensitive, almost feminized, lead singer of A-ha. The transformation happens graphically—the drawing of the hunky comic strip hero softens and changes into a drawing of Harkett as the girl looks at it. The feminization of the male occurs not as a result of female suffering (as in conventional romance) but as a result of the *will* of the feminine fantasy. The heroine avoids the traditional suffering and victimization by exerting the power of her fantasy.

In the narrative, the heroine joins her A-ha hero in the fantasy world in a complex series of reciprocal moves between the representational and the real and between photographic and graphic modes of representation. In this fantasy narrative, he joins her in the traditional feminine role of quarry, rather than the masculine role of hunter. They are chased by the villains and she escapes only by escaping from the fantasy world of the comic strip back to the real. He, however, has no such escape route and is caught and laid low by the villains. As she, back in the real world, looks at the drawing of him lying unconscious, her fantasy-power revives him. He gradually tears his way out of the comic-fantasy world until he materializes in the real world of her kitchen and collapses breathless and helpless on her floor. The final shot is of her looking enigmatically down at him as, we think, the realization dawns that she "really" possesses him, that she can will her fantasy into becoming the real.

In both videos, the romance process of feminizing the hero is condensed into two (or more) separate and simultaneous characters. In "Take on Me," the conventional cruel hero at the start of the romance is embodied in the macho hero in the comic-strip racing driver, and the feminized hero at the end of the romance is embodied in the real A-ha figure. In "Material Girl," the narrative feminization of the difference between the hero at the beginning and end of the romance is again embodied in different characters, but this time their differences are articulated in terms of wealth. Madonna, the star, rejects the rich suitor who has brought her to the studio and drives off finally in a workman's truck with the "poor" suitor. As with "Take on Me," the "Material Girl" narrative avoids any abjection of the heroine; she does not have to suffer alone in order to sensitize and finally win the hero. Madonna is in a position of power throughout. The narrative opens with the "poor" hero and a producer watching some film rushes of Madonna; he insists that Madonna is perfect and nothing needs changing. She arrives at the studio with the rich hero, and the dressing-room romance develops in parallel with her studio song-and-dance number. The "poor" hero realizes that she is playing with and parodying her desire for wealth in the song and dumps the expensive present he has brought her into the trash can and instead gives her a simple bunch of daisies. At the end he buys or rents a workman's truck and drives Madonna off in it. The final shot shows the two kissing as the rain beats on the truck windows.

The video uses money as a metaphor for power, particularly male power; so, the question of whether or not the "poor" suitor is actually poor becomes crucial. The uncertainty makes two narratives. In the first, Madonna believes he is poor and this narrative provides us with the conventional moral that money cannot buy love or happiness. Despite the overt message of the song, Madonna finds "true" love without material wealth. As noted in Chapter 5a, this is the narrative that Madonna herself prefers: she claims it is the poor guy who gets her in the end. But the second narrative casts the suitor as rich, though pretending to be poor because he knows that her song is only a masquerade and that the real way to impress her is with "sincerity"—the simple white daisies. The imagined closure of this narrative is that she falls in love with a rich man, though it is not his money that makes her love him. The interaction of this narrative with the song is more complex, for both involve a sense of play or masquerade. He plays with Madonna as she plays with the chorus boys. And in choosing the apparently poor suitor, she plays not with him but with the conventional moral—for whether he is rich or poor, she knows, and we know, that she is rich. This playing with the relationship between true love and money is so many-sided that it is impossible to determine any fixed or preferred meaning in it. Money is not just the ability to purchase; it is also a symbol of power. In taking the man who actually has the power that he pretends not to have, she is entering a relationship with quite different gender politics from that in the first narrative. The two narratives are alternately there. The textual evidence for the second is contained in two very quick shots (of dumping the expensive present in the trash can and of the roll of bills with which he pays the workman), shots so quick that many viewers miss them or, at least, do not allow them to interfere with their production of the first.

At this point in the argument, we need to note some crucial differences between the videos and the conventional romance. Neither video is closed off as neatly as romances traditionally are. In "Take on Me" it is uncertain whether the heroine and the A-ha hero will enter a real relationship together, or even whether the figure lying on the heroine's floor, the object of her possessing look, is a real or fantasy figure. In "Material Girl" the uncertainty lies in the type of "closing" romantic relationship and the distribution of gender power within it. There is also the fundamental uncertainty of how Madonna "really" relates material wealth and true love. The relative openness of the finish of each narrative leaves the viewer in a position of power vis-à-vis the text. She is invited to participate actively in the construction of the narrative and, using the same knowledge of the same conventions as did the makers of the video, to write her own script from the narrative fragments provided. What Allen (1985) calls "syntagmatic gaps" are so wide here that the amount of "writing" by the viewer is immense; both texts are thoroughly producerly, and as such require producerly readers to construct narratives from them. The texts themselves are the raw materials out of which a number of narratives can be produced.

This reader-production is guided by the conventions of romance working intertextually, but is not determined by them. Part of the pleasure is the knowing departure from the conventions, for as conventions in their regulatory function bear social power, so departing from them is a means of symbolizing a resistance to, or negotiation with, this power or, at the very least, an assertion of subordinate power. The conventional romance, with its abjected, suffering heroine, needs modifying to meet the sociocultural needs of girls in the 1980s, and these rock videos offer their readers the opportunity to do precisely that. The modification occurs partly in the narrative, particularly in the uncertainty of its closure, but most significantly in the modified reading position. The wide syntagmatic gaps that make these texts producerly do not subject the reader to the form of the narrative; rather, they leave spaces that the reader is required to fill with her own production. She is in a more empowered authorial relationship with the text than the reader of the conventional romance; different readers are able to exploit these gaps in order to produce differently articulated readings of the text that interact productively with their own social positions. The reader, located in a nexus of social forces and determinations, is able to shift the reading of a text so that its meanings and pleasures can articulate her sense of her social identity and social relations. She produces her meanings and pleasure at the moment of reading the text.

This production is a direct source of power, and gender power is another area in which the videos differ from conventional romance. Though romances provide the space within which feminine power can be articulated and finally asserted, the narrative means by which this is achieved are severely restricted, confined in the main to the lonely suffering and abjection of the heroine. This is not the case in either of the videos. In "Take on Me" the heroine uses the power of her fantasy to enter the fictional world of the hero, to share his pursuit and initial defeat by the villain, and finally not only to liberate him from the villain but also to liberate herself and him from their imprisonment in separate worlds. The feminization of the hero and her consequent power is achieved by *his* suffering, not hers. In "Material Girl," Madonna is in a position of power throughout. She is always in the position of choosing easily between the suitors, and in the song she toys with the chorus boys as she takes their jewels, money, and admiration for her own use. Stardom has always been a domain of power permitted to women within patriarchy, but Madonna shows that her possession of this power has none of the insecurity of, for instance, Marilyn Monroe's, for it depends upon her own strength, not her ability to win men's admiration. Unlike Monroe, Madonna cares nothing for the men over whom she has power.

FANTASY AND REPRESENTATION

This sense of power that the videos offer a female viewer is centered in two closely interrelated areas—fantasy and representation. The relationship of fantasy to reality, and that of the representation to the real are, to all intents and purposes, the same. Understanding their similarity requires us to reverse and deny the differences that are often set up between them in our patriarchal culture. Fantasy is often seen as feminine, whereas representation is associated with the masculine. In this view fantasy is constructed as "mere escapism," a sign of feminine weakness resulting from women's inability to come to terms with (masculine) reality. It is a sort of daydreaming that allows women to achieve their desires in a way that they are never capable of in the "real" world, a compensatory domain that results from and disguises their "real" lack of power. Representation, however, is seen as a positive act: not a means of escaping from the world but of acting upon it. Representation is the means of making sense of the world in a way that serves one's own interests. It is a political process and involves the power to make meanings of both the world and one's place within it. It is therefore "appropriately" thought of as masculine. It is seen as a site of struggle for power, in a way that fantasy is not. It is these simplistic distinctions, set up and maintained by patriarchy, that we wish to deny.

McRobbie (1984) takes a similar position when she argues convincingly that fantasy is a private, intimate experience that can be interpreted as "part of a strategy of resistance or opposition: that is, as marking out one of those areas that cannot be totally colonised" (p. 184). She makes the point that the apparently obvious distinction between fantasy and reality is open to question: "[Fantasy is] as much an *experience*, a piece of reality, as is babysitting or staying in to do the washing" (p. 184).

Fantasy is a means of representation whose privacy and intimacy do not prevent it acting just as powerfully upon the meanings of social experience as do the more public representations of language and the media. Indeed, it may actually meet the needs of subordinate subcultures better than any of the public, mass-produced modes of representation, and so may be seen to take a more directly resistive stance. Its interiority does not disqualify it from political effectivity: the interior is the political.

It is only ever a tiny minority of people in subordinated groups who organize and act directly in the political realm to try to effect changes in the social order. But the effectiveness of such activists depends to a considerable extent upon the interior resistances of others who share the same social position: without these myriad interior resistances, the activists could not justify their claims to represent a groundswell of social feeling, and their position could all too easily be marginalized and ignored.

Fantasy should not be opposed conceptually to reality, as though the two were mutually exclusive concepts. Our social reality is our experience of it: we can never experience social relations objectively, or extract *their* sense from them, for they have none, it is culture that makes sense of social relations. The difference between fantasy and a sense of reality is one of modality, for both are cultural representations: one is not real and the other false. Fantasy may be of a lower modality than more direct experience of social reality, but it is not disconnected from it, or opposed to it. The social subject moves easily along the modal scale from fantasy to more direct social experience; each feeds the other, each informs and is read into the other. The heroine of "Take on Me," who uses her fantasy to gain power over the man of her dreams, can stimulate politically progressive and positive fantasies in her viewer, and these fantasies may well chime with other traces of feminine power in the viewer's subjectivity, and may, eventually, in some cases, translate into political action within the politics of gender relationships. As part of the changing meanings of feminine-masculine relationships in the 1980s, the narrative of "Take on Me," like that of "Material Girl," may enable some girl viewers to behave differently toward their boyfriends, to understand their role within boy-girl relationships differently and thus to contribute to the gradual redistribution of gender power within patriarchy.

Fantasy is an important political part of popular culture: making a resisting sense of one's social relations is prerequisite to developing the will and the self-confidence to act upon them. The culture of the subordinate is typically a provoker of fantasy, and these two videos are no exception. In "Take on Me" four worlds are represented, each bearing a different relationship to the others along these axes of reality—representation/fantasy. Two main modes of representation present these worlds—photography and drawing. Photography appears closer to reality than does drawing; so, the photographic worlds are less "fantastic" than drawn ones. We can model the worlds thus:

THE WORLD OF "TAKE ON ME"	*World of Heroine* *(Reality)*	*World of A-ha* *("Real" Fantasy)*
fantasy/representation (drawing)	comic strip	drawn A-ha
reality (photography)	heroine in cafe/ apartment	photographed A-ha

This shows that the drawn worlds and the photographed world are each divided into two: the "real" world of the heroine (which includes the reading of comic strips) and the "real" world of A-ha (which relates to that of the heroine in terms of a different sort of fantasy). A-ha are both real people and fantasy figures to their fans, hence the designation of them as "real" fantasy. The heroine moves comparatively freely, and at her own will, among all four worlds. A-ha move easily between the representation and the reality of their worlds, but cross to the worlds of the heroine only with difficulty at *her* will.

The comic book that the heroine is reading has little to offer her—it represents only the cold, cruel hero of the beginning of a romance. Her fantasy feminizes this hero into the sensitive A-ha singer and the drawing changes from one to the other as she looks at it. Once her will has pulled Harkett across into the drawn world, she wishes to enter it herself. She then becomes a drawn representation of "herself" and, together with Harkett and A-ha, moves easily among all three fantasy worlds. A sheet of glass enables the vertical transition in the world of A-ha: when seen through it, the heroine and A-ha are represented by photographs, but as they move alongside it they become drawn representations. She and A-ha are never simultaneously "real" (photographs) until the final shot, though they are frequently both representations (drawings). Breaking the fantasy and returning to her reality involves an act of violence—tearing through the paper of the comic book. On her return to the real world, she finds herself on the ground beside the garbage pail where the cafe proprietress has thrown the crumpled comic book in a gesture that nicely symbolizes our society's disregard for feminine fantasy. At the end of the video, the A-ha hero too has to batter his way through the pages, a struggle that continues as he materializes in her "real" apartment until he lies exhausted on her floor, the helpless object of her look/fantasy.

There are two sorts of fantasy involved here. One is the fantasy of A-ha, who are real, but can enter the world of the heroine only by a willed act of fantasy on her part; the other is the fantasy of the comic book, which is an everyday part of her world that she can enter more or less at her will, but that is confined to its own level of representation. The drawn world, the represented fantasy, cannot enter the "real" world in a way that the "real" can enter the represented. The question raised but unanswered by this structural set of relationships is whether A-ha are, for their girl fans, reality or fantasy, or even whether the distinction is a valid one. I will return to this question after analyzing "Material Girl" in similar terms.

There are also four worlds in "Material Girl." There is the world of Madonna the person, along with the world of Madonna the star/performer, and the corresponding worlds of Monroe. These worlds can be modeled along the same axes as the worlds of "Take on Me":

THE WORLDS OF "MATERIAL GIRL"	*The Worlds of Madonna (Reality)*	*The Worlds of Monroe ("Real" Fantasy)*
fantasy/representation	star	star
reality ("being")	person	person

Although the structure is similar to that of A-ha's video, the ability of the heroine to control the movement among the four worlds is effected quite differently. The world of Monroe the star is represented only by Madonna's parody/pastiche of it and the power of this representation to bring Monroe's song-and-dance number to mind. Monroe's "real" world is never directly represented, though it is there as a crucial intertextual gap from which Madonna's "real" world is to be read. Monroe's absence of control over her "real" world and "star" world is significantly opposed to Madonna's control over both. The "Take on Me" heroine's "power" over A-ha is represented directly in her fantasy, but Madonna's control is represented only indirectly by its opposition to Monroe's powerlessness. Both videos require intertextual knowledge from their viewers—not only generic knowledge of romance, but more specific knowledge of stars as images and people. The history of Monroe as a powerful star and a powerless person is a story whose intertextual relations work in the same way as do the stories of romance. The question of whether A-ha is reality or fantasy to the group's fans is echoed in the question of whether Monroe's suicide and powerlessness are fact or fantasy to Madonna's fans. Of course, they are a more factual fantasy than Monroe's performances, and just as factual a fantasy as the existence of A-ha in the world of their fans. The "reality" of one world (that of A-ha or Monroe) can be made to inform the "reality" of another (that of the heroine or Madonna) only by taking on elements of fantasy and becoming what I have called "a real fantasy."

We need to look more closely at the similarities and the differences between Madonna's song-and-dance number in "Material Girl" and Monroe's in *Gentlemen Prefer Blondes*. The two songs are basically similar. Monroe sings "Diamonds Are a Girl's Best Friend," while Madonna sings "Material Girl."

Both suggest that a woman in patriarchy has to look after her own interests by using men as a source of the wealth that the system denies her by more "legitimate" means. They assert the right of the woman to use her body, the only asset granted her in patriarchy, for *her* interests, not those of men. There are differences, however, particularly differences of tone. Monroe is calculatedly looking after her own interests and ensuring that she has financial security in her old age:

> Men go cold as girls grow old
> And we all lose our charms in the end,
> But square cut or pear shape
> These rocks don't lose their shape
> Diamonds are a girl's best friend

Madonna derives much more pleasure for herself—she is not just providing for herself materially, but *enjoys* the power over men that gives her the ability to do so. Monroe shows none of the pleasure that Madonna does as she (Madonna) sings:

> Some boys kiss me, some boys hug me
> I think they're okay
> If they don't give me proper credit
> I just walk away
>
> Boys may come and boys may go
> But that's all right you see
> Experience has made me rich
> And now they're after me

The puns in "credit" and "experience has made me rich" show not only Madonna's control over language, but also that her financial demands are at one with her sexual pleasure and self-esteem. The traditional relationship of economics to sexual power is called into question: Madonna is no commodified woman to be "bought" by the economically successful man. She extracts both money and approval from the men, but because she wants to and is able to: she does not depend upon men and their money to the extent that the Monroe of "Diamonds Are a Girl's Best Friend" appears to. Madonna is no supplicant—she does not use men to fill a lack in her life.

Indeed, all that she lacks is the *need* for men. She relates to them in order to assert her independence of them. Men are there not to supply a feminine lack, but to be objects of feminine pleasure and subjects of feminine power.

DANCE AND SPECTACLE

There are also similarities and differences in their dances. In both, Madonna and Monroe reject the large red hearts offered by the chorus boys in favor of their jewels and money. But Monroe has a verse of the song sung to a female chorus, as though she were offering them advice on how to look after themselves in patriarchy. Madonna has no staged address to women: she projects an independent self-sufficiency. She is also more assertive than Monroe. While parodying many of Monroe's movements, gestures, and facial expressions, she goes further in taking money not offered and in knocking down a chorus boy and posing triumphantly over his prostrate body. Monroe wants to attract men's desire so that they will give her diamonds. Madonna merely wants their money and toys with their desire. Her gestures and expressions are less supplicatory or seductive for the men who admire her. Monroe, as was appropriate to her period, is concerned with women's ability to provide for themselves within patriarchy. Madonna asserts women's power to use patriarchal values *against* men.

Both dances are framed by a romance. Monroe tosses one of her diamond bands to her rich but ineffectual suitor in the front row of the theater, signaling her equality with his wealth, but superiority in physical sexuality. The diamonds extracted from other men are given to a rival in a gesture of feminine power over men and over her own sexuality. This power is exercised during a dance/fantasy number, but that, as argued above, does not make it any less "real." For dance, as McRobbie (1984) has pointed out, occupies a special place in feminine culture:

> Dance evokes fantasy because it sets in motion a dual relationship
> projecting both internally towards the self and externally towards

the "other": which is to say that dance as a leisure activity connects desires for the self with those for somebody else. It articulates adolescence and girlhood with femininity and female sexuality and it does this by and through the body. This is especially important because it is the one pleasurable arena where women have some control and know what is going on in relation to their own bodies. (pp. 144–145)

I have drawn elsewhere upon McRobbie's study of how girls find similar pleasures and meanings in dancing themselves to those they produce in watching films such as *Flashdance* or TV series such as *Fame*:

On one level of reading the narrative form and pleasure of *Flashdance* clearly works hegemonically: the female worker uses her skill in breakdancing to win a place in a ballet company and marry the boss's son. In the process she displays her body for patriarchal pleasure; indeed, her beautiful body is crucial to her successful move up the social hierarchy (dancing ballet rather than break, and marrying into management). Women, so the hegemonic reading would go, are rewarded for their ability to use their beauty and talents to give pleasure to me. But McRobbie has shown that this is not the only reading, and has found amongst teenage girls a set of meanings of dance and female sexuality that contest and struggle against the patriarchal hegemony. For them, dance was a form of auto-eroticism, a pleasure in their own bodies and sexuality which gave them an identity that was not dependent upon male approval. *Their* discourse of dance gave a coherent meaning to dancing in discos or watching filmic and televisual representations of it that asserted their subcultural identity and difference from the rest of society. Its meanings were meanings for them that they had made out of the forms that arguably had been provided for them by patriarchy. (Fiske 1987b)

The performance aspects of Madonna's/Monroe's dances outweigh the patriarchal construction of desire, of which traces remain in their bracketing romance narratives. Dance numbers in the classic Hollywood musicals have been theorized as interrupting the patriarchal narrative and as replacing the economy of the male gaze with spectacle. Spectacle denies the power of the voyeur over the seen object, for in the spectacle, the spectacular (in this case, the dancing female body) invites, directs, and controls the gaze, which may be masculine, feminine, or both. Madonna as spectacle invites women to find pleasure in her toying with the chorus boys just as much as she invites men to find pleasure in her sexual body, which provides the means of this toying. In spectacle, desire is replaced with pleasure, which is the satisfaction of desire, not through closure and resolution, but through openness and empowerment. The woman dancing is in control not only of the physical sexuality of her own body, but also of its meanings for herself and for others. Dance as spectacle, dance as pleasure for the self, dance as social fantasy, becomes a means of representing and therefore controlling that potentially disabling contradiction so clearly identified by Williamson (1986b): "for [Madonna] retains all the bravado and exhibitionism that most girls start off with until the onset of 'womanhood' knocks it out of them" (p. 47). At the moment when young girls become aware of their potential as women, patriarchy closes its grip upon their social relations and identities. Dance and fantasy resist this closure and assert meanings and control that are women's, not men's.

PLEASURE, POWER, AND RESISTANCE

I have argued, in Chapter 5a, that Madonna's appeal for her girl fans ("wanna-bes") rests largely on her control over her own image and her assertion of her right to an independent feminine sexuality. In this she adopts an oppositional political stance that challenges two of the critical areas of patriarchal power—its control of language/representation and its control of gender meanings and gender differences.

A fantasy that asserts feminine control over representation, particularly the representation of gender, is no escape from social reality; rather, it is a direct response to the dominant ideology and its embodiment in social relations. A fantasy that proposes an empowered heroine controlling the meanings of herself and her gender relations is an oppositional, resistive fantasy that has a political effectivity. It does not, however, have a direct political effect. The videos of A-ha and Madonna do not bring young girls out on the streets in political demonstrations, for the relationship between the domain of entertainment and that of politics is never as direct as that: they simply do not relate to each other in terms of cause and effect. But the absence of a direct effect does not preclude the presence of a more general effectivity. The assertion of women's right to control their own representation is a challenge to the way that women are constructed as subjects in patriarchy. It is a part, and an active part, of the changing ways in which women understand themselves and their social relations. Any set of social relations requires a set of meanings to hold it in place, and any set of meanings has to be produced by a social group, or formation of groups, within those social relations. Those who dominate social relations also dominate the production of the meanings that underpin them: social power and semiotic power are different sides of the same coin.

Challenging meanings and the social group with the right to make them is thus no act of escape, but is a crucial part of resisting the subjection of women within and by patriarchy. It asserts women's rights to be different from the subjectivities that patriarchy tries to construct for them. Semiotic power is not a mere symbol of, or licensed substitute for, "real" power. Its uses are not confined to the construction of resistant subjectivities, but extend also to the construction of relevances, of ways of negotiating this interface between the products of the culture industries and the experiences of everyday life. The reward, and therefore the motivation, for making meanings and relevances is a form of semiotic pleasure, the pleasure of the text. The fact that these meanings are relevant means that this power-pleasure can be transferred across the boundary between text and everyday life, a boundary that Bourdieu (1984) shows us is insistently ignored by proletarian culture. This refusal of the boundary means that the semiotic power in the text can be transformed into social power in the micropolitics of everyday life, an argument that I develop more fully in Chapter 7 of *Understanding Popular Culture*. For the moment I wish merely to argue that this matrix of pleasure-power-relevance is a crucial characteristic of popular culture, and that within it, semiotic power and micropolitical power exist on a continuum, not as alternatives. Madonna is a material girl as well as a semiotic one.

CHAPTER 6

Everyday Quizzes Everyday Life

U.S. television has broadcast more than 300 different quiz and game shows, most of them in daytime, and most of them aimed at the woman-as-consumer. A television weekday without a quiz show is almost inconceivable; quiz shows have become an essential part of the pleasures that television offers its working viewers, whether their work is performed in the home, in school, or in the waged work force. Their commercial attractions are obvious. For the producers of the goods and services to whose commodities quiz shows give star status, they provide a national shop window, and enable the producers to present themselves as "sponsors" (i.e., generous, altruistic) rather than "sellers" motivated by profit. The relationship between the sponsor and recipient appears to differ significantly from that between seller and buyer. The display (of both the goods and the "good will" of the "sponsors") is cheap—for instance, the cost of even the most expensive prize, such as a $50,000 pair of cars on the Australian *Sale of the Century*, is only a fraction of the cost of a five-day-a-week prime-time commercial. For the distributors of such programs in Australia the advantages are equally obvious: the shows help to meet the Australian content requirements, they are cheap, and they consistently reach an audience that is both large enough and has the right demographics to be sold to advertisers. Occasionally they even become prime-time ratings successes such as *Perfect Match* or *Sale of the Century*. *The Wheel of Fortune*, one of the solid, rather than spectacular, Australian shows, is currently a high-rating program in the United States, and is used as a lead-in by

NBC for its weeknight prime-time programming. *Newsweek* (February 9, 1987) revealed the economics of *Wheel of Fortune* for 1986: the show cost $7 million to produce and generated $120 million in advertising revenue.

But quiz shows' attraction for producers and distributors cannot account for their popularity with viewers. In this chapter I wish to concentrate on their role in the popular culture of the viewer, and thus to explore the seeming paradox that a popular cultural commodity can serve the interests of both its producers and consumers, even when these interests contradict each other, as, necessarily, they will. In a capitalist consumer society, the cultural interests of viewers-consumers enter a complex, conflicting relationship with the economic interests of producers. Quiz shows, which appear to address the viewer so unequivocally as a consumer of commodities, provide a good test case for exploring the power of popular culture to use the commodities, both cultural and material, of capitalist industries for its own purposes.

Some brief definitions are in order before we go any further. The social system, organized according to the economic needs of capitalism, provides the structure that determines our social experience and our social relations. Culture consists of the meanings that we make of social experience and of social relations, and the pleasures, or unpleasures, we find in them. Popular culture is the meanings/pleasures of subordinated groups in capitalism. These meanings are necessarily resistive, and need to be distinguished from those offered by mass-produced culture. Mass-produced culture, which has been so insightfully analyzed and theorized by Marxists as different as those of the Frankfurt school and those of European semiotics, offers subordinated people a dominant sense of their sub-ordination, that is, a sense that serves the interests of the dominant. Any pleasure in this sense is muted (and Marxism is notably weak in its ability to handle popular pleasure and consequently, as Hall, 1986, notes, it has tended to sidestep the issue), and is limited to the pleasures of conformity and recognition. Popular culture, however, makes meanings of subordination that are those of the subordinate, and the pleasures involved are those of resisting, evading, or scandal-izing the meanings proposed by the forces of domination. The experiences of the subordinate are diverse and dispersed, while those of the dominant are centered and more singular: thus, dominant meanings and pleasures are readily available to the sort of analysis that finds unified class (or gender or race) interests structured into and preferred by mass-produced texts. The meanings and pleasures of popular culture are multiple, transient, and located finally in the diversity of social relations that constitute subordination, and that are experienced always in some form of resisting relationship to the forces of domination. They exist in the moments of reading, rather than in the structure of the text, and are thus less readily available for analysis. Textual analysis can identify those spaces or gaps where popular readings can be made, but it cannot, of itself, describe such readings in any concrete form.

Bourdieu's (1984) productive theory of cultural capital traces the ways in which dominant culture (that of "high" art and its institutions) serves to underpin and naturalize the class differences of capitalism. Culture and material wealth are equally and similarly unfairly distributed. This theory needs extending to include a notion of popular cultural capital that does not have its equivalent in the economic domain. Popular cultural capital consists of the discursive resources by which people can articulate *their* meanings of their subordination, but not their acceptance of it. It involves popular cultural competencies that, for instance, Brunsdon (1981) finds in women soap opera fans and Grossberg (1984) in rock fans, and that are the popular equivalent of the more validated and institutionally promoted discriminatory competencies of those who "appreciate" highbrow, dominant art.

Theories of "everyday life," such as those of de Certeau (1984) explain the ordinary social practices of ordinary people as a series of tactical evasions or resistances of the order that society tries to organize them into. On one level this may involve social practices as simple as taking shortcuts across the grass instead of keeping to the paths that architects have provided; on a more complex level it involves using the resources provided by the social order (which are the only ones available) in ways that detach them from the system that produced them and that enable them to be turned back against the interests of the producers.

De Certeau (1984) uses language as a model to explain his

theory. He argues that theories of language that stress *langue* over *parole* (Saussure) or *competence* over *performance* (Chomsky) are theories that foreground language's strategic function as an agent of social control. *Parole* is an instance of *langue* at work. Theories that focus on the utterance, however, stress the tactical uses of language, the way in which its resources can be appropriated by, and used for the interests of, the weak. An utterance is the momentary, tactical language of the speaker, not an actualization of the socially determined language system. The two ways of understanding the potential of the speech act are crucially different: an utterance is the resistive appropriation of the language system; *parole* is an exemplary, rule-abiding act that gives it a concrete realization. As the linguistic system can be tactically appropriated, so can the economic. As tenants change the rented apartment and appropriate it by their transient acts and memories, so do speakers with their accents and turns of phrase make the "landlord's language" temporarily theirs. Cooking, dwelling, walking in the city, shopping can all constitute tactical utterances that appropriate the products of the strong into the service of the weak.

The differences between shopping on quiz shows such as *Wheel of Fortune* or *Sale of the Century* and ordinary economic shopping are vital. On quiz shows, one "earns" the money to spend through native wit or everyday knowledge coupled with some luck; in "real" shopping, one spends money earned by subjecting oneself to the same economic system that produces the commodities. It is money earned on *their* terms. The symbolic money of quiz shows is not bound by the economic laws that govern social difference and subordination in capitalist societies; rather, it is the product and valorization of an everyday knowledge and set of life skills that, by it, can be transformed directly into material goods or the pleasures of a holiday. This articulates openly the everyday ability of people to detach the pleasures and meanings of spending from the pain and subjection of earning.

Gans (1962), in his study of an Italian immigrant community in Boston, has shown how the subcultural use of commodities cannot be adequately explained by theories of incorporation. Disposable income was spent on display, particularly on clothes and cars, which were used to express both community membership and identity within that membership. The sense of self-esteem and identity that stylish commodities gave to the consumer, and the ferocity with which they were possessed and defended, showed that their use was the tactics of an alienated subculture, not the strategy of the dominant.

Commodities can constitute popular cultural capital, and, on quiz shows, their detachment from the restrictions of economic subjugation allows these tactical, vernacular meanings greater scope than in everyday life, where the freedom and pleasure of spending is always, finally, held in check and contradicted by the subjugation involved in earning.

Popular culture works in the interstices of our governed and controlled society. It is essentially defensive, withholding itself from the control of the social order, sometimes playing along with it, yet always ready to seize an opportunity for a guerrilla strike, for a play of tactical resistance, always alert for moments of weakness that it can turn to its own advantage. De Certeau (1984) argues that we need a new way of

> thinking about everyday practices of consumers supposing from the start that they are of a tactical nature. Dwelling, moving about, speaking, reading, shopping, and cooking are activities that seem to correspond to the characteristics of tactical ruses and surprises: clever tricks of the "weak" within the order established by the "strong," an art of putting one over on the adversary on his own turf, hunters' tricks, maneuverable, polymorph mobilities, jubilant, poetic and warlike discoveries. (pp. 39–40)

The "bargain" is just such a "trick," and "bargain hunting" is the guerrilla strike of the shopper. The bargain, the sale-priced item, is a sign of the producer's weakness, a sign of misjudging the market, that consumers had not behaved according to the rules the producer had predicted. So, getting a bargain is exploiting a weakness in the system and turning it to one's own advantage, a perfect tactical moment.

In *Sale of the Century*, the bargains offered during the progress of the competition are excessive signs of this. Their "real-world" value is given, then their bargain price (which is about 10 percent of the "real" value). The bargain price is, of course, to be paid for in metaphoric money that has been won through the contestant's wit, speed of response, and everyday knowledge. But even the price of 5–8 metaphoric dollars may cost the buyer his or her lead in the competition, so the host will often increase the temptation by adding $100–$300 real money to the bargain and simultaneously decreasing the metaphoric money needed to buy it. Such "bargaining" is a dialogue between the powerful and the weak, and in the game world of the quiz shows, the weak can only win: the bargain bought is an economic victory; the bargain resisted maintains the contestant's lead in the competition.

Similarly, when a simplified version of *Wheel of Fortune* is played in shopping malls, the metaphoric money required to play consists of receipts for goods already bought in the mall: the prizes are vouchers for more goods from the shops in the mall. Using a receipt as money is a carnivalesque inversion, a momentary freedom from the normality of economic subjection.

The New Price Is Right displays bargain hunting par excellence. The contestants are nearly all women, and the knowledge required is what our society treats as "women's" knowledge, that of the prices and comparative values of commodities. The show consists of a variety of games and competitions in which the winner is the one who best knows commodity prices and values, who is, in other words, the best shopper. But if all the show does is reproduce and repeat women's role in domestic labor, why, we must ask ourselves, should women find it pleasurable? If women are the shoppers for the family in "real" life, why should they choose to fill their leisure with more of the same?

While recognizing that the show clearly addresses women as consumers, we must also recognize the differences between the conditions of consumption on the show and those of consumption in domestic labor, for it is in the differences that the pleasures lie. The most obvious of these is the difference between the public and the private. Consumption in everyday life is essentially a private affair, its skills go largely unrecognized and unapplauded. This lack of social acclaim for women's knowledge and labor is part of their silencing in patriarchy. *The New Price Is Right* is characterized by excessive noise, cheering, and applause: the studio audience's enthusiasm verges on hysteria, the successes of the consumer-contestants are wildly applauded. There is a strong element of the carnivalesque here (see *Understanding Popular Culture*, Chapter 4), and for Bakhtin (1968), the carnival provides the occasion when the repressions of everyday life can be broken, when the voices of the oppressed can be heard at full volume, when society admits pleasures that it ordinarily represses and denies. The essence of carnival is its inversion of the rules that discipline everyday life; the necessity of carnival results from the refusal of the oppressed to submit finally to this social discipline. So the forces of carnival are the opposite of those that work to repress and control in the everyday life of the subordinate.

We can trace two main forms of liberation in the audience's enthusiasm—the first is the public, noisy acclaim given to skills that are ordinarily silenced; the second is the ability of women to be "noisy" in public, to escape from the demure respectability, from the confines of good sense and decorum, that patriarchy has constructed as necessary qualities of "the feminine."

Women, particularly those in the lower socioeconomic groups who form the core of the show's audience, are subordinated economically as well as sociopolitically. This economic subordination takes two forms: the limited amount of money available for spending and the "ownership" of that money. For women fulfilling the traditional feminine role of unwaged domestic labor, the money is the husband's: earning and providing for the family is socially linked to masculinity; spending and managing the earned money therefore becomes the feminine. On *The New Price Is Right*, money is replaced by knowledge, masculine money by feminine knowledge. The show symbolically liberates women from the economic limitations of not having enough money to buy what they would wish, and in so doing liberates them from husbandly economic power.

There is one other difference that needs addressing, and this is the one between work and leisure. Shopping as part of domestic labor has quite different meanings from shopping as part of leisure. Shopping for the family confines the women to her role as housewife-mother; shopping for fun, however, is a liberation from that role. So, shopping that is opposed to home has quite different meanings from shopping that is required by home: one is leisure, liberating and recreational, the other is labor, confining and subordinating. On all quiz shows, shopping is part of leisure and fun, and not labor: women (or men) shopping for fun as a leisure activity enter quite different social relations with the commodity system from when they shop from necessity. These relations are much less ones of subordination; in fact, they contain significant elements of empowerment for those who are more normally subordinated.

The New Price Is Right symbolically repositions the skills of consumption in the cultural life of women: it removes them from the domestic, the silenced, the subjugation of labor and repositions them in the public, the acclaimed, the liberation of leisure and fun. This repositioning or inversion is carnivalesque, and as such rests upon the pleasures of the subordinate in resisting or evading the forces that subordinate them in a moment of carnival.

Perfect Match, the ratings hit of Australian television in the mid-1980s, shows many of the features that have been discussed above; in particular, it allows everyday experiences and knowledges a public articulation in implicit and sometimes explicit opposition to the strategies of social control. (Its U.S. equivalents, *The Dating Game* and *The Love Connection*, contain most of its features between them, but neither one offers quite its complexities or its range of knowledges, and neither is such a hit in the ratings.)

The game involves the choice of a date of the opposite sex from three people that the chooser can hear but not see. Each program has two choosing games, with the genders of chooser and dates reversed in the second. The "winner" is the date who is chosen, who is then sent with the chooser on a date, usually a weekend on a tropical island or at a luxury resort. The two choosing games are separated by a segment in which a previous pair of winners return to the show and tell how successful, or otherwise, their date was. There is also a computer on the show that selects scientifically the perfect match for each chooser as a point of comparison with her or his actual choice.

The domain in which *Perfect Match* operates is that of sexuality. Foucault (1978) has shown us how the sexuality of the body has become a prime site for the exercise of social power. Nineteenth-century capitalist patriarchy used its power to define the norms (and abnormalities) of sexuality as a way of defining the norms of individual and social behavior and being. Thus, women's sexuality was confined to the requirements of the patriarchal family, and her sexual pleasure was displaced by the notion of duty (to her husband's sexuality, and to produce children). Sexuality that overspilled this control was constituted as a problem, and a whole range of medical/psychiatric discourses was developed to contain and cure it. The effect of this was that only the sexual pleasure and desires of the heterosexual male were "normal" and "natural" and thus, unlike those of the female, they could be allowed expression outside the family. This power to define normality in terms of the interests of a particular social category is social control at its most typical. It is all the more effective because what it appears to be doing is defining what is natural, not class/gender specific: there was therefore little experience of contradiction when women, for instance, accepted this definition and vigorously promoted it in the name of family morality. It is by such discursive means that, to use Foucault's (1981) phrase, "men [*sic*] govern themselves and others."

Our dominant ideology retains many traces of its nineteenth-century origins, though the challenges to it are more frequent and significant. *Perfect Match* is one of those challenges. In general, it defines sexuality as a source of pleasure for both genders, and does not grant its "moral" use within the family the ideological status of the "natural" and therefore the "right." In other words, it extends to women the definition of sexuality that had previously been reserved for men.

Women and men alternate the roles of chooser and dates, and there is no pretense that women choose by different criteria or for different ends than do men. For both, the choice is of a suitable partner for a weekend of (probably sexual) pleasure. Patriarchally constructed differences between masculine and feminine sexuality are contradicted by the structure of the show, and patriarchal privilege is discounted. Sexuality is understood as the source of equally valid pleasure for both genders, not, more "responsibly," as the basis for a long-term, hopefully marital, relationship, with the gender-power differential inevitably inherent in it. The politics of pleasure is egalitarian to the core.

This challenge to patriarchal power and social discipline is explicit in the structure of the game and implicit in the title sequence, which establishes the discourse of the show and the reading relations we are invited to adopt toward it. The sequence takes the most conventional signs of conventional romance—soft-focus pinks and pale blues, hearts, sentimental music, dewy-eyed expressions—and combines them so excessively that they become parodic or satirical. The disciplined strategic meanings of sexuality are there, but the excess produces an overspill of meaning that is available for tactical resistant purposes. The excess allows the sequence to undercut what it apparently celebrates. The struggle to liberate the meanings of women's sexuality from the control of men has been a major enterprise of the feminist movement. *Perfect Match* goes further: it offers and invites tactical resistances to the social control of sexuality for both genders. The romance is a disciplinary genre that controls masculine wildness and self interest to the same extent as it controls feminine suffering and subjugation.

Of course, the tactical resistances to sexual discipline are limited, at least in terms of their representation on the show, for its sexuality is confined to that between heterosexual, unmarried, and conventionally (i.e., patriarchally) good looking young people. A few older women and men appear on the show, but otherwise the players are young, urban, employed, financially secure enough to have active and satisfying social and sporting lives, trendily and not cheaply dressed and coiffured, and sexually attractive. This does not mean, of course, that the meanings and pleasures of the show are confined to those with similar social characteristics, for characters on television are embodiments of ideological values not iconic representations of real people. For instance, the challenge to patriarchal definitions of feminine sexuality may be mounted (indeed, may be *most effectively* mounted) by the restricted class of women represented on the show, but that does not mean that other women are excluded from the meanings and pleasures the challenge can offer.

The opposition between conventional sexual morality as social strategy and the everyday tactics of experiencing sexual pleasure despite it becomes explicit in the way that the show "plays" with the knowledge of, or insight into, people. The chooser selects his or her date from three people who each answer three questions that the chooser asks. The chooser can only hear them; the studio audience and the home viewers can see them as well. The chooser has to work with restricted information, with language and paralinguistic elements such as tone, accent, and volume. The language that gives this information is, of course, that of the utterance, the concrete here and now appropriation of the language system for the purposes of its user; it is not a *parole* seen as an actualization of *langue*. Language is used not to convey social, common meanings inherent in it as a system, but the unique, transitory meanings of its speaker. The art of using and understanding language like this is an everyday art, quite different from the linguistic arts taught in school and validated as the "proper" use of language. The players' use of language here, and their use of commodities in other shows, are both tactical appropriations of strategic systems.

And this everyday knowledge, of course, is one that the studio audience and home viewers share also, only they can add to it the visual languages of dress and the body. There is high viewer participation in the process of choice, and viewer choices are actively (and often vocally) compared or contrasted to the actual choice. These viewer and actual choices are in their turn compared to the "scientific" choice of the computer, which spells out its "perfect match." If the actual choice coincides— that is, if everyday knowledge and scientific knowledge come to the same conclusion—the doubly validated couple are each given an extra prize.

The couple then go away on their date, usually a weekend holiday, and half the couples return to a later show to tell of their experiences. This is the center of each show and one of the most popular segments, particularly when, as is often the case, the match has turned out to be less than perfect. In it the everyday knowledge, and, to a lesser extent, the scientific knowledge that informed the choice of date are set against actual everyday experience. The couple return to the studio, and, on a split screen, we see (as do they) a replay of the comments that each of them made about the other in a "private" interview immediately after the date. They then answer more questions together "live" in the studio.

The appeal of this segment is strongest when the couple did not get on well together. Part of this appeal may trace back, for those viewers who made a different choice, to the validation of *their* everyday knowledge—"I knew they weren't right for each, she/he should have chosen X"—but I suspect that the appeal rests more strongly on the validation of everyday experience against the disciplinary system. Sexuality is, above all else, a system of discipline, that is, a system by which people govern themselves and others. The discipline of sexuality, its social strategy, for young single people is that it should be used, despite its temporary pleasures, as training for marriage. The teenage magazines are full of the problems of how to find and keep the good date, and how to identify, and dump, the bad one. The evaluative system of good and bad is always, finally, the disciplinary one of long-term, responsible, mutual satisfaction that is a miniaturization of marriage. Sexuality is disciplined into the social concept of "the couple" and the resulting contract is a social one, not one concerned solely (and "irresponsibly") with immediate everyday pleasure. This discipline is so strong because its social dimension is masked and displaced onto the individual, so that when the couple "uncouples" the process is frequently experienced in terms of guilt and failure. The most powerful discipline of all is one whose disruption results not in a sense of freedom, but in a sense of guilt.

The less-than-perfect couples, who good-humoredly tell of their failures to match, who make public and enjoyable experiences that are normally private and agonizing, who can laugh at and validate experiences that we are taught should be ones of guilt and self-criticism, are refusing the discipline of sexuality. But these undisciplined pleasures always occur within and against the forces of social control. The generic conventions of quiz shows intextuate the values of patriarchal capitalism: quiz shows, commodities, and the dominant definitions of femininity (and hence of masculinity) are all the products of the same society. The urbanization and industrialization required by capitalism set up new social relations that developed steadily throughout the nineteenth century. Urbanization fractured traditional communities and produced the need for the nuclear family; industrialization set up new forms of difference between work and leisure (the concepts are quite differently related in rural economies) and between the domestic and the public; capitalism set up new relationships between production and consumption, earning and spending. And all of these differences became mapped onto equally new constructions of gender difference. So the masculine was given the meanings of the public, of work and production, of earning, and the feminine acquired the opposite meanings of the domestic or private, of leisure, consumption, and spending. Domestic work was not recognized as labor because of its association with these newly acquired meanings of femininity.

If quiz shows are popular with women (and they are), they are popular only because they bear the ideological voices of the dominant, yet also allow women the scope to resist, evade, or negotiate with these voices. Indeed, they would not be popular if they did not contain both contradictory forces, those of ideological dominance and of resistance to it. Reading relations reproduce social relations; as women's lives in a patriarchal social order involve a constant variety of tactics by which to cope with the forces that consistently strive to subordinate them, so women's textual culture must contain the same patriarchal forces against which women's readings and textual pleasures are created. Women's texts that ignore patriarchy or that show feminine values in total control over the masculine, or existing on their own apart from the masculine, cannot be popular in a patriarchal society because they lack the lines of relevance to most women's material social positions.

My account of quiz shows has not centered on their hegemonic thrust, for that does not account for their role in popular culture; it accounts only for their ability to serve the capitalist economy. Of course, the shows carry the meanings of commodity and gender that are oppressive; such meanings have to be there in order to be evaded or resisted. In the standard host and hostess pair, for example, the traditional gender stereotypes are rigorously enforced. The male is in control of the show, asking the questions and controlling the flow of knowledge. The female is the domestic, interpersonal manager who introduces the contestants, displays fashion, and enacts total happiness with her subordination. But she also fits the "show girl" image (albeit a girl-next door inflection of it);

she figures the traditional "woman on stage for display," and as such is contrasted with the everyday women contestants who compete, perform, and frequently win. On *Sale of the Century*, the contrast between the women contestants competing successfully on equal terms with men and the vapid, glamorous hostess is the contrast between the real and the plastic, between the everyday woman and an image that embodies the only femininity that men can control. It is this conflict between two meanings of femininity that generates the pleasure and that opens up gaps in patriarchal hegemony for resistant feminine readings. So, too, on *Perfect Match* there is a contrast between the way it restricts the sort of women who appear on it to those who fit the dominant stereotype (white, young, employed, conventionally attractive, heterosexual) and their behavior on the show, which breaks free from the oppression within that stereotype. *The New Price Is Right* enacts the contradictions between consumption as a sign of women's subordination and as a means of women's creativity and power over the system that attempts to subordinate them.

The quiz genre as a whole works with two different types of knowledge that are mapped into gender differences. One of these is "factual" knowledge, the accuracy of "truth" of which can be measured against external, public criteria of right or wrong. This is essentially masculine, public knowledge. *Mastermind* (with its masculine title), *Jeopardy!*, and *Sale of the Century* employ this type of knowledge.

The other type is an experiential, "intuitive" knowledge, a knowledge of people, of how they are feeling and thinking. This is the knowledge of *Family Feud* and *Perfect Match*. It is a feminine knowledge. On *Perfect Match* the "masculine" knowledge of the computer is often in direct contradiction with the "feminine" knowledge of the contestant and viewer, and is not accorded any privilege or power—the contradictions are open. The genre as a whole shows women coping equally well with both types of knowledge, able to move successfully across this arbitrary boundary between the masculine and the feminine. Men, however, appear less comfortable with "feminine" knowledges, so their participation, as either contestants or viewers, tends to be restricted to the more "masculine" type of show.

The popular appeal of quiz shows lies in the starkness of the contradictions they embody. They enable viewers to participate both in the dominant discourses and in their evasion or subversion. So those aligning themselves with social power (e.g., "knowledgeable" men) and those whose power is bottom-up rather than top-down can both find pleasurable resonances with their social situation—and, indeed, the same viewer can participate simultaneously in both top-down and bottom-up discourses. But the appeal of the shows is more popular than hegemonic, which is why they are particularly popular with children and women. On the one hand they embody nakedly the discourses that subordinate women—those of consumerism, of romance, of the family—but on the other they offer wide gaps for them to be subverted and turned back on themselves. The art of making do is the art of making the discourses of subordination into ones of empowerment for the subordinate.

CHAPTER 7

News, History, and Undisciplined Events

News may seem, on the face of it, a genre that does not accord easily with the other accounts of popular culture in this book. It appears to be determined by the reality of events and by the political requirements of a democracy. In either case, the top-down forces would seem more powerful than the bottom-up productivity that is more characteristic of popular culture.

Yet television news *is* watched for pleasure, as well as for top-down information; it is watched for its relevance to everyday life; its viewers do not simply receive the information it gives, they are productive, they do make their sense of its representations of the world. The struggle over meanings, the contest between top-down homogenizing forces and bottom-up diversifying ones, still occurs, though the balance of power may be more tilted in favor of the top. Soap opera, for instance, exists solely to be popular; it survives only because it can meet the needs of popular culture in a form that can be industrially produced and distributed for a profit. News, however, has a social responsibility, it is required to disseminate knowledge that the people may not wish to know and may find little pleasure or relevance in knowing, yet the functioning of a democracy requires that such knowledge be made available to all its citizens.

But knowledge is never neutral, it never exists in an empiricist, objective relationship to the real. Knowledge is power, and the circulation of knowledge is part of the social distribution of power. The discursive power to construct a commonsense reality that can be inserted into cultural and political life is central in the social relationship of power. The power of knowledge has to struggle to exert itself in two dimensions. The first is to control the "real," to reduce reality to the knowable, which entails producing it as a discursive construct whose arbitrariness and inadequacy are disguised as far as possible. The second struggle is to have this discursively (and therefore sociopolitically) constructed reality accepted as truth by those whose interests may not necessarily be served by accepting it. Discursive power involves a struggle both to construct a (sense of) reality and to circulate that reality as widely and smoothly as possible throughout society.

Two of the theorists who have been most influential in helping us to understand the operation of power and resistance in society are Gramsci and Foucault, and in this chapter I wish to explore how far their theories can take us in analyzing this double power of the discourse of news, and ways in which this top-down power might meet the bottom-up productivity and discrimination of popular culture.

NEWS AND HISTORY

Television news is a series of confrontations working along axes of power and resistance that are productive of a variety of popular pleasures as these lines of power meet a variety of resistances. History, too, is a terrain of confrontations, for television news is, after all, only the history of today.

Theories of news that focus on its objectivity, accuracy, or bias are based upon an empiricist notion of reality that is contradicted by my theoretical framework. The importance of such questions lies not in their role as a yardstick by which to measure the quality of the news, but in the insight they afford into the professional ideology of the newsmakers. Much more important are discursive and ideological theories that model the struggle of news not as one between accuracy and misrepresentation, but as one between different strategies of representation, between legitimated and repressed senses of the real. What, and who, determines the reality the news represents are crucial questions, but they are not ones I shall address in this chapter. Neither shall I interrogate or investigate the institutional practices that produce the news discourse we receive. My focus is on how the news and its readers handle the issues it does cover.

A useful starting point for this discursive approach is Foucault's opposition between traditional history and genealogy. Foucault (1977) promotes the writing of genealogy in contrast to that of traditional history and in doing so highlights the deficiencies of history. History, in this sense, is characterized by its production of the origins of events, of continuities that link events into a unified, coherent story, and by its pretense that it is revealing an extradiscursive truth rather than producing a discourse of knowledge and power. History produces unities, continuities, and coherences. Writing genealogy, on the other hand, involves the recognition of disparity, of the dispersion of origins and links, of discontinuities and contradictions. It sees our social past as heterogeneous, fragmented, as multiple patterns of domination replacing each other. If there is any unifying principle, it lies in the "hazardous play of dominations" that can take multifarious forms that replace each other in a "series of subjugations." Genealogy traces the succession of one pattern of domination after another. It explains not the hidden truth of history, in whatever accent this "grand narrative" may be spoken, but

> how men govern (themselves and others) by the production of truth (. . . the establishment of domains in which the practice of true and false can be made at once ordered and pertinent). (Foucault 1981: 9)

Genealogy emphasizes events in their multiplicity and uniqueness. It does not see the contradictions between them as the mask of an underlying unity that merely awaits the historian to reveal it; rather, it sees these contradictions as the precondition for the emergence of discourse. Contradictions constitute the unruliness of events that requires the emergence of the rules and power of discourse to govern them by organizing them into a truth.

I wish to appropriate this opposition between history and genealogy to suggest that Marxist, in particular Gramscian, explanations of news are adept at tracing its operation as history—its writing of a unified story, its revelation of hidden meaning, its construction of a grand narrative behind the apparent randomness of events, and the hegemonic recruitment of this narrative into the service of the dominant classes. This model is persuasive up to a point, but leaves unexplained crucial elements of the news, elements that a genealogical model foregrounds more clearly. Within the news, the contradictions and the discontinuities of events remain and finally resist its attempts to write a coherent history out of them. Television news contains within itself the opposition between its desire to write history and its requirement to write a genealogy: genealogy is necessitated by the resistances of events to the attempts to unify them into a history.

This points us to two articulations of the same problem. The first is the definition of what counts as history, what counts as news—that is, which social domains and institutions are selected to constitute the domain within which knowledge of the truth can be produced. The second is the discursive strategies involved in the telling of this story, the production and reproduction of this truth, and how we can understand these strategies in their relationship to that crucial discursive matrix of knowledge-power-pleasure.

NEWS AND CONTROL

The two approaches to news that we may tag the "Gramscian" and the "Foucauldian" provide us with two ways of modeling news's struggle to exert control. The Gramscian is close to "history" in that it emphasizes news's attempt to construct social meanings and therefore control and direct the ideological effectivity of the events it reports. News, as an agent of social control, has been well and thoroughly analyzed by a number of scholars (e.g., Hartley 1982; Fiske and Hartley 1978; Hall 1973) and, while drawing upon those analyses, I do not wish to elaborate them here; rather, I wish to emphasize news's discursive energy, its struggle to write history and deny genealogy, its attempt to exert discursive or narrative control over the unruliness of events.

News is like history in its discovery of, and emphasis on, links between events, structuring them into a monosemic, cause-and-effect relationship. This continuity is presented, however problematically, as inherent in the events themselves and not as a function of history-news as a discursive practice. Yet, American network television news does not efface its own discursivity; on the contrary, in many ways it foregrounds it— its graphic and electronic devices, its constant stressing of its own institutional authorship ("Steve Shepard for ABC News, Frankfurt," and so on) that goes with its signature, its self-constructed difference from the news produced by other institutional authors (such as NBC and CBS). It also foregrounds its own textuality as a "weave of voices" (Barthes 1975a), as "heteroglossia" (Bakhtin 1981). But it does this in a way that it hopes will not deconstruct this textuality and call it into question, but that will authenticate it by reference to an apparent "truth" that is located in reality itself. How far this hope is fulfilled is, of course, another, and finally more important, question.

There is a contradiction in news practice that coincides precisely with a contradiction revealed by Foucault's account of how history works. News-history sets up a "hierarchy of discourses" (MacCabe 1981) that attempts to discipline its "weave of voices" or "heteroglossia," and both Barthes and Bakhtin argue the eventual failure of any attempt to exert textual power through establishing a hierarchy among the voices that constitute the text. News's attempt at creating a hierarchy is explicit, and therefore not uncontradicted. It is actualized in the different narrative roles accorded to its different voices and their correspondence with spaces that are both material and symbolic. The central space is that of the studio anchorperson, who does not appear to be author of his or her own discourse, but who is spokesperson for an objective, "unwritten" discourse of truth. Paradoxically, the personality of the anchor is used to guarantee the objectivity of the discourse. Personality traits such as "reliability" work as embodiments of objectivity. The location of this discourse in the familiar, institutional studio is a signifier of its sociocentrality and its ideological conformity. No radical, disruptive voices are heard in these accents or from this space.

Further "out" is the reporter, who signs off as both an individual and an institutional voice. The reporter's function is to be in touch with "raw reality" and to mediate between it and the final knowledge of truth emanating from the studio. Different reporters can make different contributions to the same "truth"; they need individual signatures so that their "truths" are seen as subjective, "nominated" (Barthes 1973) and therefore limited, and thus lower in the discursive hierarchy than the "truth" of the studio.

Further out still is the noninstitutional reality—the eye-witness, the involved spokesperson, the "actuality" film, the voices that appear to speak the real, but that can never be allowed to speak for themselves. There is a vital contradiction here. The knowledge of truth exists only in the studio, yet the authentication of that truth depends upon the eyewitness or the actuality film, which embodies the authenticity of the truth it is not allowed to speak, the truth that can be produced only by the discourse of the studio. This actuality film, of course, is frequently not of the events of the news. A story of kidnappings in Lebanon (see below) is "authenticated" by film of an ordinary, peaceful Beirut street, or a story about the disappearance of Terry Waite by file footage: what matters is not the content of the film, but its status as "actuality." By repressing the events of the film and exploiting only its status as authentic discourse, news exerts its repressive discipline, for the events of this "actuality" are a potential source of contradiction, of disunity. News wants only the "authenticity" of such film, not the intransigent "eventuality," for that forms the matter of genealogy rather than of history.

There is a parallel here with Foucault's argument that the truth that history constructs is situated in history itself, that is, in its own writing of continuity and coherence: events are distanced from history and from truth, yet history needs events in order to authenticate, but not disrupt, its truth. The greater the truth, the further it is from events.

News's attempt to control "actuality," like history's to control "events," has been termed "claw-back" (Fiske and Hartley 1978), a metaphor that refers to the extent of the struggle needed to haul events into the safe, sociocentral sense of the studio. The news's foregrounding of its textual devices is an attempt to authenticate the process: it says that "the truth" can be written only by our vast institutional author that can mobilize all these voices and organize them in a hierarchy leading to a final knowledge of the truth that is greater than any one of them, or than any other way of structuring them, because it produces a unified, continuous, uncontradictory common sense. Similarly, history foregrounds its own methodology, its own sources, not in order to reveal its discursive practice of making truth, but rather to authenticate and guarantee the "truth" that its discourse produces. News works precisely according to MacCabe's (1981) modeling of the operation of the classic realist text; indeed, it probably exemplifies his model more clearly than any of the fictional texts to which he actually applies it.

EVENTS AND DISCOURSE

Presented below is the news/history of a snowstorm as broadcast by ABC last night (January 22, 1987).

Snow

(ABC News, January 22, 1987)

Sound Track	*Screen*
STUDIO	
Good evening. As someone in South Carolina says, "The weatherman isn't kidding." From the deep South to the upper Northeast it has been a major storm and there is very little that has not been affected. It is winter after all and here's what it was like: first Rebecca Chase is in the	Conventional studio shot of anchor: Graphic over his shoulder of map of United States with white cloud over east coast, headed "WINTER STORM." Full screen of graphic map, snow symbols over southeast move up coast to

South where they had one of the heaviest snowfalls in years.

REPORTER

Most of the south wakes up to a beautiful but treacherous layer of snow. With as much as a foot of snow in some places, people got to work the best way they could, although in Atlanta most businesses and schools never opened. Utility crews, however, were on the job as the wet snow pulled down power lines and trees leaving 50,000 without power. And Hartsfield International Airport, the nation's second busiest, also shut down most of the morning until runways were cleared.

The same storm system which dropped five inches of snow on Atlanta, four inches on Tennessee, also spawned twisters near Tampa, Florida. And in Wilmington, North Carolina, the problem was flooding. Forecasters now are warning that the snow which shut down the South today could turn to ice tomorrow.
Rebecca Chase, ABC News, Atlanta.

REPORTER

This is John Martin. At 6:39 this morning heavy snow was falling against the Capital Dome here in Washington. Even so, the government brought in 300,000

northeast leaving blue area behind them. "ATLANTA" superimposed.

Small frame insert zooms out of Atlanta to bottom left, it contains footage of snowstorm, then expands to full screen.
C.U. car wheel spinning in snow.
Bus slewed across snowy highway.
C.U. bus wheel deep in snow.
Passengers leaving bus.
Skier on highway.
Utility crews working.
Utility crews working.

Snow at airport.
Snow at airport.
Snowplow at airport.

City under snow.
Suburban street under snow.
Trees fallen on cars.
Trees fallen on cars.
Flooded river.
Flooded river.
C.U. street sign "The Atlanta Journal," pull back to snowy highway.

Repeat graphic map of United States.
"WASHINGTON D.C." superimposed.
Small frame insert zooms out of Washington to bottom left, it contains footage of snow falling on Capitol Dome, then expands to full screen.

employees: within a few hours it sent them home

C.U. sign "Department of Justice Building," pull back to people in snowy street. Pedestrians in snow.

Some people tried to carry on: about 2,000 opponents of abortion gathered at the White House. President Reagan encouraged them from inside to fight on:

Marchers with banner "March for Life."

VOICE OF REAGAN

"It's evident to me that you're not going to let a little weather stand in the way of this noble cause."

Demonstrators in snow, zoom to organizers on platform.

REPORTER

So they marched in the great Washington snowstorm of 1987, the worst since 16 inches fell in 1983. This time more than 11 inches fell by midday. Cars jammed Constitution Avenue, airports closed, workers scrambled for transportation. But despite all that, many people marvelled at the snow:

Marchers in snow.

Traffic jam in snowy street.
Traffic jam in snowy street.

Deserted airport.
People boarding bus.

VOX POP

"Oh yes it's wonderful, it's great, beautiful. It's (laughs) great."

Woman and man in street, talking to reporter.

Children sledding.

REPORTER

John Martin, ABC News, Washington.

Repeat graphic map of United States.
"NEW YORK CITY" superimposed.

REPORTER

This is Bill O'Reilly in New York. As the snow fell, the radio supplied the narration:

RADIO VOICES

"Heavy wind-driven snow will continue into this evening . . ." ". . . and the national weather service has placed a winter storm warning that affects the tri-state area . . ." ". . . so we have a messy situation . . ."

REPORTER

To deal with the near blizzard conditions, an army of 450 plows tried to keep city streets clear. It was tough going, especially since the suburban Long Island Railroad is on strike causing thousands more to drive to the city. It was impossible going at New York's airports. They closed, forcing some international flights to divert as far away as Kansas City, and stranding thousands of passengers.

VOX POP

"We're from Utah trying to get home. We've been out in the wet snow, freezing. Here we are, drenched, no hotels, no transportation . . ."

REPORTER

In Boston, Philadelphia and other northeast cities it was more of the

Small frame insert zooms out of New York to bottom left; it contains footage of children in snowy street, then expands to full screen.
Men pushing car in street.

Snow plows in street.
Snow plows in street.

Traffic jam in street.
Car slewed onto sidewalk.

Snow at airport.
People waiting in terminal.
C.U. airport departure screen.

People sitting on floor of terminal.

Man talking to reporter.

Woman under umbrella in snow.
Pedestrians in driving snow.

same, clogged streets, closed airports, slippery streets. It was clearly no time for a stroll.	Child in stroller being pulled through snow.
Bill O'Reilly, ABC News, New York	
STUDIO	
You heard a mention of airports. . . . Because of today's storm at least 10 major airports on the east coast were shut down. And the storm has had a ripple effect. . . . there was no problem with the weather at Chicago's O'Hare Airport, but when much of the East is closed, many of the travellers at O'Hare have no place to go.	Conventional studio shot of anchor. People in terminal, "O'HARE AIRPORT CHICAGO" superimposed. C.U. airport departure screen.

We notice first that the "natural" continuity of the storm as it moves up the East Coast is mobilized to provide a unity and a coherence among the shutting down of government, a right-to-life protest march (complete with the disembodied vocal support of Ronald Reagan), and an industrial dispute on a suburban railroad. The unity of the storm is constructed by the graphics, which give us a satellitelike view of its progress (and what discourse can be higher in a hierarchy than one emanating from a satellite?) so that we *know* that it is, in fact, the same storm in Atlanta as in Washington as in New York. Its path is echoed by the order of reports in the story; like it, they move from South to North in a neat reversal of political news: once more nature opposes culture. Its disruptiveness forms the continuity among the disruptions of economic shutdowns, industrial disputes, and protest marches, but the point of news/history is not that disruptions happen—news/history is made of the struggle between the forces of order and those of disorder—but that the discursive control over these disruptions, the ability to locate them within a sense-making apparatus, is the power of news/history writing at work. News/history is a discourse of power.

Conversely, to write a genealogy of these discontinuous moments that news has swept into its discursive field of force would disunify them, would emphasize the differences between the shutdown of government (by those with social power) and the shutdown of a railroad (by those with subordinate power, the power of resistance to power) between the sanctioned resistances of a right-to-life protest (right wing) and an industrial dispute (left wing), between the voice of the government sending its employees home because of the storm and the voice of the president applauding marchers for carrying on despite it, or between the official discourse of the storm as a disruptive, threatening event, and the voices (and pictures) of the people enjoying it. Three days later, another storm caused the government to shut down again. That evening's news showed a senator complaining that the shutdown had cost the taxpayers $8,000,000, while the camera showed us the same taxpayers enjoying the freedom from the discipline of work and economics that the senator's discourse was propagating, a discourse through which "men govern (themselves and others)" but that also produces their own moments of resistance to this governance. (This same story also contained an interview with a visiting Jamaican diplomat, who joked that the Strategic Defense Initiative was misplaced: rather, the government should research ways of preventing the Russians from dumping nine inches of snow on Washington.) The continuity of the storm can be used to link events within and against an enormous field of diversity.

The Gramscian model would tell us that the conventions of news are constructing the storm, the shutdown of government, protesting marchers, striking railroad workers, and the Russians as relatively equal threats to the status quo. The storm acts as a metaphor that naturalizes the social and political threats of the events, and thus dissolves any sense of their oppositionality into the commonsense "truth" that the status quo will cope with them, and further that it will emerge not only unthreatened, but actually strengthened by them: disruptions and threats work finally to demonstrate the system's ability to accommodate them. The Gramscian model would explain the shots of people having fun in the face of disruptions by seeing them as traces of the hegemonic struggle: they evidence the precariousness of the power of the Protestant work ethic and its consequent fear of popular pleasure, they show that its ability to win people's consent is constantly under question and that any consent that it may win is never complete, is always grudging, always contains the knowledge of what has been repressed.

Foucault, however, would say that any power, and here we are talking of discursive power, exists only by virtue of resistance, that resistance is not an obstacle to power but an essential component of it. For Foucault, power is not adequately explained in Gramscian terms—that is, in terms that assign priorities to economics, class, and ideological domination—for power is not simply the means by which different sociopolitical interests attempt to establish and maintain their class interests, a power whose necessity will vanish once the struggle has been won. The ultimate power for Foucault is the power of knowledge, and social control is exercised through the control of knowledge or truth. The role of discourse in the production of knowledge is not the same as its role in the production of common sense in Gramscian theory, though the differences are, as I understand them, ones of emphasis rather than of substance. Hegemony investigates the production of common sense by asking what sense is established as common and whose class interests it serves. Foucault turns rather to his idea of "a will to knowledge," a will that is not class specific, and the subsequent power is the power to control knowledge/truth rather than the power to control class interests. Because of our "will to knowledge," the production of a truth is inherently pleasurable, whether that truth be a dominating or a resisting one:

> The pleasure that comes of exercising a power that questions, monitors, watches, spies, searches out, palpates, brings to light: and, on the other hand, the pleasure that kindles at having to evade this power, flee from it, fool it or travesty it. The power that lets itself be invaded by the pleasure it is pursuing: and opposite it, power asserting itself in the pleasure of showing off, scandalizing, resisting. (Foucault 1978: 45)

The pleasure in the official power to shut down government is resisted and scandalized by the pleasure of sledding, of enjoying the beauty of the snow, pleasures associated with the body, which for Foucault is one of the prime sites of power and resistance—the power to control its meanings and pleasures is not foregrounded in "history," though Foucault's genealogies have centered on it.

There is no one set of social interests served by the unifying of snow, pro-lifers, industrial disputes, a closed administration, and the pleasures of sledding: the coherence of the news is discursive power at work, rather than more narrowly defined sociopolitical power. This does not mean that the two are unconnected, clearly they are not, but rather that power is not to be explained by a model of a "grand narrative," whether it be Marxist, neo-Marxist, capitalist, or liberal-pluralist in inflection. Rather, power must be understood discursively in terms of its ability to impose a particular knowledge over resisting, competing knowledges. Power and resistance are not just opposite sides of the same coin, each requiring the other; rather, they are interchangeable lines of force. Resisting is itself a form of power. Power is not necessarily a top-down force and resistance a bottom-up force, for the bottom-up power of the socially subordinate can be met with the resistance of those who in terms of economics or politically institutionalized power may be said to be dominating.

The understanding of power is to be sought in its moments of exertion, which may be historically and socially situated, but whose sociohistorical situation does not, of itself, provide adequate explanation of what is going on. Another, more political story broadcast yesterday—but now yesterday has become January 23 (to be true to my preferences, I must make the history of writing this piece part of its meaning)—shows the same forces at work.

Kidnappings

(ABC News, January 23, 1987)

	Soundtrack	*Screen*
STUDIO		
	In Lebanon tonight there is still no word of the actual whereabouts of the hostage negotiator Terry	Conventional studio shot, still frame of Terry Waite behind anchor.

Waite. But as ABC's Charles
Glass reports, he does appear to
be safe.

REPORTER

In London today, the Church of
England tried to put an end to
rumors about the long
disappearance of its envoy, Terry
Waite. The church released a
statement saying Waite was safe
and locked in discussions with
the captors of Americans Terry
Anderson and Thomas
Sutherland. The British Press had
fueled the rumor machine with
speculation. Waite may have
been kidnapped and the
Lebanese Christian radio
station, notoriously unreliable
on Muslim affairs, took exactly
the opposite view, saying Waite
was close to freeing the hostages.

Still of ecclesiastical-looking
   building, diagonal slash
   "London," zoom in on
   window.
Picture of Waite superimposed
   on window.
Pictures of Anderson and
   Sutherland superimposed.
Front page of British newspaper,
   headlines "Terry Waite
   Kidnap Fear."
Busy radio studio.
Still of man listening to radio,
   reduced to square, top of
   screen.

RADIO VOICE

Information to the Voice of
Lebanon says it's very possible
that Anglican Church envoy
Terry Waite is in the Bekaa area
and that he may bring back with
him two hostages.

Graphics of spoken words roll
   onto blank area of screen.

REPORTER

While Waite talked in secret,
Muslim West Beirut was the
scene today of an apparent
double kidnapping of two
fairheaded men, according to
eyewitness reports, who may
have been West Germans. This
would bring to four the number of

Street scene, moving traffic.
C.U. of "Pavilion Club," pull
   back to street scene.

West Germans kidnapped in Beirut since the arrest in Frankfurt of Mohammed Ali Hamadei, one of the alleged hijackers of TWA Flight 847 in 1985. Most West Germans, said to number about 150 people here, have fled from West Beirut, either to Christian East Beirut or by sea to the island of Cyprus. In Cyprus, United States helicopters are standing by, reminders that there are now three possible outcomes for the Waite mission: the helicopters could bring out Thomas Sutherland and Terry Anderson if Waite succeeds; Waite could come back emptyhanded; or, least likely, find himself a hostage.

Charles Glass, ABC News, London.

STUDIO

So now, as Charles Glass makes clear, the West Germans are feeling the kind of pressure, not only in West Beirut but at home, that the Americans have been feeling for a very lengthy period of time. And on Sunday in Germany there is a general election. Is there a relationship between the general election, Hamadei, who the United States wants extradited here, and the people who are disappearing in Lebanon? Many people in Germany are absolutely convinced. Here's ABC's Steve Shepard.

Street scene, shoppers and cars.

Street scene, shoppers and cars, bare shop windows.
M.C.U. men talking in street.
M.C.U. military checkpoint in street.
Family on dockside.
Helicopter hovering.
Two helicopters flying.

C.U. Waite looking up into sky.

Conventional studio shot, C.U. anchor.

REPORTER

At a morning news conference, Chancellor Helmut Kohl refused all questions on the German hostage crisis. Socialist Leader Iohannes Rau, Kohl's main rival, also refused comment today except to offer Kohl his support during the emergency. But Germany's press is more talkative. Just about every television news program and newspaper has an opinion on the crisis:

Establishing shot of news conference, slash "West Germany."
C.U. Chancellor Kohl at conference.
M.C.U. Rau in street.

Opening sequence of German TV News.

"Gain time and keep all options open" says one paper.

"Leniency will lead to more kidnappings" says another.

Montage of German papers, superimposed graphics:
"Keep Options Open"
"Leniency leads to Kidnappings"
"Don't Extradite"
"Try Hamadei in Germany."

Many say "Don't extradite Mohammed Ali Hamadei to the United States: try him here instead."

But so far, for fear of endangering the hostages, nobody is making the kidnappings an issue in this Sunday's election. The main themes as usual are the economy and peace.

Kohl in crowds, electioneering.
C.U. Kohl speaking.
M.C.U. Kohl speaking on podium.
Applauding audience.

West Germany is immensely rich. A Mercedes isn't a status symbol here, it's a taxi.
The German mark is strong and the German people can afford the luxury items that fill their stores.

Car assembly line.
C.U. Mercedes on assembly line.
Two Mercedes taxis in street.
Woman looking in jeweler's window.
Fashionably dressed woman in street.
Shoppers in front of luxury shops.

The Heuser family is typically middle income. In Germany that's enough to buy his son computer discs and pay for a vacation in California. Helmut Heuser not only supports Chancellor Kohl's economic program but his strong military posture as well:	Two young boys playing with a construction toy at home. Home computer. C.U. computer screen. Middle-aged man and wife at home.

HELMUT HEUSER

Therefore we know exactly what it means to be free and what it means to be not free.	C.U. of man, "Helmut Heuser" superimposed.

REPORTER

But Germany's socialists want defense cut and social spending increased, while the growing Green Party wants that and a less materialist society:	Marchers demonstrating, red banners, German slogans in red. Different marchers demonstrating. Different marchers demonstrating.

SPOKESPERSON

People are beginning to say, "I'm not really happy, I'm deep inside depressed, I'm not happy, why do I need two videos, why do I need two cars?" and that debate is what we always hoped would happen one day.	C.U. woman speaking, "Petra Kelly, Green Party Candidate" superimposed.

REPORTER

But with the economy booming and forty years of peace to look back upon, most Germans today don't seem very anxious for a changed government. Until the hostage crisis, Kohl was heavily favored in the upcoming election.	Reporter talking to camera, "Steve Shepard, Frankfurt" superimposed. C.U. Kohl speech making. Longshot: Kohl speech making, huge slogans behind him. Kohl waving to applause.

Kohl still looks a winner unless
something happens in the next
few days to the hostages in
Beirut.

Steve Shepard, ABC News,
Frankfurt.

The discursive strategy of the news here is to find a unity, a
series of continuities, among events that include the disappearance of a British hostage negotiator, the German capture of a
Lebanese suspected of hijacking an American airliner,
kidnappings in Beirut, American helicopters in Cyprus, the
West German general election, with its issues of economic
materialism and peace, the American experiences of TWA
Flight 847, and, unspoken but present, of Carter, the Iranian
hostage crisis, and the presidential election of 1980.

As with the snow history, nature is recruited to provide
continuity. Events in Lebanon yesterday are geographically
continuous with TWA Flight 847 in 1985 and those in Teheran
in 1979: all are part of "the Middle East." History then joins with
geography to naturalize the links between Germany and
Lebanon, so that the election story in Frankfurt can be
continuous with that of kidnappings in Beirut. Using history
and geography to unify and deny the multiple contradictions
in the concept of nation is a pervasive discursive strategy that
is not confined to the news. There is, of course, a certain irony
here, in that the "origin" of many events in the Middle East lies
precisely in the fact that one nation has no geography to give it
a material realization. Again, Gramscians would argue that as
the snow was used to deny contradictory meanings of events
of that day, so too geography is used to deny socially active
contradictions in the concept of nationhood, and that the same
discursive strategy lies behind giving ideologically allied
nations a geographical unity, so that Britain, West Germany,
and the United States are unified because they form "the West"
rather than the "capitalist bloc."

But, again, these links do not provide a sufficient explanation
of what is going on in this story writing. The unruliness of
events and their power to resist news's attempt to write them
into history is apparent once again. The studio anchor says:

Is there a relationship between the general election, Hamadei, who the United States wants extradited here, and the people who are disappearing in Lebanon? Many people in Germany are absolutely convinced.

But the reporter's story not only fails to make those links, it explicitly contradicts them: "For fear of endangering the hostages, nobody is making the kidnappings an issue in this Sunday's election." The phrase "for fear of endangering the hostages" is news/history writing at work, constructing hidden continuities among events that the "actuality" reporting contradicts. It reveals the hidden meaning upon which the grand narrative depends in order to write events in Lebanon in 1987, events in Germany in 1987, and events in the United States in 1979/80 into the same history.

As the report continues, it covers the main themes of the election—the economy and peace—and exposes more contradictions and the enormous discursive effort it has to deploy to unify them. The prosperity of West Germany is used to distance the Middle East, to alienate it, and to unify German events with events in other Western democracies. The contrast between German peace and prosperity and the poverty and lawlessness of Lebanon offers a singular truth behind Germany's dilemma and links it to America's. A genealogy of these events would set them in a relationship of dispersed, multiple links. It would refuse the news's repressive practice by which German prosperity is denied a discursive link with the poverty of the Middle East, and by which explanation-bearing connections and contrasts between the shop windows of Frankfurt, full of luxury goods, and the shop windows of West Beirut, stripped bare even of the basic necessities, are repressed in order to promote the singular, political meaning already made. But the contradictions of these events remain, disrupting and resisting the power of news to produce its own knowledge. More explicit than the Palestinians' lack of a geographical articulation of their nation, and thus even more disruptive of the discursive power of the news, these are events in a genealogy rather than facts in a history. As such, they form a source of multiple pleasures. The pleasure in the power of discourse to make its own knowledge of truth, to scandalize it by denying its continuities, to recover repressed and multiple contingencies. The links between the shop windows of Frankfurt and those of Beirut are dispersed, fragmented, dependent on a multiplicity of causes, and therefore not part of the news's history and its singular continuity of cause-and-effect kidnappings.

This continuity is extended so that West Germany in 1987 is made into part of the same story as America in 1980, and Kohl doing and saying nothing before his election is continuous with Carter doing and saying much, but failing, in his election. So the next day's news will tell us that West Germany will not send its highly trained antiterrorist squad to rescue the hostages, as the camera shows them swinging on ropes through a concrete jungle of sheer-walled buildings like direct descendants of Tarzan crossed with Errol Flynn—a not inconceivable mythological origin for Carter's doomed rescue mission.

The history that the news is writing is an attempt to subject the unruliness of events to the rules of news discourse, an enterprise I am equating with that of traditional history. This discursive power needs further investigation.

The Gramscian model can take us a long way. The conventions of news discourse and the conventions of history writing have developed in institutions produced by, and integrated into, capitalist societies. They therefore necessarily have inscribed within them lines of hegemonic force: they tell the story of the past not only to make sense of the present, but to make common sense of the present. And common sense is the organization of a complicity around the interests of the dominant classes that effaces all traces of its mode of production. It wins the more or less willing consent of subordinate groups to a set of meanings that serve the interests of others, and that thus work to deny social differences, especially differences of power. It is thus common (American) sense that Kohl would not say or do anything before the election: it is common sense to give chronologically and geographically related events a singular cause-and-effect explanation that extends their continuity beyond themselves so that it comfortably encompasses events disconnected by both the Atlantic and a decade. So we could continue, exploring how the construction of a particular common sense of "the Free West" serves dominant American interests, of how dominant ideological forces that we label those of the Protestant work ethic are established as the commonsense values by which to understand a snowstorm and the events associated with it.

And we can add to this that the news necessarily retains traces of the repressed ideologies, the subordinate common senses whose intransigent presence requires hegemony to struggle so hard and so relentlessly to maintain its position. The visibility of these resistances is, of course, related to the degree of threat they are seen to pose: the sight of popular pleasure temporarily liberated by a snowstorm in a moment of carnival is not much of a threat—as the snow recedes, work will inevitably reassert its discipline and control. (The news's coverage of people having fun would be very different if snow had not provided a limited and licensed moment—if people had arbitrarily decided that having fun was, in principle, a better way of spending their weekdays than working.) This voice of resistance is more containable, less threatening, and thus more visible, than the voice that speaks explanations of the kidnappings in the contrasts between the shop windows of the Western world and those of West Beirut. The threatening voice is the one that speaks Helmut Heuser not as the metonymic proof that capitalist democracies work, but as the symbolic agent-provocateur of Middle Eastern hostility. The resistances, whether semiotic or political, are essential components of hegemonic force, and the impact of the commonsense consensus that is being fought for can be understood only in its relationship to the competing, subordinate senses that have to be temporarily and thus continually silenced.

Recent studies (e.g., Lewis 1985) of the reception of television news have shown us that this hegemonic force may well be less effective than earlier theorists have suggested and feared: viewers can and do extract events reported in the actuality segments from the discursive framework of the news story and thus free them from those constructed coherences. They can and do resist claw-back. But such studies do not challenge the hegemonic model itself; instead, they shift the emphasis within it from the power of hegemony to the forms of resistance, and welcome though this shift may be, it does not go far enough.

KNOWLEDGE, POWER, AND PLEASURE

We need to understand that there is a dimension of news discourse over and above its hegemonic or ideological function. The graphic representation of a snowstorm moving up the right-hand side of a map of the United States cannot, Foucauldians would argue, be adequately explained in terms of the hegemony of the bureau of meteorology; rather, it is a discourse engaged in the production of knowledge and as such requires us to understand it in terms of the matrix of knowledge-power-pleasure. The framed images of the storm growing out of Atlanta or Washington or New York are not the agents of class power, but of discursive power. They are there to be enjoyed not for what they say, but for their ability to say it. Similarly, the studio anchor exerting his power to claim a relationship between the Beirut kidnappings and the West German general election when the reporter in Frankfurt says that "nobody is making the kidnappings an issue in this Sunday's election" is more than a hegemonic agent, he is a discursive power producing knowledge, a truth in power relations with competing truths.

Knowledge, power, and pleasure melded together form the line of force by which "men govern (themselves and others)." There is a pleasure in exerting power. The power of the news exerted in its discursive control of the snowstorm is made available to the viewers by its foregrounding of its own discursive apparatus. The diagram of the nation, the snow symbols moving up it, the zooming enlargement of "Washington" as the story reaches it—all these engage the viewer in the discursive practice of producing knowledge. The pleasure involved in the power to produce a knowledge is greater by far than the pleasure offered by any specific knowledge that may be produced.

Similarly, in the German kidnapping story, the strain involved in the studio's forging of continuities evidences the power required to subdue undisciplined events and subject them to the rules of news and history. Essential to the pleasure in this power is the pleasure of resisting it, the pleasure of knowing the unruliness of events. The discursive yoking of the shutdown of the government with the continuation of the right-to-life protest is genealogical rather than historical: the power/pleasure of the discourse to produce a historical single knowledge is fragmented in a multiplicity of pleasures as a multiplicity of resistances engage with it. Pro- and anti-right-to-lifers would mobilize this dispersion of links quite differently; indeed, it is impossible even to outline the range of potential meanings that can be made out of this conjunction of events, and thus the number of knowledges into which they can be recruited as authenticators. We cannot specify the actual forms of resistances and their power/pleasures involved, though we can, and must, predict their occurrence. For discursive pleasure relies not on the meanings that are made, but on the power to make them, and an essential component of this power is the bottom-up power to make meaning in explicit resistance to the top-down power of news/history. There is a real pleasure in "scandalizing" the top-down sense of Reagan's support for the marchers by questioning the depth of a support that is expressed only in a disembodied voice from a presumably warm and comfortable office, when what the voice says is that suffering in the storm is evidence of the sincerity of the protest.

When Steve Shepard in Frankfurt says, "West Germany is immensely rich. A Mercedes isn't a status symbol here, it's a taxi," the balance between the top-down power and the bottom-up power of resistance is more even. While admiring West Germany's wealth and using it to connect West Germany with the United States by a produced "knowledge" that capitalism really does work, the excessiveness of the discourse invites resisting knowledges, possibly xenophobic and anti-German, but possibly radical and antibourgeois. Bottom-up power enables the production of resisting knowledges, some of which may produce a "truth" that encompasses those contrasts between the German and Lebanese shop windows that the news discourse has attempted to repress. The news discourse gives us the history of today's apparent kidnappings, links them to previous ones and to the hijack of TWA Flight 847, and provides the narrative closure for this minihistory by telling us that most West Germans have now fled West Beirut. But the camera tells us an entirely different story. It shows us shots of normal Beirut streets, crowded with traffic and pedestrians.

They are clearly poorer than the streets of Frankfurt we are to see later on, but they are normal streets. News discourse uses only the "authenticity" of these shots, and represses their competing, contradictory truths—that Beirut is a city where (different) people live (different) lives, not merely an anarchic hotbed of terrorism. These repressed truths point to the economic and social contrasts between the West and the Middle East as requiring a far more complex knowledge of the relations between them than the one offered by news/history. It is this singular narrative, with its casting of the Middle East into the discursive role of villain and the West as hero-victim, that is challenged by the refusal of events to submit themselves to the discipline of history.

These traces of undisciplined events that history represses but genealogy recovers not only allow us to produce resisting knowledges, but give us access to the process of producing knowledge. The pleasure in this is a double-voiced pleasure, for it lies not only in the production of a knowledge-truth, but also in the recognition that this knowledge-truth is a subjugated truth playing a resisting, scandalizing role in that "hazardous play of domination" by which men govern. The possibility is there that some future genealogy will reveal the emergence of a new dominating knowledge of the Middle East and that this instance of a resistant knowledge may turn out to be the new dominant knowledge in its emergent form. But, then again, it may not: there is no necessity in history, no grand narrative of the oppressed and powerless overthrowing the systems that oppress and disempower them.

News/history smooths over the contradictions between the Western and Middle Eastern shop windows by implicit reference to the unities that good is better than evil, that peaceful persuasion is better than terrorist force. But in a genealogy these contradictions constitute a source of power: far from being the silenced victim of the dominating discourse, they are the preconditions for its existence. There would be no need for a governing knowledge that capitalist democracies are good if there were not a multitude of contradictory events that challenge and resist it. There would be no pleasure in the power of the news to produce a knowledge of truth were there no evidence of the competing knowledges that need to be subjugated to it.

News's struggle to subjugate unruly events to its own rules can never be won, and can never produce a hegemonically smooth surface. Its own discourse has been formed precisely because of the impossibility of achieving its own ends. If discourse works to construct power-knowledge-pleasure within a play of domination, then it must necessarily acknowledge the resistances that not only determine the form that it takes at any one historical moment but also require its very existence.

The pleasures of television news, then, are the pleasures in the production of knowledge, pleasures that involve opposing lines of force. It is not just that news provides the means with which to disagree with it (though it does just that), but rather that its status as discourse requires that it do so. The numerous studies that demonstrate the very low recall that people have of the content of last night's news should not lead us to conclude either that television news is inefficient or that viewers are thick. The discrepancy between people's inability to remember news and their desire to watch it (all U.S. network news programs rate between 11 and 13, and in Britain and Australia the evening news will occasionally creep into the top 10 programs) would seem to indicate that it is the watching of the news rather than the information it conveys that holds the key.

Gramscians and Althusserians would argue that the pleasure of watching the news is an ideologically produced one. The form of the news, this argument runs, demonstrates that the framework of the dominant ideology is adequate for making sense of the world, and therefore of our subjectivities. It is the pleasure of familiarity that confirms and validates dominant ideological practice and produces the willing consent of the subordinate to the system of domination. The willingness of the consent and the pleasure in the practices that produce it are obviously interdependent.

A Foucauldian approach would identify a number of problems with this ideological notion of pleasure. One of the most fundamental is that it disempowers people: it assumes that pleasure is found in subjection and that the pleasure increases as the subjection increases and is therefore made more comfortable. The more completely people consent to the conditions that subordinate them, and the more enthusiastically they embrace the subjectivities constructed for them by the dominant ideology, the greater their pleasure. While there may well be a pleasure in accommodating oneself as comfortably as possible to dominant ideological practices, it is a muted pleasure and one that cannot account for resistance or opposition. It is also a singular account of pleasure that implies that the pleasures felt by all subjects in the same ideology are largely the same. It is a theory of pleasure that either ignores social differences or grants them very little power. A singularity of explanations, a singularity of history, serves the interests of the status quo: the voice of change can be heard only in social diversity and the differential distribution of power. This hegemonic model also grants disproportionate power to the forces of domination, and consequently underplays those of resistance. Its explanations of why people find pleasure in watching programs that disempower them, that misrepresent their social relations, and that serve interests that are opposed to theirs lie finally in theories of ideology as false consciousness or as unproblematically the agent of class domination. The consequence of this is the "cultural dope" (Hall 1981) theory, that people are helpless in the face of the forces of their ideological construction. The paradoxes within a definition of pleasure that denies self-interest mean that most Marxist theorists have sidestepped the problem altogether.

Other fundamental weaknesses of the Gramscian model are two closely related ones: the first is its inability to account for the contradictory voices in news, and in all popular programs, except by a theory of inoculation (Barthes 1973), which argues that potentially radical contradictions are injected as carefully controlled doses that serve only to strengthen the dominant order. It cannot account for the contradictions that escape control and that work to resist it rather than support it. It assumes the success of the textual practice of constructing and promoting the dominant ideology and cannot account for its "failure."

Similarly, it cannot explain news's (and, increasingly, television's) foregrounding of its own discursivity. Shows like *Moonlighting* and *Miami Vice*, TV sports, and MTV, all, like news, offer up television's textuality, its constructedness, as a source of pleasure. TV offers the pleasure and power of making meanings on top of, and in opposition to, the ideological pleasures of accepting ready-made meanings of self and of the world.

Cultural-ethnographic studies of television are increasingly showing that viewers make their own socially pertinent meanings out of the discursive resources of television, not in the structureless equality beloved of liberal pluralism, but always in a relationship of domination-subjugation, of power and resistance, of power from above and power from below.

This power is not adequately explained by reference to structures of economics, party politics, or even ideological practice. It is a power to produce knowledge, a set of truths that form the means by which people govern themselves and others. This power necessarily exerts itself in opposition to diverse competing knowledges and truths that bear different modes of governance. History seeks to efface these competing truths, genealogy to recover them as evidence of the dispersion of events and of disparities between them. As power is two-directional, so its associated pleasures are double-voiced. As members of a governed society we find pleasure in participating in the power to produce the knowledge that governs; equally, as governed, disciplined members of that society we know the pleasures in resisting that power, in producing competing knowledges of the world. The voice of the senator complains in the name of the taxpayer that the government's shutdown has cost $8,000,000 of taxpayers' money; the camera shows us those same taxpayers enjoying the liberation from social control that the snow has brought. Both pleasures are there, the pleasures of exerting the disciplinary truth of the taxpayer and of experiencing the liberating truth of the fun of undisciplined play.

This problematic is finally one of exerting discursive and social control over the unruliness and diversity of social life. Arguments that news should be more accurate or objective are actually arguments in favor of news's authority, and seek to increase its control under the guise of improving its quality. News, of course, can never give a full, accurate, objective picture of reality, nor should it attempt to, for such an enterprise can serve only to increase its authority and decrease people's opportunity to "argue" with it, to negotiate with it. In a progressive democracy, news should stress its discursive constructedness, should nominate *all* its voices and refrain from its desire to impose a knowledge of the world upon all its readers. It should recognize that truths compete with each other for power within a social system. It should be more willing to delegate the power to make knowledge and truth to its readers, and thus to invite active, engaged, argumentative viewers. Because news deals, in a high modality, with the very stuff of social conflict and social differences, it is politically healthy for news to encourage its readers to negotiate (often stubbornly) with it, to use its discursive resources to provoke and stimulate viewers to make *their* sense of, and validate *their* point of view on, the social experiences it describes. The pursuit of objectivity, with its final unarguable "truth" located in an assumed universal, empiricist reality, is precisely the wrong enterprise for news in a democracy; it is an enterprise that is totalitarian to its core.

The differences between news and fiction are differences only of modality. Both are discursive means of making meanings of social relations, and it is important that readers treat news texts with the same freedom and irreverence that they do fictional ones. Such an active, argumentative reading strategy is harder to adopt for news, because the professional ideology of news itself invests heavily in promoting its authoritative status in our society. It becomes an important task for the critic, then, to demystify news's discursive strategies and to discredit its ideology of objectivity and the truth.

DISCUSSION

The following is an edited transcript of a discussion provoked by the presentation of the material in this chapter at the symposium "Television and History" at the National Humanities Center, North Carolina, March 1987.

Questioner A: There seems to lie behind your argument a residual naturalism, particularly in your treatment of events and resistance. It's as though you put *natural* events against the way news talks about them, and as though you posit a *natural* resistance to power. How natural do you think events and resistance really are, and if resistance isn't natural, where does it come from?

John Fiske: Thanks for raising this—I am aware that I lay myself open to this sort of charge of naturalism in my paper, and welcome the opportunity to try and wriggle out of it. The first point I would make in my defense is that Foucault must share some of the blame. When he talks about events, when he talks about the need to "eventualize" history, he comes very close to suggesting that events do have their own essence, their own meanings—and I take it that's what you refer to by "naturalism." I don't intend to buy into that. The undisciplinarity of events, their unruliness, stems not from their nature or their essence, but from their potential to be mobilized in other discursive formations: they can always be made to mean differently by being taken up by different discourses. News discourse has to repress these discursive alternatives, it tries to censor out the unrealized discursive potential of events. But, of course, it can never be totally effective in this. Traces of repressed discourses, traces of this suppressed discursive potential, always remain, and it's these intransigent traces that constitute what I have called the "unruliness" or the "indiscipline" of events. They refuse to submit themselves finally to the discursive rules and discipline of news/history.

Questioner A: Aren't you in danger here of conflating the sociopolitical resistance of people against oppressive systems of power and the resistance of events to their structuring in discourse? I would have thought that the two resistances were quite different.

John Fiske: I think we need to be clear about their differences theoretically, but also to stress their interconnections politically. What I mean by that, is that it is theoretically proper to recognise that what I like to call "semiotic resistance" differs from politically active resistance, but that it is politically naive and inept to maintain that distinction to the point of devaluing semiotic resistance or even to suggesting that it's an agent of incorporation, a sort of internal bread and circuses that ends up by winning people's consent to the status quo. I conceptualize it quite differently from that. Semiotic resistance is the power of people in their various social formations of subordination and disempowerment to resist the colonization of their consciousness by the forces of social power. The power to think differently, the power to make different sense of social experience, of oneself and of one's social relations, is the power to resist the ideological and hegemonic practice of constructing us all as subjects of bourgeois patriarchical capitalism. Semiotic resistance stems from the fact that people use the discursive resources of a society quite differently from the way that the dominant forces do. They talk, they think, they joke, and all the time they are making *their* sense of their particular form of subordination, they are exploiting their power to use discourse differently, resistingly. And the indisciplinarity of events gives them points of purchase, weak spots in the discourse of domination, at which they can exercise this power. Now the connection between this and social resistance is much harder to think through, but I'd just like to make a couple of quick observations on it. The first is to ask that if people don't *think* differently, where on earth can social change come from? If our consciousness can be so thoroughly colonized that we always accept *their* meanings of *our* experience, from where can we get the motivation to change? And second, I would like to point out that organized resistance in the political domain is always the work of a tiny activist minority, but that in the long run, its effectiveness depends on millions of people thinking differently, people who have resisted the colonization of their consciousness, people whose interior semiotic resistances provide a groundswell of support that prevents the activists from being marginalized as eccentric extremists, and makes them into spokespeople. I am very suspicious of political arguments that devalue internal or semiotic resistance—it seems to me that it is an essential prerequisite of social change—not, I hasten to add, a sufficient *cause* of social change, thinking differently will not in itself bring that change about, but a necessary terrain for other, more public agencies of change to work within.

Questioner B: Listening to John Fiske's paper has raised a number of questions in mind, and I'm not quite sure if I can formulate them coherently. But they're something to do with the discontinuities of Foucault's genealogy being in some way postmodern, that the form of news itself, its fragmentariness, its collage of images culled from all over, its banging together of disconnected stories—all these are in some way postmodern too. And also floating around in my mind is the feeling that in some way news always denies history, it always turns everything into the present, and that has echoes of post-modernity too. So I suppose what I'm saying to Fiske is that under the guise of a Foucauldian reading, you have actually produced a postmodern reading, and what would Foucault have to say to that?

John Fiske: What a series of interesting points you make in that question, or comment, rather. Let me address them in a random order as they come to mind. First, Foucault and postmodernism—we need to be quite clear that Foucault's constant emphasis on power and on discourse provides a unifying core to his work, particularly his late work, that is quite antithetical to postmodernism. In fact, it's quite contradictory to his own distrust of the "grand narrative," though his discontinuities are, as I understand it, organized within structures of power and control, of top-down power meeting bottom-up power, of social control being exerted, evaded, resisted, scandalized, of social power and discursive power being pretty well indistinguishable. Or, at least, that's the way I read him, that's the dimension of his work that I mobilize and reuse in mine. And I emphasize bottom-up power and evasions and resistances more than he does, particularly I emphasize bottom-up discursive power in a way that I don't think he does at all. I not only draw on Foucault, I take liberties with him—but what the hell, that's what ideas are for, aren't they?

So I do take your point; my emphasis on the discontinuities of genealogy, on the necessary absence of a "grand narrative," on the contradictions and fragmentariness of news, on the failure of the narrative structure to impose its final disciplinary coherence—all these points are easily assimilable into postmodernism. And the point you make about history, or rather historicity, is a good one too. The use of file tape of Terry Waite looking up at the helicopters in Cyprus (or is it in Cyprus? We don't know) mixed with footage of the Beirut street after the kidnapping (or is that more file footage? We just don't know), mixed with live studio commentary—all this is a wonderful postmodernist denial of historicity, treating the past simply as a resource bank of images for casual reuse, a collapse of everything into the present. The postmodern experience is one of synchronicity; it plunders the past for its images and in using them denies their historicity and makes them into a kind of eternal present: and what strikes me as I think about the points you raise, is that file footage works precisely in this way—its use in today's news denies historical difference, it negates diachronicity and collapses all into a postmodern present. And thinking through this further, it also strikes me that this is a mechanical or material equivalent of a mental or invisible process that is central to the way that news works and history works in us—take the example of Carter's fruitless attempt to rescue the Iranian hostages and the Reagan-Carter election of 1980, all these are a sort of invisible file footage in our memories whose fragments are part of the collage of images from Frankfurt and Beirut: they're wrenched out of their past and collapsed into the images that constitute our present. The news is a collage of fragmented images, and each image spawns more, calls up more, each image is a simulacrum—a perfect copy that has no original. The news is images of images of images, the final hyperreality.

Questioner B: Yes, I go along with that—it seems to me that there is something irredeemably postmodern about the news—but if there is, doesn't this contradict the whole thrust of your argument, and your deployment of Foucault and Gramsci to support it? You argue, if I get it right, that news is an attempt to make meanings out of, and thus to establish discursive control over, events that are unruly, undisciplined and that resist this attempt. So there are two sorts of control and resistance at work in your model—the attempt to control the meanings of events is one which is resisted by the traces of alternative meanings that are repressed by the discipline of discourse—a resistance of events, if you like—and then there's a resistance of readers, who may oppose the sense of news and find the right, the power to make their own—a resistance of readers as well as a resistance of events. But if the news is a postmodern collage of fragmented images, it doesn't need resistance, there's nothing there to resist.

John Fiske: I think you've hit the nail exactly on the head. I was not offering a postmodernist reading of the news, but was deliberately presenting the news as a sort of field or terrain where various forms of power operate and meet other forms of power or resistances. But Baudrillard does suggest that the refusal of meaning is the only form of resistance possible in a society like ours which suffers from information overload—we are just bombarded with information-rich images every moment of our lives, and the only way we can cope with this, the only way we can resist the power of this information to take over our lives is to accept the images only as signifiers, only as surfaces, and to reject their meanings, their signifieds. So perhaps the news is simply a succession of surface images, of signifiers, for the viewers to experience—people can't recall last night's news, because there is nothing to recall, there are only images, only signifiers to experience. While this may be postmodern, it is, according to Baudrillard at least, a form of resistance. I don't know, it seems a bit despairing somehow. I'm reluctant to go that far, I don't really want to find myself caught in a postmodernist nihilism, however liberating or exhilarating it might appear. I think I'll hang on to notions of power for a bit longer at least!

Questioner C: It is good that Fiske is taking us beyond the imposition fetish and classbound oversimplification of a strictly Gramscian approach to the news. Images are indeed not simply the "expressions" of class interest; to insist that the domain of images conforms to a master narrative reeks of political nostalgia for the days when the white-hatted class could be imagined to ride down out of the factories to face off against the black hats. But the concept of power/resistance is getting mightly elusive as it is dragged in to become the ether of Foucauldian studies, that all-pervading element which accounts for everything and nothing. To move from the couplet power-resistance to the triad knowledge-power-pleasure is progress, but there is danger in thinking that the triad exhausts the possibilities. Just what sort of pleasure are we talking about in news watching? Is there not also dread? Fascination? Curiosity? The blank look? Is there not a danger that the aha! discovery of pleasure as the juice of everyday life has led to a sort of critical promiscuity in which whatever people are doing is rendered both valuable and comprehensible by assigning it an apparently uniform quota of the pleasure element? Do I detect, if not a master narrative, the resurgence of a master concept?

I should add that the sharp distinction between history and genealogy eludes me. It's not so easy to wriggle away from the metanarrative habit; is Fiske imposing yet another one, history versus genealogy? Straw man is facing off against straw man, when in fact man rides horse. Are historians today seriously defending stuffy old "history" in the sense Fiske is beating down? And where is this ideal-type "genealogy" which breaks definitively from master narrative? Surely not in *Discipline or Punish*, which takes for granted a linear historical sequence. The uncritical deployment (as Foucault would have said) of Foucault, for all the talk about the need to look with utmost specificity at micropower and resistance, leaves out the actual messy flux and contest of politics wherein discourses clash in specific settings and get brokered, deflected, flattened, reworked, compromised, etc. Instead of that turbulent mess Foucault gives us epistemic sequences: Discourse A replaces Discourse B, through clashes unspecified. When you get to the grain of actual historio-graphic work, this is not satisfactory. I suspect that TV news also comes across more cluttered than Fiske's supertexts might suggest.

John Fiske: I think this question—contribution, rather—is incisive and focuses accurately on some of the key issues in my paper. The most important ones seem to me to be pleasure-power-knowledge, history-genealogy, and power-resistance.

Yes, I'm aware I may have overemphasized pleasure, possibly exposed it to the risk of becoming a "master concept," but I can offer some historical defense of this. Scholars on the left, among whom I class myself even if some others might wish I wouldn't, have far too long emphasized ideological and hegemonic practices as the key to understanding popular culture. While Althusser may theorize resistance, all his theoretical energy is devoted to revealing the insidiousness of ideological practices, and the Frankfurt School have no room in their scenario for resistant or evasive practices. As Stuart Hall has pointed out, this produces a left-wing elitism that implicitly or explicitly devalues the people with whom it is politically aligned: an uncomfortable position, to say the least. One result of this is the way it has blinkered Marxist theory to the notion of popular pleasure, and particularly to the idea that popular pleasure must necessarily contain traces of resistance: there is no popular pleasure in being ideologically duped or hegemonically victimized. The power of ideology or hegemony simply is not that great. To theorize pleasure in the way I think we need to, we must go beyond Foucault, because, like Althusser, he theorizes and celebrates resistances, but spends all his energy on tracing the discursive apparatus of power. I want to theorize popular pleasure as occurring at that interface between the power-bearing apparatuses and the intransigent social experiences of the subordinated groups. Popular pleasures are socially located, socially determined, and are found in pertinent strategies either of evasion or of resistance, but they cannot exist outside of, or in harmony with, the forces of power and social discipline. Psychoanalytic theories of pleasure seem to me to be able to explain only the processes of domination, and, as such, fit easily with an Althusserian perspective —as is evidenced by much feminist film theory. I want to develop a socialist theory of pleasure that locates it within the structures of domination, but on the side of the subordinated. So I wish to explain the popularity of popular texts by focusing on where their social or ideological power breaks down, on the opportunities they must give to the variety of subordinated groups that constitute their audiences to make their own socially pertinent meanings out of their textual or discursive resources. There is a double pleasure here, the pleasure of the socially pertinent meanings—the subordinate, as opposed to the dominant, meanings of subordination and powerlessness, and the pleasure of being involved, being productive, in the making of these meanings.

And this brings me to the history-genealogy couplet, as I use it. I use "history" to describe a homogenizing approach to the past, an attempt to write it into a master narrative continuous with the dominant ideological constructions of the present. And I don't share the questioner's optimism that this sort of history is no longer being produced. Because it fits so well with realism, our period's dominant mode of representation and thinking, I believe it has become sedimented as the commonsense view of what history is. Genealogy is a much less developed concept, and I am aware of the paradox in Foucault, that he promotes genealogy but tends to produce history, albeit one that emphasizes discontinuities over continuities. I share, too, a certain disquiet that Foucault's shift away from materialism toward discursive power has left behind any account of *how* social change occurs—he charts the shift of discursive power from regime A to regime B without really investigating why this shift occurred at all. It's all part of his openness to the charge of "naturalism," but I suppose he would defend it by arguing that too intensive a search for the causes of social change inevitably becomes a search for a history, for a grand narrative.

But that's not really the point I want to make; what I want to argue is that the concept of a genealogy is worth exploring and developing because it may open up to us those repressed meanings of events and experiences that the forces of social power attempt to discipline out of existence, or at least to delegitimate, but which in their intransigent resistances to this discipline may be an important source of popular pleasure. Popular pleasures depend upon exploiting those meanings that history attempts to suppress, but whose existence genealogy acknowledges. That's why I want to use and explore the concept and the opposition, however simplified, between it and history.

And I think, if I can make one final point, that you suggested that the news is more "cluttered" than I allowed for: yes, I agree again here—I wished in my paper not to produce a supertext out of the clutter, but to show how that clutter could be mobilized in ways that have no precedence over any other ways, in ways that don't produce *the* supertext, but one out of many potential subtexts. Oh, and thanks for the word "clutter." I'd not thought of it before—I think it's a very productive one and I fully intend to steal it from you and use it in the future!

CHAPTER 8

Popular News

The familiar division of television's programming into information and entertainment carries with it the implication that information is objective, true, educational, and important, whereas entertainment, by opposition, is subjective, fictional, escapist, trivial, and, frequently, harmful. Ultimately, information is judged to provide "good" television and entertainment "bad," so to be entertaining comes to mean to compromise standards, to pander to the low. The logical extension of this simplistic opposition is that the final choice facing us is between good, accurate, responsible television that may be unpopular, and bad, compromised, irresponsible television that people actually want to watch.

TV news is the terrain over which such cultural struggles are waged—open to attack from one flank for compromising standards of accuracy and social responsibility in order to attract audiences, and from the other for being boring, irrelevant, and eminently forgettable. It would be better for TV news if it confidently asserted that its position in the repertoire of news media is one that makes its popularity its defining characteristic. It should, therefore, be evaluated less by informational criteria and more by those of popular appeal. We should demand of our television news that it make the events of the world *popular*, that it subject them to popular taste and attempt to make them part of the popular consciousness of society. To encourage a wide diversity of people to want to watch it, and to remember and think about its events, TV news must meet the key criteria of popular taste, those of relevance and pleasurable productivity.

RELEVANCE

Relevance is largely a matter of content, as the experiences of the viewer's life are matched to those represented in the text, but it has an important formal dimension as well—it is not just the selection of stories, but the manner of their telling that determines their relevance. Open, popular texts make their content available to a wider range of uses; they admit the production of a wider range of relevances than do more closed, authoritative ones. Relevance requires connections between the text and the social experience of the reader that precedes it: reading is not merely a decipherment (de Certeau 1984) of signs, but the bringing to bear upon the text of previously existing knowledges. Reading is a cultural practice, not a set of skills.

It may be helpful here to conceive of culture (by which I mean the making of meanings of self and of the world, the practice of thinking and feeling in certain ways rather than others) as occurring on three interlinked levels. The macro level can be identified as that of Western democratic capitalism. Its ideological framework provides a common level of culture that makes it far easier for an American, say, to understand a Briton or a West German than a Palestinian. But within this broad, abstract framework national cultures, national identities, indeed, nations themselves are constructed as different, as distinctive. The differences among Great Britain, the United States, and West Germany are politically, culturally, and historically constructed differences within an overarching framework of similarity. The TV news of each nation (that is, the national news, not regional, local TV news) operates largely within this mid-level of a national culture.

But within each national culture are a vast number of subcultures that constitute the terrain of the popular; these subcultures maintain their differences from each other and, typically, from the national culture. A subculture exists only because of its need to maintain social difference. At the most micro level, these subcultures are the oral, face-to-face communities among which we move in our daily lives.

Popular television programs are open to relevances at each level. *Dallas*, to give a well-studied example, is clearly relevant to the macro level of Western capitalism, and, equally clearly, is, on the mid-level, a specifically American inflection of it. (*The Onedin Line*, conversely, is recognizably a British, non-American example of the big business soap opera.) On the whole, there are very few contradictions between the macro and mid-levels of culture; the mid-level makes concrete in different ways the more generalized abstractions of the macro. It is between these and the micro levels that most contradictions occur, and *Dallas* is particularly open to different, often contradictory relevances as it is brought into contact with a wide variety of popular allegiances at the micro levels (see *Understanding Popular Culture*).

While popular culture may well construct relevances at all levels, the crucial one is the micro. If there are no relevances between a text and the everyday lives of its readers, there will be little motivation to read it, and less pleasure to be gained from doing so. News may well be watched out of a vague moral sense that we ought to know what is going on in the world, but if it lacks these microconnections, it will be watched half-heartedly and will be rapidly forgotten—which, indeed, is the fate it frequently suffers.

Our normal evaluation of news concentrates on its operation at the macro and mid-levels of culture and ignores the conditions under which it is read at the micro levels. For instance, in late 1987 and early 1988 the Israelis were worried about the pictures given to the rest of the world of the Arab uprising on the occupied West Bank. They felt that the media stories were anti-Israeli, and they wanted to control or regulate them to ensure a more "balanced" (i.e., pro-Israeli) portrayal. Understandable though such a desire may be, it ignores the fact that reading is the making of connections between existing cultural knowledges and the text, and that the cultural knowledges of Americans will differ from those of Israelis. Control of the image does not extend to control of its reading.

The point is that these knowledges and social experiences that constitute mid-level culture preexist any text and pre-determine any reading. They are deeply sedimented and resistant to change, held in place as they are by their close connection with the macro level. Within this mid-level there are specific knowledges about the non-American world that determine the cultural practice by which an American will read images of Israel or Europe. These knowledges were laid down in the American school system toward the end of the last century, as part of the attempt to build an identifiable national culture. The schoolbooks of the period consistently portrayed the United States as virtuous and natural, and Europe (and, by implication, the rest of the world) as corrupt, decadent, and unnatural. The United States was portrayed as free, peaceful, and stable, while Europe and the rest of the world were tyrannical, wartorn, and unstable. The knowledge of the nation was formed by negative knowledges of the rest of the world. In this view, then, the mid-level motive for watching a newscast would not be to understand the Middle East so much as to understand America.

The images of the Israeli army and the stone-throwing youths of the West Bank will be read by Americans in terms of their connections to the knowledges of their mid-level culture, so they are more likely to seem relevant to the national memory of the English army failing to control the irregular minutemen than with American troops in Grenada or Vietnam. Relevance is, of course, highly ideological. So, too, in a culture as passionately committed to free speech and a free press as is America's, the nightly images of Israeli military palms blocking the lenses of U.S. TV cameras become particularly highly charged, for they are concrete instances of the American knowledges of the differences between the United States and the rest of the world. The American meanings of free speech and of censorship precede and overpower any historically specific Middle Eastern ones. Insofar as the conditions under which a text is read differ from those under which it is produced, the meanings produced from it will differ. The military censorship of the media in the current conditions on the West Bank has its own meanings: images of that censorship in an American living room will have American, not Israeli, ones, and are more likely to be linked to concurrently similar images from South Africa. Israel and South Africa may be very different, but the similar images from them when received in the same American living room are likely to provoke meanings whose similarities outweigh by far the differences between the conditions under which they were produced.

But if this mid-level culture of America is profoundly reactionary, chauvinist, and isolationist (as it is), in describing it I have not described all of the reading process. Texts are also read according to their connections with the micro levels of culture at which is to be found the enormous variety of everyday, popular cultures through which the wide diversity of American society is lived. The closer culture operates to the macro level, the more homogenizing, centralized, and reactionary it is; conversely, the closer it moves to the micro, the more it becomes heterogeneous and diverse, and it is its diversity that allows for the possibility of readings that oppose or differ from those that fit the dominant ideology.

Popular culture is made along a shifting set of allegiances, or felt collectivities, that are mapped onto, but transect, the objective structure of a society. Thus U.S. black urban youths who have experienced repressive policing may well form subjective allegiances with the Palestinian youths on the Left Bank that enable them to make sense of the TV news in terms of their own experience, while simultaneously making sense of their social experience in terms of the TV images from Jerusalem. Members of the National Guard, however, or readers of *Soldier of Fortune*, will be more likely to ally themselves with the Israeli military, and thus to make quite different sense both of the images and of themselves. For a midwestern farming community, to take another case, the images may have little connection with their everyday culture, in which case their mid-level meanings of how awful the non-American world is are the ones most likely to be produced. Because of their lack of relevances on the micro level, such meanings are likely to be comparatively casual and forgettable, for it is the relevance to the everyday that produces important, engaged meanings—it is these relevances that make news matter, that make it more likely to be talked about and thus to be made an active part of the culture of everyday life.

PRODUCTIVITY

Talk is one of the main ways in which meanings are produced and circulated at the micro level; indeed, this level of culture is essentially oral, not literate, not text-based. Talking about television is an important way of negotiating the interface between it and everyday life, of selectively making it part of popular culture. Television's popularity is related to the ease with which it can be incorporated into oral culture. Meanings produced at the moment of watching are often reworked and recirculated socially in conversation, and are themselves influenced by previous conversations, for talk is social relations in practice. Indeed, some viewers defer the production of any meaning from a television program until they can discuss it with their peers. Oral culture does not just reproduce and recirculate the meanings of mass culture: it is a material part of the conditions under which that mass culture is received and thus of its meanings.

There is a connection between the affective dimension of television—that is, the intensity with which its meanings and pleasures are experienced or the importance given to them in everyday life—and the extent to which it is talked about. Television that is talked about has some identifiable features of both content and form, though in practice no distinction is made between them. Relevances of content may be relatively literal (as in soap opera, which is probably the most talked-about genre of all) or more metaphoric (as the relevances constructed by Australian school students between prison on television and school in real life; see *Understanding Popular Culture*, Chapter 6). Relevance may be sought through content, but the productivity of popular culture is more a matter of form.

The more formally open and internally interrogatory television is, the more it will be talked about. Soap opera is full of questions—it always leaves open and undecided the feelings of its characters, their possible courses of action, the judgments to be made of them and their behavior. Sports programs give the viewer a range of background knowledge to bring to bear upon the game, and to call up the fan knowledge many viewers already possess; this knowledge is frequently used to contradict the "reading" of the game given by the on-screen experts. Like soap opera, TV sport is open, full of contradictions: both invite viewer engagement, disagreement, and thus popular productivity.

Oral culture is participatory—distinctions among author, text, and reader, or between text and life, are blurred and minimized. Quiz or game shows, talk shows, and shows like *Divorce Court* or *People's Court* invite and receive participatory audiences because they appear to be unwritten, unauthored, their outcomes are uncertain, they involve ordinary people, they appear to be "live," and thus part of life rather than a textual construction—they exhibit all the key features of oral rather than literate culture.

POPULAR NEWS

TV news is uneasily poised. On the one hand, it needs to meet the literary values of the mid-level culture, for news literacy is part of a more general cultural literacy. News needs to meet the criteria of social importance and social responsibility, however hard they may be to define. Such criteria can never be politically or socially neutral, so the political debates begin when we start, as we must, to select which information about the world we include, and how and to whom we disseminate it. There is also concern about the extent to which the flow of information should be dictated by the needs of capital. As it is, the rest of the world receives far more information about the United States than the United States does about the rest of the world. The power of American cultural capitalism means that the United States is overwhelmingly an exporter rather than an importer of culture and information: size and parochialism are not mutually exclusive. These concerns, essentially ones of content, are finally educational—the criteria that decide what it is that a nation's citizens should know about the world are fundamentally similar to those that determine a school curriculum: they are important, vitally important, but they are not the only criteria for a popular broadcast news.

It is interesting to note here that Britain has two news sources specifically aimed at children, with specifically educational aims. The newspaper *Early Times* and the TV show *John Craven's Newsround* both aim to give children the background knowledge that will enable them to read the "adult" news. They provide the cultural knowledges that are normally assumed by the adult media, and that, ironically, they are often criticized for not providing.

These are knowledges within the mid-level culture; they meet the criteria of education and social responsibility, criteria that broadcasters have always found difficult to reconcile with the practices and pleasure of popular taste. They have tended, in general, to resolve this conflict by moving toward the criteria of entertainment and popular pleasure and away from those of education and social responsibility. This trend is most marked in the United States, particularly in *USA TODAY* (in both its newspaper and television forms), and is accelerating in the United Kingdom and Europe as satellites and cable systems open up previously publicly regulated systems to more and more commercial competition. The desire to preserve "responsible, informational" public systems against the "vulgar entertainment" of the commercial is understandable, but often misguided: there is, after all, little point in applauding a socially responsible news service that nobody chooses to watch, or, worse still, one that only a small minority chooses to watch, for then the division between the politically informed elite and the politically uninformed majority would grow even wider. As we begin to understand more about popularity, so we should allow this understanding to reshape our news values and what we demand from the news in our popular media.

Rather than opposing "popular" news to "responsible" news, we should seek to develop a repertoire of news services, in which the main aim of the popular news might well be that of catching attention and stimulating interest. If this interest appears relevant to the social situation of the viewer-reader, he or she may then turn to other forms of news to satisfy the desire for further information. News has different meanings and serves different purposes in different sections of society: it is therefore appropriately circulated in a variety of forms by a variety of media. A weekly or monthly current affairs journal with a comparatively small specialized readership differs from a large daily newspaper; a daily newspaper with national aspirations and readership differs from one with a local or regional readership. Newspapers differ from TV, and on TV cable news differs from broadcast news, public channels from commercial, current affairs shows from news bulletins, national news from local.

Of all these news media, it is the broadcast nightly news that is the most widely received and commonly believed to be the most influential. It is broadcast news that needs to be popular, that needs to balance popular tastes and pleasures with educational, socially responsible criteria. The main function of broadcast news, then, should not be to disseminate information considered to be socially necessary, but rather to make such information *popular*—which means to make it matter, to encourage it to be taken up within micro-level cultures.

To achieve this it cannot abide solely by the criteria of objective, necessary information—these criteria can be met elsewhere in the news media repertoire or in the school classroom. If the function of broadcast news is to encourage the popular circulation of information about the nation and the world, then our criteria for evaluating it must include those of entertainment. We should not criticize it for "pandering" to entertainment, but rather should evaluate *how* entertaining it is, and *what* information it makes entertaining. In other words, we need to evaluate it according to the criteria of popular culture.

Broadcast news should aim to stimulate its audiences to take up its information and insert it into the culture of their everyday lives. It should aim to be talked about, which means it must discard its role of privileged information-giver, with its clear distinction between the one who knows (the author) and those who do not (the audience), for that gives it the place and the tone of the author-god and discourages popular productivity. Rather, it should aim to involve its viewers in making sense of the world around them, it should encourage them to be participants in the process, not recipients of its products: it should, in de Certeau's (1984) terms, aim to make them readers rather than decipherers. Instead of promoting a final truth, then, it should provoke discussion (like soap opera) or disagreement (like sportscasting).

Ironically, TV news is ideally suited to this—it is the professional practices of journalism and their ideology of objectivity that militate against it. News has, potentially at least, all the elements of popularity built into it, and it fights against them in order to conform to a professional ideology that is essentially literate, homogenizing, and textually authoritarian —and therefore inappropriate. Central to this ideology is objectivity. Objectivity is authority in disguise: "objective" facts always support particular points of view and their "objectivity" can exist only as part of the play of power. But, more important, objective facts cannot be challenged: objectivity discourages audience activity and participation. Rather than being "objective," therefore, TV news should present multiple perspectives that, like those of soap opera, have as unclear a hierarchy as possible: the more complex the events it describes, the more the contradictions among the different social positions from which to make sense of them should be left open and raw. The anchor and reporters should be less concerned about telling the final truth of what has happened, and should present, instead, different ways of understanding it and the different points of view inscribed in those different ways. So, too, they should not disguise their processes of selection and editing, but should open them up to reveal news as a production, not as transparent reportage.

The people cope well with contradictions; popular culture in industrial societies is largely constructed out of them, for the social experience of the subordinate is contradictory to its core—the social system that nurtures and rewards them also oppresses them; they simultaneously play along with it and oppose it in a form of constant lived irony. The abrasive faces of the contradictory spark meanings that escape the control of the dominant, that become available to be made into the popular. It is contradictions, the unresolved relationships among different social experiences, that provoke discussion and encourage the oral reproduction of meanings that is so central to popular culture. This is not a mere recirculation of meanings already presented, it is a reworking of the stuff from which meanings are made, a restructuring of social relations and discursive relations that is the responsibility and creativity of the reader and not of the producer of the text.

This, of course, is risky business, for the meanings that people make will often evade social control—they may be offensive, oppositional, embarrassing. But it is this that will make them popular, active meanings, and will make the events of which they make sense seem to *matter*. News's constant attempt to close down contradictions and resolve them into a final objective meaning (the "true facts") actually kills those events, distances them from the viewers and makes them easily forgettable and, as many a survey has shown, frequently forgotten (Gunter 1987).

News should eschew not only objectivity, but also narrative closure. Instead of attempting to find a narrative end-point from which to look back and understand what has gone before (and all journalists are trained to do this), it should, like soap opera, leave its multiple narratives open, unresolved. Instead of saying, "This is what happened today," it should say, "These are the events we are in the middle of." It should not present itself as the record of what has occurred, for that is the literate narrative of books and films, but rather as the ongoing, unresolved narrative of soap opera, for that is television's equivalent of the oral narratives through which we make sense of our daily lives. Soap opera is so readily incorporated into everyday life because its formal structures represent the liveness, the nowness, the unwrittenness of oral culture.

When news stresses its immediacy, it is actually stressing its recency, not its liveness: any liveness it may have had has been closed off into the past tense, so the best it can do is to stress how recently past (but not live) its events are. Soap opera, like oral culture, like the events that news is actually dealing with, draws no firm line between past and present and therefore suggests the continuity of this past-present with the unwritten future, a continuity that is broken by news's concern with telling us the final truth of what *has* happened. The journalistic search for a point of narrative closure is a search for a point from which the only view is backward.

This is a legacy from print journalism, with its roots in literate culture, but the electronic media become popular to the extent that they distance themselves from the literate and approximate the oral. It may be appropriate for newspapers or journals to speak of current affairs with a voice of authority, to narrativize them so that they make coherent sense—even, perhaps, to present that sense as the objective truth. In so doing they are aligning themselves, appropriately enough, with literate, disciplined, controlled culture. They invite educated, disciplined readers who will read *with* them, not mindlessly agreeing with what they say, but cooperating with the discursive strategies by which they say it.

But the popular reader is undisciplined. He or she dips into and out of the text, selecting fragments to pay attention to because they fit his or her criteria of relevance, not because they are preferred by the textual structure. So Lewis (1985) found that some of the viewers of a political news story in the United Kingdom gave their attention to a live film insert and ignored the narrative framing and explanation given it by the rest of the text. From a literate point of view, they "got it wrong." But such a "misunderstanding" of the textually preferred meaning of an event is a typical reading practice of the popular, for it frees that event from the meanings of those with textual power, and opens it up to meanings that are relevant to the various formations of the people. A "misreading" of this sort is a necessary practice of the popular. It is part of the popular disrespect for the text, a way of treating the text as a resource, not as a revered object or as an authoritative message-bearer.

Frequently the events that news covers will be distant from the everyday lives of its viewers, and it will not be able to construct, in the way that soap opera does, multiple points of pertinence from which viewer-specific relevances can be made. But if its content is to be dictated more by educational than popular criteria, then its form should reverse these priorities. It should aim to make those events deemed by educational criteria to be of national significance as popular as possible. To achieve this it must not preach or teach; rather, it must invite participatory readings and lay itself open to viewer-selected, viewer-produced, viewer-circulated meanings of its content— for only this viewer productivity can make those events part of the micro-level culture of the everyday.

When the events of the news become woven orally into the fabric of everyday life they are made to *matter*. It is more important in a democracy to stimulate people into making national and international events matter in their daily lives than it is to teach them about the "truth" of those events. Popular news must escape the control of those who wish to promote a certain set of meanings of the world. Popular news must not be propaganda, even in its original sense of the propagation of the (Christian) truth; it must not serve the sociopolitical interests of any set of social forces because, in so doing, it risks failing to meet the two criteria of the popular—relevance and productivity.

Currently, there are many complaints about the quality of TV news. There are similar complaints about the low level of participation in political life, and about low levels of knowledge about politics and national history. It is all too tempting to make a commonsense truth out of this—that a poor television news is responsible for the low levels of political participation and knowledge. Of course, there must be some connection between the two; TV news is one of the sources of political knowledge and one of the potential motivators of political activity. But the relationship between the political life of a nation and its television news, particularly in the realm of the popular, is never one of cause and effect—in either direction—nor is it self-evident that the criteria by which the news is judged to be "poor" would, if applied rigorously, make it popular. Indeed, many of the criticisms of television news criticize those of its characteristics that make it more readily accessible to popular cultural uses.

The more valid criticism of television news is that it is not popular enough. Far from wishing to improve its objectivity, its depth, or its authority, I would wish to increase its openness, its contradictions, the multiplicity of its voices and points of view. Television news is already like soap opera, but it needs to extend these similarities if it is to engage its topics relevantly and importantly with the everyday lives of the people.

CHAPTER 9

Searing Towers

Verticality liberates. Humans distinguish themselves from other animals by rearing upward on their hind legs, despite the consequent problems in the lower back. So, as Lakoff and Johnson (1980) detail so thoroughly, the spatial relationship of *up* to *down* becomes a concrete metaphor for a variety of social, moral, and physical properties. We conceive of class differences not horizontally, from left to right (for that would break the capitalist taboo of naming the politics of social difference), but vertically, from higher to lower. So class aligns itself with all the other value differences made concrete in the up-down metaphor: thus high morals, highbrow taste, and high social position not only appear to fit "naturally" together, but are equally "naturally" rewarded with happiness (high versus low spirits) and high earnings. *Up* becomes a spatial metaphor that agglomerates unrelated values into a conceptual unity that is as politically active as it is logically incoherent: high social position does not necessarily go with high morals (as the Reagan-Bush administration has demonstrated so clearly), but so powerful is the naturalizing force of the up-down metaphor that any contradictions within it are either rendered senseless and thus ignored or read as regrettable exceptions that do not question the naturalness of the system.

It becomes obvious and "natural," therefore, that the lower classes have lower moral standards and lower tastes; they are associated with sickness (we *fall* ill) and with unconsciousness (we *fall* asleep), and their low skills and low jobs justify their low incomes. When we relate this back to our belief that animals are low and humankind is high, and then secure it with the ultimate metaphor—God, Heaven, and life are *up*, the Devil,

Hell, and death are *down*—we begin to realize the conceptual and political labor performed by the deceptively simple "natural" difference between up and down.

The elevator transporting us up the 103 floors of Sears Tower, the tallest building in the world, is thus a political machine, for altitude is power. Who, to make the point, can name the longest building in the world, and how much of a tourist attraction would it be? It is not just Trivial Pursuit freaks who can name Sears Tower, the World Trade Center, and the Empire State Building. The Eiffel Tower characterized Paris and immortalized its builder simply by its height, and when Jo Bjelke-Petersen, the obsessively expansionist premier of Queensland, planned to build the tallest building in the world in Brisbane, he was eccentric only in his desire to locate it in a second-rate Australian city. In capitalism, enormous height goes with commercial and political power. In earlier Western societies it was religious power that commanded the heights, so, until the Eiffel Tower, the tallest buildings in Europe were all (naturally) cathedrals. But, despite the high values and high regard given to altitude, humans are actually firmly rooted in *terra firma*; at best we rise only a few feet above the animals and live out our lives on the horizontal plane. Gravity means that natural life is two-dimensional, and thus breaking through into the vertical is always an aberration, always an excitement. However frequently we fly, the moment of takeoff is categorically different from pulling our car away from the curb, and executive suites are rarely on the first floor—despite its convenience. Only menials and functionaries inhabit the below-ground floors. There are, of course, carnivalesque inversions of any rule, so high achievers at work will descend from their offices in the sky to spend their leisure in dives and low bars, where they experience the low life, the pleasures of the body, and can brush fingers with the underside of society.

LOOKING DOWN

De Certeau (1984), in one of his poetic theorizations of height, writes:

To be lifted to the uppermost summit of the World Trade Center is to be lifted out of the city's grasp. One's body is no longer clasped by the streets that turn and return it according to an anonymous law: nor is it possessed, whether as player or played, by the rumble of so many differences and by the nervousness of New York traffic. (p. 92)

He likens the experience to that of Icarus—the momentary achievement of freedom and power followed by the inevitable return to the quotedien. He finds, on the 110th floor, a poster: "It's hard to be down when you're up." He notes, too, that the desire to look down on the city long preceded the means of satisfying it, so that Medieval and Renaissance painters produced birds-eye views of cities that no human could enjoy. Today, many tourist brochures are odd combinations of such views imposed (often confusingly) upon a more objective, scientific street map. The map is the humanly unachievably perfect representation, freed from the physical constraint of a singular point of view, from which even satellite photographs suffer. The map is the text that no reader disobeys, whose author is ubiquitous and anonymous in authority, and therefore unchallengeable.

Looking at Chicago from Sears Tower turns it into (almost) a map and the voyeur from the Skydeck into (almost) the map maker. It promises us the birds-eye point of view that is beyond human achievability. There is magic and power in the air. Lévi-Strauss (1969) tells us that science is to civilized thought what magic is to primitive—they are both ways of extending the power of people over their environment, of culture over nature. There is, then, nothing paradoxical in the phrase "the magic of science"—it is simply a recognition of the coexistence within all of us of the primitive and the civilized.

Sears Tower is a work of scientific magic. Its publicity bombards us with miraculous facts: it is 1,454 feet high; it has a working population of 12,000; its 28 acres of exterior surface and 16,000 windows are cleaned by automatic hoists 25 feet long, 10 feet wide, and 16 feet high, which weigh up to 18½ tons each—replacing the 2,930 man hours it would take to clean the building each month. It consists of 76,000 tons of steel, enough concrete to build an eight-lane highway five miles long, and its

114 rock caissons are sunk as deep as the Statue of Liberty is tall. The facts proliferate. They are, actually, excessively ordinary, but they are presented as icons of wonder and amazement: paradoxically, while purporting to explain the Tower, their real function is to mystify it. In a scientific society, facts, detached from their engineering or scientific contexts, become miraculous.

We are deluded if we allow ourselves to believe that our scientific society has thought processes that are more rational and thus more advanced than those of tribal peoples. An Aborigine who understands that a dream is the past coexisting with the present is thinking neither more nor less scientifically (or magically) than the tourist reading to his wife that the Tower's electrical wiring would stretch from Chicago to El Paso. Sears Tower is a plethora of superlatives, and superlatives are the means of approaching the gods, for it is only by them that the godlike can be described. Even its main artwork, the sculpture "Universe," is notable for its awesome facts and superlatives:

> Installed in 1974, the work is composed of five moving elements turned by motors, and measures 55 feet wide and 33 feet high! It is Calder's largest "moving mural." (undated brochure)

The exclamation point suggests the awed tone of voice that contradicts the mundanity of the data, but underscores the ludicrous arrogance of the title. Calder, we are told in another brochure, is himself a superlative ("America's greatest sculptor"), and, significantly, he was an engineer turned artist, which "accounts for the unique qualities of his art." Art is where humankind is most like God in creating and controlling a world, and aesthetic creativity is often mystified into the most spiritual of human abilities, so a sculpture that denies any difference between engineering (or scientific thinking) and art (or mystical thinking) is precisely appropriate in a tower that is presented as a miracle of technology.

> Sears Tower is the world's tallest building! The 103rd floor Skydeck (the highest occupied floor) rises 1,353 feet above the ground. Two express elevators soar to this altitude in just over one minute. (undated brochure)

But before experiencing all these facts, exclamation points, and superlatives, tourists are gathered around a transparent model of the tower, a three-dimensional automated map whose various points light up in response to the disembodied commentary emanating, like the voice of God, from nowhere and everywhere, as it explains not only how the tower was built, but also how people live in it. The tower is revealed to us as a vertical city, full of shops, restaurants, offices, banks, and sidewalks. It has public areas, with trees, waterfalls, and sculptures, and a transport system in which commuters have to change between express and local elevators to reach their destinations. The tourists, clustered around the model, see all this in miniature, as, when they reach the Skydeck, they will see the rest of the city. Sears Tower, the vantage point, is the only part of the city hidden from them, but the model more than makes good the deficiency; it miniaturizes the city into the Tower so that the Tower becomes a microcosm of downtown Chicago (or anywhere)—people constantly on the move between working and consuming. Any other forms of social relations are relegated, like the suburbs, to the periphery.

As we soar to the 103rd floor there is no respite from facts, for the disembodied voice tells us, again, how high and fast we are ascending; we are no more allowed escape from technological awe than the worshippers in the medieval cathedral were able to avoid the bombardment of holiness that its every physical detail hurled at their senses. But in the ascent, something happens—the first signs of pleasure begin to show among the tourists. Some jump or bend their knees to magnify the acceleration and deceleration. There's a sense of excitement (and terror) that was totally absent as we were obediently awestruck in front of the model. As we emerge from the elevator we are suddenly, and surprisingly, windswept—an uncontrolled act of nature mentioned in no brochure or commentary, for it lies beyond technology; it is an undesigned effect of the compression of air in the elevator shaft.

The technological awe of the towering experience is, like any religion, a system of control and authority that attempts to extend itself around the Skydeck, but with little success. The recorded voices on each face of the deck are widely ignored; the maps that identify specific features of Chicago are referred to only briefly, for this is "official" information, it is external knowledge that is integral to the system of the city, and is thus quite alien to the Icarean pleasure identified by de Certeau.

The city is a mix of freedom and constraint. It is designed to promote certain ways of behaving, of moving, of thinking. It is the ultimate text, produced and reproduced by the forces of capital and law and order, designed for the most efficient exercise of what these forces believe should constitute everyday life. Yet its very complexities make it also the place of greatest disorder, its multiple systems of control and discipline open up gaps where life can be lived out of control, beyond discipline.

The city for de Certeau (1984) is a discourse, a structuralist language system. It is a rational organization that must repress all physical, mental, and political irrationalities; it must repress histories and traditions with the "nowhen" of its synchronic system, for histories and traditions carry the unruly experiences of the people, which oppose rational organization. Finally, like a discourse of power, it creates a universal and anonymous *subject*, which is the city itself, an amalgam of its organized citizenry and its buildings and plans. City planning is not just architecture or geography, it is the design of people as city-subjects purged of the historical and social specificities of what de Certeau calls "the many different, real subjects—groups, associations, or individuals" (p. 94).

Using the terminology of *Discipline and Punish* (Foucault 1977a), de Certeau (1984) analyzes the city as a system of

> panoptic administration . . . of mechanisms and technical pro-
> cedures "minor instrumentalities" capable merely by their
> organization of "details", of transforming a human multiplicity into
> a "disciplinary" society and of managing, differentiating, classifying,
> and hierarchizing all deviances concerning apprenticeship, health,
> justice, the army, or work. "These often minuscule modes of
> discipline," these "minor but flawless" mechanisms, draw their
> efficacy from a relationship between procedures and the space that
> they redistribute in order to make an "operator" out of it. (p. 96)

A city, then, consists of "spatial practices [that] in fact secretly structure the determining conditions of social life." As a discourse is a system for disciplining meaning, and therefore those who use it, so a city is a system for disciplining life and those who live it.

But such disciplinary strategies are never totally successful; they are always vulnerable to tactical raids in everyday life. Surfers can and do evade disciplinary attempts (both discursive and behavioral) in their use of the beach, Madonna wanna-bes can and do use the discourse of patriarchy to question it, and city dwellers can and do turn its disciplinary mechanisms into their own freedoms. But to create freedoms within these systems, one has to inhabit them. It is natives who live most freely in a city, or anywhere else, tourists and visitors are more subjected to its official discipline as they follow the routes mapped out for them (routes that natives spurn—they have their own ways of moving) just as the speaker of a foreign language will be constrained to use it more correctly (i.e., less freely) than a native speaker. Sears Tower is not full of Chicagoans—they have their own ways of creating freedoms and empowerments within and against the disciplinary apparatuses of the city—it is full of tourists seeking a more instant sense of freedom and empowerment. Chicagoans are more likely to have experienced Manhattan from the World Trade Center than their "own" city from Sears Tower or the Hancock Building.

The city is textualized by the height. It is made not into a book, with its disciplinary linear sequence of words, but into a newspaper or tabloid sheet, its readers able to skim it in any order in search of a moment of interest, a new "angle" on the familiar. The birds-eye readers see the hidden, the rooftop gardens, jogging tracks, and swimming pools normally exclusive to their owners. They chart the traffic jams, their extent and their causes, in a way that is impossible on the ground. They see the city more powerfully, with fewer restrictions; they see (look over) it and see (understand) it in a way that the horizontality of the everyday denies them. They are Gullivers in Lilliput, adult children in Toyland—all miniaturized worlds aggrandize the normal: model makers are imaginary giants. The city is a text to be read, a toy to be played with.

Reading from a height "permits us to transcend sensation and see things *in their structure*" (Barthes 1982:242). Chicago from the Tower is a city of the horizontal and the vertical, of frantic movement and the solidly stable. Its movement is horizontal—its vast railway yards and coiling highway intersections, the invisible waterways on Lake Michigan, the network of streets, canals, and bridges almost directly underneath. And in between them the immobile towers of its skyscrapers: in a reverse of the normal, it is the sky that is filled with immovable steel and concrete, whereas the ground is in constant motion and flux. From the Eiffel Tower, Paris offers itself visually prepared to be read by a process of decipherment that blends perception with intellect. The birds-eye voyeur sees structural relationships that underlie the city and its topography. Chicago's poise between the Great Lakes and the Great Plains, its straddling of rivers and inlets, the organizing geography of the city, can be read only from on high. And the geography is overlaid with a panorama, which for Barthes is a view to be read, not perceived. A panorama is, on the one hand, a continuous, uninterrupted analog of nature, not a text but a raw experience; on the other hand, it seeks to be deciphered, it is full of signs that require recognition, that can be understood only through a familiarity with their ground-level existence. They are the equivalents of familiar words recognized in a new text. Perception-plus-intellect is the marriage of the concrete and the abstract, the deep structure and the surface sensation. It is a way of knowing the city that only altitude can offer.

Height also terrifies. Vertigo is a necessary condition of power even for accustomed high fliers. There is a comfort and ease in accepting the discipline of the social, in living by *their* ready-made meanings handed down to *us*, in not risking one's coiffure in the rush of air caused by a rapid ascent away from the horizontal. But all freedom, all power is risky and the risk is essential to it.

No reader is completely free, no text offers itself up entirely to the readers' discretion. The city is the icon of entrepreneurial capitalism—whatever else it may mean, it must always mean this. Sears Tower is not just the apogee of human technology, magic, it is the apogee of entrepreneurial capitalism, and in that role it attempts to control the meanings of the freedom it offers. Such freedom, it attempts to say, is possible only within the individualism upon which capitalism depends. So the history of Sears, the superlative company whose development is almost synonymous with the opening up of the West, is inter twined with the facts of the tower: the wonderment slides easily from one to the other. Sears, at this level nothing more than an abstract financial concept, is given a steel and concrete signifier that is both the sign and the presence of the company. The Tower is simultaneously icon and index.

And binding them all together (the Tower, Sears, Chicago) is the invisible essence of the city and the significant absence from its maps and texts: its people. The people are absent from the model of the Tower, absent from the view from the Skydeck, absent from the technological miracles of its construction, absent from Calder's "Universe." For the people are absent from capitalism. Capital is abstract, conceptual, immaterial: the people form the body of labor that actually produces the wealth of capitalism, but their existence is unacknowledged because to acknowledge it would be to admit to their exploitation. The city of Sears Towers may be a city of wonders, but it is a city without people. Herein lie intransigent contradictions. The people escaping from the repressive horizontality of the city miniaturize it to the point where there is no room for them. Its spatial strategies can be so easily risen above precisely because, miniaturized, they can no longer function as technologies of power administering people.

Because capitalism has evacuated the people as a set of oppositional social allegiances, it has to produce its own "people" to fill the vacuum. So, at the bottom of the tower, before seeing even its model, the tourist must undergo "The Chicago Experience"—a seven-minute slide and sound show in which 12 computerized projectors present over 1,000 images of Chicago in ever-changing combinations alongside the sound of the "real-life" voices of its "people." And these "people" are as much the products of capitalism as the Tower itself—they are far removed from the people of popular culture, the oppressed who resent their oppression and whose everyday creativity consists of making their freedoms, their meanings, their pleasures in its gaps, of turning its resources to their purposes, of evading its administrations.

The people of "The Chicago Experience" are those the system creates for us to populate its city with as we look down on its streets and buildings. Listen to them:

I think Chicago works because it has people willing to make it work.

The spirit of Chicago is to take a chance, to do it right and put it together, and to be willing to sometimes take the risks that are necessary where other centers are not.

The strength of any city is its people, it is founded and progresses on the basis of how strong the people are, and the great thing about Chicago is it not only survives but thrives, and it thrives on the basis of the people who work to make it.

These are the voices not of a people, but of perfect city-subjects—Sears Corporation miniaturized into individuals dedicated to work, progress, risk taking, and success. But within such unified subjectivity lies a controlled unthreatening diversity:

What I like about Chicago is that it is a blue-collar, no-nonsense town. I like it because people have definite opinions . . . because there is so much ethnic diversity, because it has such vitality.

Any conflictual dimension to the class and racial differences alluded to here is totally repressed. Social differences produce not conflicting interests but vitality and strong minds—just what capitalism needs. The only black voice admitted into this Chicago-subject is that of a blues musician, who talks of the fun and enjoyment of the music, again repressing all the meanings of social oppression out of which it grew. Effacing the history of the blues effaces the history of the blacks in white America and of the presence of Chicago's huge and oppressed black underclass, in the same way the definition of blue-collarness as the source of clear, strong opinions effaces the history and the presence of the proletariat.

The diversity of Chicago, then, is the diversity required by capitalism—a source of social energy to be exploited and turned into more capital. It is not surprising, then, that the stylistic diversity of Chicago's corporate architecture is seen as the analog of the social diversity of its city-subjects, for such diversity is only a masquerade of difference:

The wonderful thing about the architecture is its diversity, is that it has so much character compared to a lot of cities where every building looks like every other building . . . but if you make a 360-

degree turn in downtown Chicago you can see buildings that represent just about every period and are representative of the character of the people here.

The ultimate and literal naturalization of such diversity into a fertile, organic unity is achieved by the man who likens it to the differences between seasons and concludes:

I don't think I could take any place that was the same all the year round . . . this is what I like about working here, nothing's ever the same.

The commentary closes with a voice hymning liberal pluralism and consensus:

I love this city and I hope it continues to thrive and grow and bring all our diversities together in the kind of harmony that makes this one of the greatest cities in the country. Chicago is wonderful.

The city-subjects of "The Chicago Experience" are like its architecture—miracles not of technological, but of social engineering. The other skyscrapers are not only what Sears Tower soars above, they are also what it grows from. So, too, these city-subjects are individualized models of Sears Corporation, that it rises above but also grows out of. There is plenty to escape from in our elevator.

LOOKING UP

Whatever its physicality, its massiveness of steel, glass, and concrete, a city is, finally, an abstract concept. Chicago is not its buildings, it railroads and freeways, its parks and lake shores, it is not even its people and the multiplicity of their histories— it is an idea, an abstraction that we might call "Chicagoicity." It is a play of meanings escaping any specificity, geographical, historical, or social, yet encompassing all of them.

Meanings, not just these of Chicago, may always be in motion, never finally definable, but in everyday life we need to anchor them. To hold them still however momentarily, we need to be able to conceive of a sense of a meaning that exists, rather than a constant process of meanings being made, rejected, and remade. We need to organize the play of meanings around focal points of reference, we need to anchor the abstract generalities of understanding in the material facts of "nature" by the process that Lévi-Strauss calls "the logic of the concrete." This logic, which he sees as a universal mental process, is at work as it metaphorically transposes class, moral, and other differences into the concrete difference between *up* and *down*.

In our systems of representation, this transposition is reproduced in the shift between the verbal and the visual. Verbal systems deal easily with the abstract—their problems lie always in making their representations specific and concrete. Visual systems are the opposite, they deal easily with concrete specifics but have problems in generalizing. When Barthes (1982a) argues that the significance of the Eiffel Tower for Paris lies in its unavoidable visibility, he is pointing to this logic of the concrete, the transposition from the abstraction of the word *Paris* to the concrete visual of the Eiffel Tower. A community is an abstract concept, however material its history and geography, so "Parisian-ness" is made concrete by being able to see the Tower, the Tower creates a spatial and therefore material community:

> The Tower is there, in front of all, framed by my window; and at the very moment the January night blurs it, apparently trying to make it invisible, to deny its presence, two little lights come on winking gently as they revolve at its very tip: all this night, too, it will be there, connecting me above Paris to each of my friends that I know are seeing it: with it we all comprise a shifting figure of which it is the steady center: the Tower is friendly. (Barthes 1982a: 236–7)

Sears Tower may be inappropriately described as "friendly," but its function of organizing a community into a visual, spatial, and therefore *material* experience is similar to that of its Parisian counterpart. Of course the visual is not confined to the actual moment of seeing—the Parisian can visualize the Tower when it is out of sight, when he or she is in Africa or Australia; what matters is its presence, and visualization is the recognition of presence and the situation of oneself in relation to that presence. Visualization makes abstractions concrete.

Sears Tower makes Chicagoicity visual. It anchors the drifting, shifting concepts, and in so doing it functions similarly to but differently from the Eiffel Tower for Paris. For Barthes, the significance of the Eiffel Tower lies precisely, if paradoxically, in its absence of meaning. It is an empty signifier, it is nothing except *there*, pure presence, therefore, it "means" everything. It anchors the community of Paris without defining it, it concretizes the meanings of the city without limiting them. It is creative, not definitive; provocative, not repressive. Like Sears Tower it transgresses the separation between seeing and being seen, it is to look at and from and so is

> a complete object which has, if we may say so, both sexes of sight. This radiant position in the order of perception gives it a prodigious propensity to meaning: The Tower attracts meaning, the way a lightening rod attracts thunderbolts; for all levels of signification it plays a glamorous part, that of a pure signifier, i.e., a form in which men unceasingly put *meaning* (which they extract at will from their knowledge, their dreams, their history), without this meaning thereby ever being finite and fixed: who can say what the Tower will be for humanity tomorrow? But there is no doubt it will always be something. (Barthes 1982a: 238)

The emptiness of the Eiffel Tower means that it can be more easily made into popular culture: it offers itself as a cultural resource that can respond to social and historical differences. Sears Tower, however, is ideologically filled, a signifier encumbered with signification. Its physical solidity is a sign of its semiotic fullness, and contrasts with the skeletal airiness of the Eiffel Tower, its visible emptiness. Sears Tower is more recalcitrant: the freedom offered by its verticality is always there, but it is encumbered in the way that the Eiffel Tower's is not. Sears Tower is inescapably corporate capitalism. There is something playful, irresponsible, carnivalesque about the Eiffel Tower that refuses rationality and the discipline of the everyday: it is there to escape, to vacate; it is liberatingly empty.

Sears Tower has no sense of fun: it is a totally solemn building, packed with meaning and discipline. Only in its verticality, its visibility, and the view from its summit does it resemble the Eiffel Tower. In other respects it resembles a cathedral. Each organizes a community in the name of a higher rationality—capitalism or Christianity—a disciplined community at odds with the grass-roots allegiances of popular culture. The spire of a cathedral is to look at, not from. Its vaulted ceilings draw the eye up in awe, and miniaturize the looker: in a cathedral one is made small in the eye of God, the people are as effectively repressed as they are in Sears Tower. The cathedral may, contra Sears Tower, emphasize the mystical over the technological, but it still merges the two in a reciprocal interchange of power. If Sears Tower is a miracle of technology, Chartres Cathedral is the technology of the miraculous.

But even in the repressive apparatuses of the cathedral there are gaps for the popular to insert itself. Folk devils and popular paganisms erupt among the angels and saints, the grotesque challenges (however weakly) the beautiful, disorder is never quenched by the grand design. But similar popular opportunities exist only in the height of Sears Tower, only when one *cannot* see it, when it becomes only a point, not an object, of view. Only then is there a popular escape from its repressive meanings, though we must note that the pleasure of this escape is so empowering and liberating that no cathedral dared offer it to its congregants—though many will now, perforce, to their secular tourists. So, too, the tourists in Sears Tower will endure with a mix of apathy, awe, and skepticism the overt propaganda of "The Chicago Experience" and worship of the model as the price to be paid in order to experience the birds-eye view. Popular culture must contain that which is to be resisted or evaded. Both these disciplinary experiences are, appropriately, on the lowest accessible floor of the building, as though to emphasize the repression of *down* against the liberation of *up*. In the fixed society of feudal Christianity, *up* was for God only; in the meritocratic society of yuppie capitalism, *up* is the reward for those who most successfully conform to its ground rules. Looking up at a cathedral spire leads one's thoughts away from earth toward heaven; looking up at Sears Tower is seeing the material "heaven" achievable in this life. Both the cathedral spire and the Eiffel Tower lead one away from the ground (albeit for very different purposes), but Sears Tower, from below, is totally rooted. Only from within does it offer an Icarean moment of liberation. The Eiffel Tower is unnecessarily excessive, its technology irresponsible and carnivalesque, but

Sears Tower magnifies the norms and structures of capitalism as a cathedral does those of Christianity: nowhere does it exceed them and offer up this excessiveness for resistant, offensive, or popular meanings.

SO WHY IS IT POPULAR?

Popular culture is a culture of contrasts, and in this book I have traced some of the ways its contradictions are played out in specific instances. The ones I have chosen have, on the whole, been those in which the voices of the popular can be heard most clearly in their speech against (contradiction) the voice of dominance. Capitalism, even in its late consumerist form, is still primarily a system of production that grounds its control of the social order in its control of the production and distribution of resources. Its control in these domains is well nigh unchallengeable, though theorists like de Certeau (1984) and cultural ethnographers such as Willis (1981) have shown how resistant popular practices refuse to lie down and die even in such tightly controlled contexts as the workshop or the classroom. But in general popular culture finds its most fertile soil in the fields of leisure and consumption, for that is where the power-bloc is, despite its attempts to the contrary, at its most vulnerable. Beach going, video arcades, television quiz shows, and Madonna exist only because of their availability to be made into popular culture. The ability of the various allegiances of the subordinate that constitute the popular to produce their culture in opposition to that of the power-bloc is therefore most easily traced in them, for in them popular practices are least repressed and therefore most visible. In other cultural practices, however, the dominant have more at stake—politically, morally, ideologically, as well as economically—and here the contradictions are more overtly repressive and popular practices more covert, more sporadic. TV news opens itself up to popular expropriation more reluctantly than quiz shows; the opportunities for resisting practices in shopping malls are more constrained than in video arcades. And Sears Tower offers the people the fewest opportunities of all. Its economic function is massively dominant, and, unlike that of a mall or a TV show, hardly dependent on its popularity. This is not to say that the economic health of Sears Corporation needs no base in popular culture—clearly it does—but that the popularity of the Tower has a negligible economic effect. There is, indeed, a certain ironic support for my argument in the fact that, as I write, Sears Tower is up for sale because of the economic problems of the corporation.

So what are the pleasures it offers? They are of two main sorts—popular pleasures and hegemonic ones. Of these, the popular can also be thought of as twofold—ones of semiotic security and ones of liberation. Having forced this categorization I immediately wish to retract it, for pleasures are not experienced as categorically distinct from each other, but merge one into the other despite their contradictions.

In our societies, popular culture, however oppositional or evasive, is always the popular culture of capitalism, and however much capitalism subordinates and oppresses people, it also offers them real benefits and rewards, however unfairly distributed. In most historical periods there is only a minority of popular formations that wish to revolutionize capitalism radically, or to leave it and live under a different social system altogether. Popular resistances are selective, not wholesale—progressive, not radical.

There are pleasures, even for the most subordinated, in aligning oneself with the system that subordinates one. These are the pleasures by which hegemony wins some of the consent of some of the formations of the people to some of the common sense of capitalism. The skyscraper is a product of capitalism, particularly of its American corporate version. The aesthetics of the Manhattan skyline are an aesthetics of capitalism: they are as ideological as those of the Renaissance.

The awesomeness of Sears Tower is as attractive as that of Chartres Cathedral—if one is to be oppressed one might as well be oppressed magnificently; one can thus participate in one's own oppression with a hegemonic pride. But such pleasures, however powerful, however essential to any social system, however much part of people's experience, are not popular pleasures. They stem not from allegiances of the people, but from the interests of the power-bloc. They are, eventually, the pleasures against which popular pleasures situate themselves

Having said that, however, we must not think we have exhausted such pleasures by describing their hegemonic thrust. There is a sense in which their hegemony lays itself open to popular skepticism. In conversation with tourists on the Skydeck, I came across a variety of reactions to "The Chicago Experience," most of which showed some form of alienation or distance from it. The closest people came to enthusiasm or engagement was when they were admiring its technological sophistication—here the words "clever" or "smart" were most frequently used—"Pretty cool, the way they did it." While the technological form met unanimous approval when it was commented on at all, the more explicitly ideological content raised a greater variety of responses. Some thought it was boring or stupid, others gave it a grudging approval—"good" or "okay" were common words—but they were typically spoken in a disinterested or even dismissive tone of voice. Others were explicitly skeptical—"That's what they'd like us to believe" or "They picked the people real carefully, didn't they?" "There's a lot they don't tell you in these things—gangs and things, the blacks would tell it different . . ." There was pleasure in disbelief, a sense of pride in not being taken in that could be seen as an example of the hedonistic skepticism that Bourdieu (1984) identifies as typical of proletarian taste. This pleasure in not being duped can be experienced only when the attempt is made and recognized: it is when the hegemonic thrust is explicit that it becomes most vulnerable.

Resistance is easiest and most pleasurable when what is to be resisted is clear and unambiguous. Jameson (1984) has suggested that one of the characteristics of late, multinational, corporate capitalism is that its institutions have become so vast and unimaginable as to become almost invisible (see *Understanding Popular Culture*, Chapter 2). A multinational corporation does not have the same presence as the nineteenth-century factory owner in his house on the hill, and is thus harder to conceive of antagonistically. The semiotic uncertainty of abstractions make them appear less immediately threatening, less overtly dominating: there does not appear to be anything very solidly *there* to align oneself with or against. At least Sears Tower is *there*, it gives corporate capitalism a concrete and steel presence: at least "The Chicago Experience" allows bourgeois ideology to speak with unusual clarity.

The popular skepticism, however, was directed much more against the latter than against the former. The technological miracles achieved by capital were not seen as dominating, divisive, or repressive in the way that the bourgeois definition of "the people" was. Technology appeared a capitalist achievement in which the people felt able to participate: as consumers they doubtless possessed cars, TVs, and stereos that differed only in scale, not kind, from the world's tallest building from which they were looking. Indeed, the domestic technology of cars and entertainment systems offer similar senses of both freedom from constraint and control over some, at least, of the conditions of one's social existence, even if only in the domains of leisure. The technology of the Tower did not contradict the tourists' experience of technology in their everyday lives: bourgeois meanings of the Chicago-subjects and of their experiences of the city, however, clearly did, at least for some. There is a popular pleasure in the way that the Tower and "The Chicago Experience" make material and apprehensible elements of late capitalism that are more typically abstract, distant from the everyday and thus ineffable. Experiences that are graspable can at least be coped with, by rejection, acceptance, or negotiation, and can thus be both meaningful and pleasurable depending on which tactics of coping are adopted in which context. Such semiotic security is pleasurable, for it allows the subordinate the knowledge of what it is they have to cope with.

The liberating experience of altitude has already been discussed, and it may underlie the people's ready acceptance of the technological miracle, for it was, after all, only the technology that made the God's-eye view possible. There would have been little, if any, popular pleasure in the technology if our experience of it had been confined to the model. Popular pleasures are participatory, and it was only the elevator and the altitude in which people could participate.

One of the characteristics that differentiates popular culture in capitalist societies from folk culture is its constant search for the new and the different (see *Understanding Popular Culture*, Chapter 7). The ephemerality of popular tastes and fashions is an expression of the constantly changing experiences and formations of the people, which are quite different from the more stable and repetitive social conditions that produce folk art. Sears Tower plays upon this desire for the new by insisting on its uniqueness and its difference (measured to the nearest foot) from other tall buildings. The uniqueness of the altitude offers a purely hegemonic pleasure, for it is aligned with the competitiveness of corporate capitalism—it expresses only Sears's sense of superiority over its corporate competitors. The popular pleasure of altitude is unaffected by the few hundred feet by which Sears Tower "beats" the World Trade Center, or the many hundreds of feet by which it beats the Eiffel Tower. The novelty that is popular is the novelty of altitude; it lies in the difference between *up* and *down*, between the vertical and the horizontal, not in that between one towering experience and another.

References

Allen, R. (1985). *Speaking of Soap Operas*. Chapel Hill: University of North Carolina Press.

Allen, R. (ed.) (1987). *Channels of Discourse: Television and Contemporary Criticism*. Chapel Hill: University of North Carolina Press.

Althusser, L. (1971). "Ideology and Ideological State Apparatuses," in *Lenin and Philosophy and Other Essays* (pp. 127–186). New York: Monthly Review Press.

Armstrong, N., and Tennenhouse, L. (eds.) (1987). *The Ideology of Conduct: Essays in Literature and the History of Sexuality*. New York: Methuen.

Bakhtin, M. (1968). *Rabelais and His World*. Cambridge: Massachusetts Institute of Technology Press.

Bakhtin, M. (1981). *The Dialogic Imagination*. Austin: University of Texas Press.

Barthes, R. (1973). *Mythologies*. London: Paladin.

Barthes, R. (1975a). *S/Z*. London: Cape.

Barthes, R. (1975b). *The Pleasure of the Text*. New York: Hill & Wang.

Barthes, R. (1981). "Theory of the Text," in R. Young (ed.) *Untying the Text*. London: R.K.P.

Barthes, R. (1982a). *A Barthes Reader* (S. Sontag, ed.). New York: Hill & Wang.

Barthes, R. (1982b). *Empire of Signs*. New York: Hill & Wang.

Baudrillard, J. (1981). *For a Critique of the Political Economy of the Sign*. St. Louis: Telos.

Baudrillard, J. (1983). *In the Shadow of the Silent Majorities and Other Essays*. New York: Semiotext.

Bennett, T. (1983). "A Thousand and One Pleasures: Blackpool Pleasure Beach," in Formations (ed.) *Formations of Pleasure* (pp. 138–145). London: Routledge & Kegan Paul.

Bouchard, D. (ed.) (1977). *Language, Counter-Memory, Practice: Selected Essays and Interviews by Michel Foucault*. Oxford: Blackwell.

Bourdieu, P. (1968). "Outline of a Sociological Theory of Art Perception." *International Social Sciences Journal* 2: 225–254.

Bourdieu, P. (1984). *Distinction: A Social Critique of the Judgement of Taste* (R. Nice, trans.). Cambridge, MA: Harvard University Press.

Bowlby, R. (1985). *Just Looking: Consumer Culture in Dreiser, Gissing and Zola*. London: Methuen.

Bowlby, R. (1987). "Modes of Modern Shopping: Mallarmé at the *Bon Marché*," in N. Armstrong and L. Tennenhouse (eds.) *The Ideology of Conduct: Essays in Literature and the History of Sexuality* (pp. 185–205). New York: Methuen.

Brooks, B. D. (1983). Presentation at the conference, "Video Games and Human Development: A Research Agenda for the '80s." Harvard Graduate School of Education, May.

Brunsdon, C. (1981). *"Crossroads*: Notes on Soap Opera." *Screen* 22 (4), 32–37.

Chambers, I. (1986). *Popular Culture: the Metropolitan Experience*. London: Methuen.

Chodorow, N. (1978). *The Reproduction of Mothering*. Berkeley: University of California Press.

Cohen, S., and Young, J. (1973). *The Manufacture of News*. London: Constable.

Consumer Guide (ed.) (1982). *How to Win at Video Games*. Cheltenham: Bulger.

D'Acci, J. (1988). *Women, "Woman" and Television: The Case of Cagney and Lacey*. Unpublished dissertation, University of Wisconsin—Madison.

de Certeau, M. (1984). *The Practice of Everyday Life*. Berkeley: University of California Press.

Douglas, M. (1966). *Purity and Danger*. London: Routledge & Kegan Paul.

Douglas, M., and Isherwood, B. (1979). *The World of Goods: Towards an Anthropology of Consumption*. London: Allen Lane.

Drummond, P., and Paterson, R. (eds.) (1985). *Television in Transition*. London: British Film Institute.

Eco, U. (1986). *Travels in Hyperreality*. London: Picador.

Enzensberger, H. M. (1972). "Constituents of a Theory of the Media," in D. McQuail (ed.) *Sociology of Mass Communications*. Harmondsworth: Penguin.

Ferrier, L. (1987). *Postmodern Tactics: The Uses of Space in Shopping Towns*. Paper presented at "Moving the Boundaries" symposium, Perth, W. Australia, November.

Fiske, J. (1987a). "British Cultural Studies," in R. Allen (ed.) *Channels of Discourse: Television and Contemporary Criticism* (pp. 254–289). Chapel Hill: University of North Carolina Press.

Fiske, J. (1987b). *Television Culture*. London: Methuen.

Fiske, J. (1989). *Understanding Popular Culture*. Boston: Unwin Hyman.

Fiske, J., and Hartley, J. (1978). *Reading Television*. London: Methuen.

Fiske, J., Hodge, R., and Turner, G. (1987). *Myths of Oz: Readings in Australian Popular Culture*. Boston: Unwin Hyman.

Formations (ed.) (1983). *Formations of Pleasure*. London: Routledge & Kegan Paul.

Foucault, M. (1977a). *Discipline and Punish*. London: Allen Lane.

Foucault, M. (1977b). "Nietzsche, Genealogy, History," in D. Bouchard (ed.) *Language, Counter-Memory, Practice: Selected Essays and Interviews by Michel Foucault*. Oxford: Blackwell.

Foucault, M. (1978). *The History of Sexuality*. Harmondsworth: Penguin.

Foucault, M. (1980). *Power/Knowledge*. Brighton: Harvester.

Foucault, M. (1981). "Questions of Method." *Ideology and Consciousness* 8 (Spring).

Gans, H. (1962). *The Urban Villagers: Group and Class in the Life of Italian-Americans*. New York: Free Press.

Greenfield, P. (1984). *Mind and Media*. London: Fontana.

Grossberg, L. (1984). "Another Boring Day in Paradise: Rock and Roll and the Empowerment of Everyday Life." *Popular Music* 4, 225–257.

Gunter, B. (1987). *Poor Reception: Misunderstanding and Forgetting Broadcast News*. Hillsdale, NJ: Lawrence Erlbaum.

Hall, S. (1973). "The Determination of News Photographs" in S. Cohen and J. Young (eds.) *The Manufacture of News* (pp. 176–190). London: Constable.

Hall, S. (1981). "Notes on Deconstructing 'The Popular,' " in R. Samuel (ed.) *People's History and Socialist Theory* (pp. 227–240). London: Routledge & Kegan Paul.

Hartley, J. (1982). *Understanding News*. London: Methuen.

Hartley, J. (1983). "Encouraging Signs." *Australian Journal of Cultural Studies* (2).

Hebdige, D. (1979). *Subculture: The Meaning of Style*. London: Methuen.

Hobson, D. (1982). *Crossroads: The Drama of a Soap Opera*. London: Methuen.

Hodge, R., and Tripp, D. (1986). *Children and Television*. Cambridge: Polity.

Jameson, F. (1984). "Postmodernism, or the Cultural Logic of Late Capitalism." *New Left Review* 146 (July/August), 53–92.

Lakoff, G., and Johnson, M. (1980). *Metaphors We Live By*. Chicago: University of Chicago Press.

Leach, E. (1972). "Anthropological Aspects of Language: Animal Categories and Verbal Abuse," in P. Maranda (ed.) *Mythology*. Harmondsworth: Penguin.

Leach, E. (1976). *Culture and Communication*. Cambridge: Cambridge University Press.

Leiss, W. (1978). *The Limits to Satisfaction*. London: Marion Boyars.

Lévi-Strauss, C. (1969). *Myth and Meaning*. New York: Schocken.

Lewis, J. (1985). "Decoding Television News," in P. Drummond and R. Paterson (eds.) *Television in Transition* (pp. 205–234). London: British Film Institute.

MacCabe, C. (1981). "Realism and Cinema: Notes on Brechtian Theses," in T. Bennett, S. Boyd-Bowman, C. Mercer, and J. Woollacott (eds.) *Popular Television and Film* (pp. 216–235). London: British Film Institute/Open University.

McQuail, D., Blumler, J., and Brown, J. (1972). "The Television Audience: A Revised Perspective," in D. McQuail (ed.) *The Sociology of Mass Communications* (pp. 135–165). Harmondsworth: Penguin.

McRobbie, A. (1982). "*Jackie*: An Ideology of Adolescent Femininity," in B. Waites, T. Bennett, and G. Martin (eds.) *Popular Cultures: Past and Present* (pp. 263–283). London: Croom Helm/Open University Press.

McRobbie, A. (1984). "Dance and Social Fantasy," in A. McRobbie and M. Nava (eds.) *Gender and Generation* (pp. 130–161). London: Macmillan.

McRobbie, A., and Nava, M. (eds.) (1984). *Gender and Generation*. London: Macmillan.

Mercer, C. (1983). "A Poverty of Desire: Pleasure and Popular Politics," in Formations (ed.) *Formations of Pleasure* (pp. 84–100). London: Routledge & Kegan Paul.

Mitchell, E. (1983). Presentation at the conference "Video Games and Human Development: A Research Agenda for the '80s." Harvard Graduate School of Education, May.

Morse, M. (1986). "Post Synchronizing Rock Music and Television." *Journal of Communication Inquiry* 10 (1), 15–28.

Nava, M. (1987). "Consumerism and Its Contradictions." *Cultural Studies* 1 (2), 204–210.

Pressdee, M. (1986). "Agony or Ecstasy: Broken Transitions and the New Social State of Working-Class Youth in Australia." Occasional Papers, S. Australian Centre for Youth Studies, S.A. College of A.E., Magill, S. Australia.

Propp, V. (1968). *The Morphology of the Folktale*. Austin: University of Texas Press.

Radway, J. (1984). *Reading the Romance: Feminism and the Representation of Women in Popular Culture*. Chapel Hill: University of North Carolina Press.

Samuel, R. (ed.) (1981). *People's History and Socialist Theory*. London: Routledge & Kegan Paul.

Sanders, N. (1982). "Bondi The Beautiful: The Impossibility of an Aesthetics." *Occasional Papers in Media Studies*, N.S.W.I.T. 16, June.

Schudson, M. (1984). *Advertising: The Uneasy Persuasion*. New York: Basic Books.

Silverstone, R. (1981). *The Message of Television: Myth and Narrative in Contemporary Culture*. London: Heinemann.

Sinclair, J. (1987). *Images Incorporated: Advertising as Industry and Ideology*. London: Croom Helm.

Stedman-Jones, G. (1982). "Working-Class Culture and Working-

Class Politics in London, 1870–1900: Notes on the Remaking of a Working Class," in B. Waites, T. Bennett, and G. Martin (eds.) *Popular Culture: Past and Present* (pp. 92–121). London: Croom Helm/Open University Press.

Thompson, R. (1983). "Carnival and the Calculable," in Formations (ed.) *Formations of Pleasure* (pp. 124–137). London: Routledge & Kegan Paul.

Volosinov, V. (1973). *Marxism and the Philosophy of Language*. New York: Seminar.

Waites, B., Bennett, T., and Martin, G. (eds.) (1982). *Popular Culture: Past and Present*. London: Croom Helm/Open University Press.

White, D. (1979). "Michel Foucault," in J. Sturrock (ed.) *Structuralism and Since*. Oxford: Oxford University Press.

Wilden, A. (1971). *System and Structure*. London: Methuen.

Williamson, J. (1978). *Decoding Advertisements*. London: Marion Boyars.

Williamson, J. (1986a). *Consuming Passions: The Dynamics of Popular Culture*. London: Marion Boyars.

Williamson, J. (1986b). "The Making of a Material Girl." *New Socialist* (October), 46–47.

Willis, P. (1981). "Class and Institutional Form of Counter-School Culture," in T. Bennett et al. (eds.) *Culture, Ideology and Social Process*. London: Batsford Academic/Open University Press.

Wollen, P. (1982). *Readings and Writings: Semiotic Counter Strategies*. London: Verso.

About the Author

John Fiske is Professor of Communication Arts at the University of Wisconsin-Madison. He has written widely on the subject of popular culture and is the author of *Reading Television* (with John Hartley), *Introduction to Communication Studies*, *Myths of Oz* (with Bob Hodge and Graeme Turner), and *Television Culture*, and is the general editor of the journal *Cultural Studies*. Born and educated in Great Britain, Professor Fiske has taught previously both there and more recently at Curtin University in Western Australia. He is an inveterate consumer of popular culture.

Index